CHINA

On Your Own

D1738576

OPEN ROAD PUBLISHERS, Vancouver

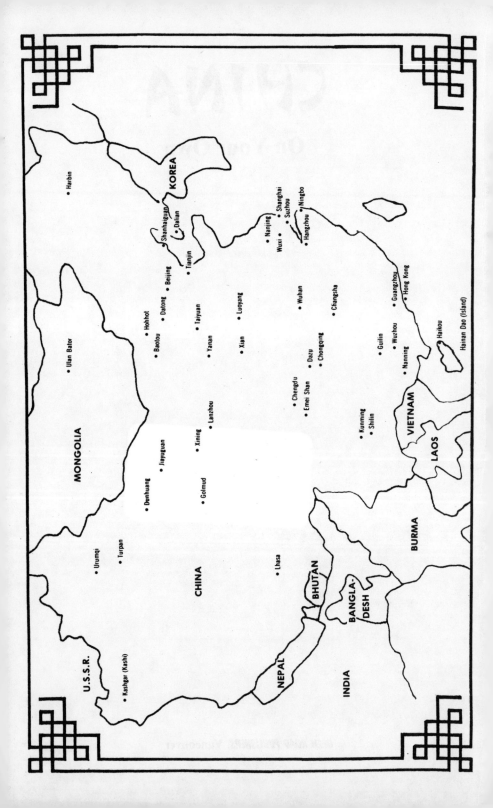

CHINA

On Your Own

FRONT COVER

Top left: A Kazak family, Bogda Shan (Xinjiang Province) (K)

Top right: A Uygur at Sunday bazaar, Kashgar (Xinjiang Province) (K)

Bottom left: Cliff-face sculpture of Buddha, Yungang caves, Datong (Shanxi Prov.) (K)

Bottom right: An offshoot of the Grand Canal, Wuxi (J)

ISBN 0-9691363-1-5
Copyright © 1985 Russell and Penny Jennings and Michael R. Kelsey
First Edition, December, 1982
Second Edition, May, 1983
This Revised Edition, September, 1985
Reprinted, October 1986

Canadian Cataloguing in Publication Data

Jennings, Russell, 1943-
"China On Your Own"

Includes index.
Bibliography: p. 240
ISBN 0-9691363-1-5

1. China - Description and travel - 1976-
Guide-books. I. Jennings, Penny, 1941-
II. Kelsey, Michael R. III. Title.

DS712.J46 1985   915.1'0458   C85-091378-0

PUBLISHER:
  OPEN ROAD PUBLISHERS
  P.O. BOX 46598, STATION 'G'
  VANCOUVER, B.C., CANADA V6R 4G8   Telephone (604) 736-0070

DISTRIBUTORS: See back page

Typeset by Acadia Printing Ltd., Vancouver
Printed by Colorcraft Ltd., Hong Kong

4

CONTENTS

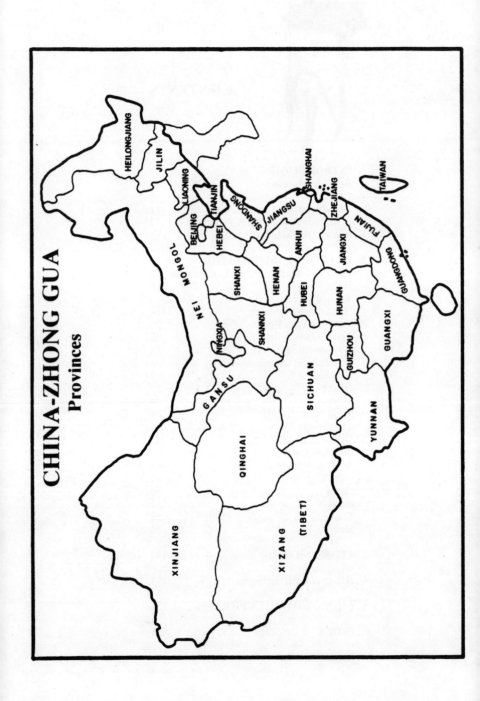

CHINA-ZHONG GUA
Provinces

HEILONGJIANG

JILIN

LIAONING

NEI MONGOL

BEIJING

TIANJIN

HEBEI

SHANDONG

JIANGSU

SHANGHAI

ZHEJIANG

TAIWAN

SHANXI

HENAN

ANHUI

JIANGXI

FUJIAN

SHAANXI

HUBEI

HUNAN

GUANGDONG

NINGXIA

GANSU

GUIZHOU

GUANGXI

QINGHAI

SICHUAN

YUNNAN

XINJIANG

XIZANG
(TIBET)

6

CONTENTS (Continued): CITIES

ACKNOWLEDGEMENTS

To the following travellers for their support:
Pam Dermody
Dale Dubberley and Carolyn Paver
Ken Fraser
Randy Heward
Kay and David Kos
Kenn Looten
Berndt Luchterhand
Derek and Liz Vann
Ruth Westergaard and Bruce Williams

INVITATION

Travel opportunities and travel regulations in China are changing. We would appreciate additions and deletions to be sent to us so we can advise other travellers.

Acknowledgement will be given in the next edition. Please forward your information to your nearest co-author.

Russell and Penny Jennings
Open Road Publishers,
P.O. Box 46598, Station G,
Vancouver, B.C., V6R 4G8
CANADA

Michael Kelsey
Kelsey Publishing Co.
310 East 950 South
Springville, Utah,
USA, 84663

LEGEND

Symbol	Name	Chinese
	Hotel	Binguan; sometimes called Fan Dian
	Church	Jiao Tang (Geo Tong)
	Mosque	Qin Din Si (Chin Din Si)
	Temple	Si, or Miao (large temple) or Guan (Daoist temple)
	Gate	Men
	Cave	Dong
	Tomb	Ling
	Public Security Bureau	Gong Anghee
	Ruins	
	Airport	Ji Chang
	Harbour or boat dock	Gang
	Building	Jian Zhu Wu, or Lu (tall)
	Lake and sea	Hu and Hai, respectively
	Railway line	
	Railway station	Juo Che Zhan
	Park, Garden, Forest	Gong Yuan, Yuan, Lin respectively
	Wall, Great Wall	Qiang, Qiang Chen respectively
	Paved country roads	Malu
	Dirt road	Lu
	City Streets	Lu or Jie Dao
	Mine	
	Mountain peak, Mountain ridge	Shan Feng
	Paved mountain trail	
	Mountain trail	Shan lu
	Mountain campsite	
	Pass	Guan
	Route (no trail)	

On the town maps, the numbers beside the roads are bus numbers.
On the hiking maps, the high numbers indicate the elevation in metres. 9

Beijing: Escape tunnel in "underground city" (J)

INTRODUCTION

China is the world's third largest country after USSR and Canada.

Do your "homework" before going to China. Read about the history, customs, food, architecture, the Silk Road, religions, politics, archaeological sites, the national minorities and the arts. Read anything on China you can find in book stores and libraries.

Because you will be travelling China on your own, you will not have a tour leader to explain what you are seeing or answer the myriad of questions that will come to mind.

Now is the time to visit China, before Western influences affect the lifestyle (housing, food, clothing) of the people.

The authors travelled independently on flexible itineraries, booking and paying for food, accommodation and transport on route. They arranged for their visas in Hong Kong.

TRAVEL COSTS

The Jennings' average daily expense totalled US $15.00 per person, the bulk of which was transportation. Michael Kelsey's daily average was US$8. Michael's travels included some camping in the mountains and some hitch hiking when transport was not available. All authors travelled hard class on the trains, booked dormitory rooms where possible and ate in 'local' restaurants.

THE CHINESE AND US

The Chinese are tolerant and helpful. We are their guests. Individual travel is new to China. Their knowledge of our language and culture is limited. Do not get exasperated and thump tables to get attention; do not make unfair demands when ordering food or buying tickets for transportation.

The Chinese are trusting. Do not betray their trust by doing what some travellers have done, renting a room for two and crowding as many as ten travellers into it.

The Chinese respect us. Respect them. Do not, as some travellers have done, clean your teeth or wash your feet in Beijing's fountains.

They dress conservatively in clean attire. We must do the same.

ATTITUDE OF CHINESE OFFICIALS

They are tolerant and helpful despite our lack of knowledge of their language and customs. They recognize the fact that individual travellers clog the flow of people at ticket offices at train stations and bus stations and at hotels.

Tour groups, on the other hand, are easier to welcome as guests. They are well-dressed and orderly and never cause trouble. And they bring in more foreign currency.

ON YOUR OWN VERSUS A TOUR

Independent travel in China is a challenge. Its rewards include close contact with the local people as you travel with them on trains, buses and boats and share their tables in restaurants. You also enjoy lower travel costs compared to being on a guided tour. However, you have a language problem. Making travel arrangements will be time consuming and probably frustrating. Patience will be your greatest resource.

We do not condone independent travel for everyone. Travelling China is not a relaxing holiday. If you have not experienced travelling in third world countries, think again before you make China your first foray into a foreign country.

You must expect to experience a lack of comforts: crowded trains and buses, lack of privacy in some hotels, primitive toilet facilities in many places, crowded restaurants and unabashed stares by curious Chinese onlookers in most places you go. Most travellers feel it is all worthwhile for the rewards are great in this newly opened country.

Others may prefer a tour.

As a member of a tour group you have guides, instant companions and pre-arranged accommodation and transportation. Experiences are different, the rewards many.

GOING BY YOURSELF

If you plan to visit China as a lone traveller but hope to meet others in a similar position, chances are that you will. If you go from Hong Kong to China in October or in late March or April you will meet many others in Hong Kong, while in China you will meet dozens of others in hotel dormitories in the more frequently visited cities.

AGE and ATTITUDE

AM I TOO OLD TO TRAVEL CHINA ON MY OWN?

Age is a state of mind. No one is "too old". What you may want is more comfort. Although this book is directed at people wanting to travel on a budget we are adding the following section for the young and not-so-young who would prefer to travel China independently on a first class basis. Here is how to do so:

You can travel soft (first class) on the trains and/or fly, and have CITS make your sightseeing, transportation and accommodation arrangements.

However, you still need patience, perseverence, reasonably good health, the tenacity to board overcrowded buses and the ability to carry your own bags. Age is not important; a positive state of mind is.

ACCOMMODATION and FOOD: Upon arrival in a city you will need accommodation. (Refer to our hotel list). The large hotels have elevators. A double room will cost between Y24 and Y40 for two. Many rooms do not have private facilities; you will find the bathroom and toilet down the hall. The toilet is Western style. The hotels have restaurants. A Western breakfast (eggs, toast, coffee/tea) is an available option. Chinese food is served for other meals. A 24-hour laundry service is usually available.

ILLNESS: If you require medical assistance, advise the hotel clerk. If entry into a hospital is necessary you will take a taxi. Ambulances are not always available in China. You will pay a nominal fee for the medication used.

SIGHTSEEING: The CITS office may be in your hotel. The staff speak English. Ask them about city tours; they can book a tour, usually for the next day. Alternatively you could visit a tourist site by taxi then dismiss it and hail another one for the return journey. Or you could have the taxi wait. Some taxis have meters; some drivers give receipts. You do not tip taxi drivers. If travelling by cycle trishaw you have to bargain.

If you need help at a tourist site or train station, look around for a young Overseas Chinese. He may be from Hong Kong and so speak English. They are distinguishable by their brighter coloured clothes, their modern clothing styles, and the type of bags they carry. By bags we mean sports bags, day packs and backpacks, usually of coloured fabrics.

PRE-ARRANGING TRANSPORT AND ACCOMMODATION: Contact CITS. Ask them about onward transport as soon as you arrive in the city. They need about 48 hours to get your tickets. They can book trains and planes and arrange your accommodation in a distant city. They charge a nominal fee of about Y2.

TRAINS: You may prefer a soft class seat in the day time and soft berth during an overnight train trip. Soft class has four bunks to a compartment. A pillow, linen, blanket and towel are provided. There is a small table with a lamp on it. A vacuum flask of hot water is provided and filled continually. All your luggage goes into the compartment with you; there is ample space under the seats and a large shelf above. For privacy, you can close the compartment's sliding door. The toilets will be at either end of the carriage. One will be Western style; the other, Asian (squat down) style. Food orders will be taken by the conductors; you can eat in your compartment. The conductor gives plenty of warning as to when to disembark. The cost of a soft class berth is comparable to the airfare for the same distance.

PACKAGE TOURS FROM HONG KONG: As an introduction to China you may feel more comfortable if you arranged in Hong Kong for a short four-day tour to say, Guangzhou, Foshan (Buddhist statues) and Zhaoqing (limestone crags), Guangzhou. After returning to Guangzhou toward the end of the tour you could remain in Guangzhou (Canton), extend your visa then visit other parts of China independently. A four-day tour as described would cost about HK $1500 (US$265). It includes a flight from Hong Kong to Guangzhou, food, accommodation, sightseeing and the train ride back to Hong Kong which you would decline. Or maybe you could use it later. Speak to a Hong Kong agent such as Trinity Express or China Travel Service. See index for address.

TOURS, ACCOMMODATED/ESCORTED: After looking over this booklet you may have concluded that travelling China on your own is not for you. If you prefer to travel with a tour, check with your local travel agency for tour groups that are leaving from your home country. You may benefit from lower fares that apply to groups.

If you wish to stay away longer, thereby not return with the group, ask your travel agent to arrange a "land cost only" tour. He could fly you on the same airplane with the group but you would be paying a higher airfare. However, the tour operator may be using an excursion fare that would allow you to stay longer without extra charge on the airfare.

Another possibility is for your agent to arrange with a Hong Kong based tour operator to book you on a tour. You would be joining other nationalities who fly into Hong Kong independently for the tour. However, you are taking the chance that you are the only person to book to leave for China on the particular day. You would be travelling alone but would be met at airports and/or train stations by representatives of China International Travel Service.

The cost of this type of travel arrangement becomes rather prohibitive for many people; it is less expensive to join an already existing tour group. Some companies that would have the answers are:

CHINA TRAVEL SERVICE, 77 Queens Road, Central, Hong Kong. Telephone:5-259121/Telex: 73344 HKCTX HX. Branch Office: 27 Nathan Rd., 1st floor, Kowloon, Hong Kong. Telephone: 3-667201;

CULTURAL TRAVEL, 905 Car Po Commercial Building, 37-43 Pottinger St., Hong Kong. Telephone: 5-420652/Telex: 75617 CHAND HX;

TRINITY EXPRESS, China Tour Centre, 614, New World Centre, Kowloon, Hong Kong. Telephone: 3-683207/Telex: 50704 TRIEX HX.

THINGS TO DO BEFORE YOU LEAVE HOME

PASSPORT: Check the validity of your passport.

VISA PHOTOS: Have visa photos taken. Three are needed for the China visa that you obtain in Hong Kong. Booth photos are acceptable for visas.

HEALTH: Check with your local health department and ask whether any shots are mandatory. If you need shots, the medical practitioner will record them in a yellow booklet you will be given called INTERNATIONAL CER-TIFICATE OF VACCINATION.

INSURANCE: Buy medical insurance coverage. A travel agency can provide this. Some travel insurance will cover your flight home if further treatment in your home country is recommended by a physician in the country where you incurred illness or an accident.

AIRFARES: Check with travel agencies about airfares. Remember that a travel agency represents all airlines and so can give you a comparsion of fares. Your airfare will be determined by a number of factors: length of stay, whether one way or round trip, whether charters exist, or excursions, stand-bys, seat sales, or non-stop flights, whether you can change your dates after departure or whether you can switch to another airline on the same route without penalty.

DENTIST: Have a dental check.

WILL: Make a will.

POWER OF ATTORNEY: Arrange a Power of Attorney for a next of kin to handle financial matters.

PHOTOCOPIES: Make photocopies of pages 1 to 5 of your passport and of your International Vaccination Certificate (if you need to carry one). Leave a set of photocopies at home and carry a set with you.

TRAVELLERS CHEQUES: Leave at home a copy of your Travellers Cheques numbers. Carry a copy of your Travellers Cheques numbers with you, but keep them separate from your T.Cs. Many travellers carry their Travellers Cheques, cash, passport and vaccination certificate in a money belt or a body pouch hung around their neck. Most travellers carry some bills in a hard currency such as U.S. dollars to make changing of small amounts of money more convenient.

RECONFIRM: Reconfirm your flight reservation by phone 72 hours prior to departure. Find out what time you should check in at the airport.

DOCUMENTS: Keep your passport, vaccination certificate (if required), air ticket and immigration exit form on your person.

CUSTOMS: At the Airport Customs office, fill out a form, listing details of your camera or other equipment that you are taking out of the country. This will preclude you from having to pay duty upon your return.

HONG KONG

ARRIVING: After going through immigration and customs, visit the airport tourist office for maps and advice about accommodation. Change a minimum amount of money into Hong Kong dollars and cents at the Airport Exchange counter. You get a bad rate of exchange here. Change more money when you reach downtown Kowloon. To go downtown take Bus No. 201 from the airport. You need the exact change; check the sign at the bus stop for the exact fare.

ACCOMMODATION: Accommodation to suit all pockets is available in the Nathan Road-Salisbury Road area. The Chungking Mansion is a rabbit warren of family run guest houses. You have many guest houses from which to choose. The YMCA is in Salisbury Road. The Lucky Guesthouse is at 5/A 4a Humphrey's Avenue, around the corner from the mosque. This place might have the cheapest accommodation in Hong Kong. Not shown on the map are many expensive first class hotels in the area of Chunking Mansion such as Imperial and Ambassador.

DEPARTING: If you are not already holding an air ticket for a flight out of Hong Kong you can buy a flight at a reasonable cost through the Traveller's Hostel. Sample fares are:

Hong Kong — **Shanghai,**   HK$1010 one way.
Hong Kong — Beijing,   HK$1000 one way via Manila
Hong Kong — Taipei,   HK$820 one way.
Hong Kong — Manila,   HK$850 one way.
Hong Kong — Bangkok,   HK$800 one way.
Hong Kong — Tokyo,   HK$900 one way.
Hong Kong — U.S.A.,   HK$2280 one way.
Hong Kong — Europe,   HK$2450 one way.
Hong Kong — **Australia**   HK$3100 one way.

DEPARTING BY BOAT: Ferry to Guangzhou from HK$75; ship to Shanghai from HK$460. (Approximately HK$7.35 = US$1).

You can buy airfares and boat tickets from Traveller's Hostel (see index) or from Traveller Services, Room 704-5, Metropole Building, 57 Peking Road, Tsimshatsiu, Kowloon, Hong Kong. Tel. 3-674127.

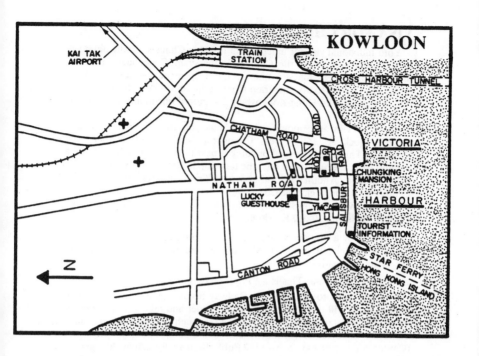

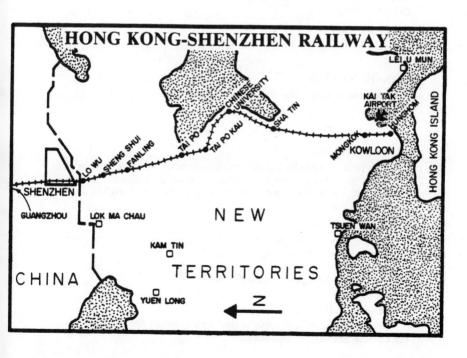

VISA FOR CHINA

Your individual visa for independent travel in China is usually obtained in Hong Kong. However, the Chinese Embassy in Copenhagen issues one month visas. Other Chinese Embassies in Europe issue one week transit visas which enables one to take the train from Berlin to Moscow, Irkutsk and Beijing then quickly to Hong Kong where a standard one month-five week visa is issued.

For your visa and bookings into China you can go to the Traveller's Hostel, Block A, 16th Floor, Chungking Mansion, 40 Nathan Road, Kowloon. This multi-storeyed building is next to the Holiday Inn. If you are coming from the airport by bus, the bus stop is 100 metres south of Chungking Mansion. Another helpful agency is Trinity Express, 614 New World Centre, Kowloon. Tel. 3-683207.

For your visa you must give three photos. There is a photo booth in the YMCA, Salisbury Road, Kowloon.

The cost of a visa for China varies according to what is included (e.g. transport, hotels) or excluded. Although we are listing some examples here, ask about alternatives.

1. The HK $450 Visa. This is a "Pay Today, Go Tomorrow" visa.

You are taken to the Kowloon Railway Station by a China Tour representative. He will travel with you to the border and take your passport and have your visa stamped in it. Then you go through Chinese Immigration and Customs, have lunch (included) and continue by train to Guangzhou (Canton). You may have to visit the Public Security Bureau in Guangzhou to obtain your Aliens Travel Permit. Regulations concerning the need for an Aliens Travel Permit are changing. You will be advised of the current procedure in Hong Kong.

2. The HK $500 Visa.

Cruise to Shanghai, 3 days. The price includes visa, boat ticket, eight meals.

3. The HK $350 Visa.

Includes visa, boat ticket to Guangzhou and hotel.

4. The HK $300 Visa.

Includes visa and boat ticket to Wuzhou (10 hours).

5. The HK$150 Visa

This is popular with those in a hurry. You obtain your visa overnight or in 24 hours and make your own train or boat arrangements to reach Guangzhou. The train is more popular. Most independent travellers use this method.

6. The HK $90 Visa.

This visa, popular with those not in a hurry, takes about 3 days. As in No. 5 you make your own travel arrangements.

7. The HK$450 Visa. It is valid for 3 months.

OVERSEAS CHINESE

"Overseas Chinese" can apply in their home country for a visa. Apply to the Chinese Embassy or Consulate.

NOTE: In Canada, a visa for independent travel can be obtained from TIN-BO VACATIONS, 719 Somerset St. West, Ottawa, Ontario, K1R 6P7 Tel: (613) 238-7093. Send your passport, one visa application form, two photos, Cdn$50 and a suggested itinerary. (You need not adhere to your itinerary). The visa takes 3 days to issue.

CHINA VISA EXTENSION

A visa is normally issued for one month or 5 weeks. When inside the country you can go to any Gong Anghee (Public Security Bureau) and get a one month extension without difficulty. If you want to stay longer than two months you can then either leave the country (return to Hong Kong) and get a new visa, or you can travel to outlying regions and get more extensions. Cities which are rumored to be good places to get long extensions are Xining, Turpan and Dunhuang. If you are doing a really long trip, keep asking other tourists about the locations of Gong Anghees which are sympathetic to travellers. A common rule is that the less frequented Gong Anghees are more friendly to foreigners than the big city offices. Beijing and Xian have the worst reputations. There is a nominal fee of Y5 to extend.

HOLIDAYS and FESTIVALS

There are four official public holidays:
1st January, New Year's Day. (According to the Western Calendar).
1st May, Labor Day.
1st and 2nd October, National Days, commemorating the founding of the People's Republic of China.
The above are primarily family days.
Due to more liberal attitudes taking hold in China, celebration of Chinese New Year now takes the form of street processions that include men on stilts and singers. This has occured in Beijing and may spread to other cities. Chinese New Year occurs usually in January or February. It varies according to the lunar calendar.

Note: The Guangzhou (Canton) Trade Fair is held twice a year, between 15 October and 15 November, and between 15 April and 15 May. Accommodation in Guangzhou is at a premium and transport (train, ship, hydrofoil, air) between Hong Kong and Guangzhou is heavily booked. You may be denied an individual visa to visit Guangzhou as your first city in China. You may have to go by ship to Shanghai.

PLANNING YOUR ROUTE

In planning your route, different factors arise. Are you seeking an overview of the country or does your interest lie in archaeology, anthropology, horticulture, religious sites or gastronomy? For most people on their first trip to China, they want a sampling of everything. This is how it was for us.

Refer to our page on Duration of Train Journeys to establish your travelling times. You can reduce travelling time by taking domestic flights.

One idea is to travel in a clockwise direction from Guangzhou to include say, Guilin, Kunming, Xian, Beijing, Shanghai then by boat to Hong Kong or train to Guangzhou. We have listed only the major cities. You could stop at intermediate cities such as Shilin (Stone Forest), Emei Shan (the mountain), Datong (Buddhist caves), Suzhou (gardens) and Hangzhou (silk). Another plan would be Guangzhou, Guilin, Chongqing, boat to Wuhan, Xian, Beijing, Shanghai and then south.

As a "rule of thumb", out of every three days in China, one day is spent travelling. For this exercise a day means the full 24 hours.

CLIMATE

Mid-September to Mid-November (Autumn): Best Months (fine weather). Warm in south, cool in the north.

December, January (Winter): Mainly dry. Cool and mild in the south but bitterly cold in the north. Because the north is visited by the dry, cold winter winds from Siberia, the temperatures in the north are lower than regions of the same latitude in other parts of the world.

April (Spring): A good month to travel, after September/October. Dry in the north but some rain in the south. During early spring dust storms can occur in the north.

June, July, August (Summer): Hot, humid and rainy. The heaviest rainfall throughout China is in July. The rains come from the southeast where moist air has gathered over the sea.

The recommended time to go into the grasslands is during the summer. By September it can be very cold with a strong north wind blowing across the flat terrain. You can rent warm fur collared coats from the hotel in Hohhot for Y1 if you go during the cooler months. It is well worth the investment!

PLANNING YOUR ROUTE

Where to go to find:

BEACHES
Beidahe, Qingdao, Putuo Shan Island.

CAVE HOMES
Sanmenxia, Gongxian, and along the Huang He (Yellow River).

CITY WALLS
Kaifeng, Nanjing, Xian, Shanhaiguan, Datong.

CITY RUINS
Kashgar (Kashi), Turpan, Dunhuang.

GARDENS
Beijing, Hangzhou, Suzhou, Yangzhou, Shanghai (Yu garden).

GREAT WALL
Badaling (65km north of Beijing), Jiayuguan (western end), Shanhaiguan (eastern end).

IMPERIAL PALACES
Beijing, Chengde, Shenyang, Qufu, Taian (Tai Shan).

MUSEUMS
Beijing: Museum of Chinese History, and the National Palace Museum.
Nanjing: Nanjing Museum
Shenyang: Imperial Palace Museum
Xian: Provincial Museum
Turpan: Turpan Museum

RELIGIOUS SITES
Christianity (Churches): Shanghai, Dalian, Jilin, Harbin, Kaifeng, Qingdao
Confucianism: Qufu (birthplace of Confucius)
Buddhism (temples): Lanzhou, Louyang, Xian, Lhasa, Xining (Taer Si), Zhongwei, Taiyuan, Suzhou, Ningbo, Hangzhou, Kunming, Chengdu, Datong PLUS temples at the nine sacred mountains of Heng Shan Bei, Tai Shan, Heng Shan Nan, Hua Shan, Song Shan, Putuo Shan, Jiu Hua Shan, Wu Tai Shan, Emei Shan.
Buddhism (cave statues): Datong, Dunhuang, Louyang, Leshan, Maijishan, Dazu, Gongxian, Bingling Si, Taiyuan, Turpan, Kashgar (Kashi) and along the SILK ROAD.
Islam (Mosques): Xian, Turpan, Kashgar (Kashi), Yinchuan, Urumqi, Xining, Kaifeng.

TOMBS
Beijing (Ming tombs north of Beijing), Zunhua (Qing tombs), Gongxian, Xian, Nanjing, Dengfeng, Qufu, Shenyang, Anyang.

Entrance to Imperial City, Beijing

BASIC ROUTES

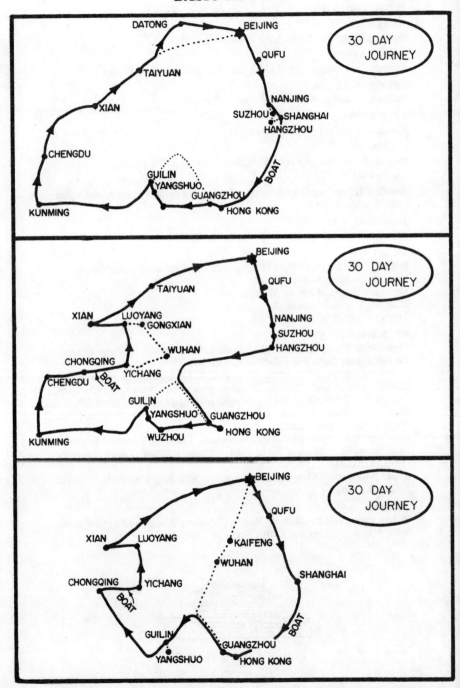

Add-on routes

A. FROM CHENGDU TO KATHMANDU — 10 DAYS(CHENGDU TO LHASA BY AIR)
B. CHENGDU–LHASA–CHENGDU — 6 DAYS(BY AIR)

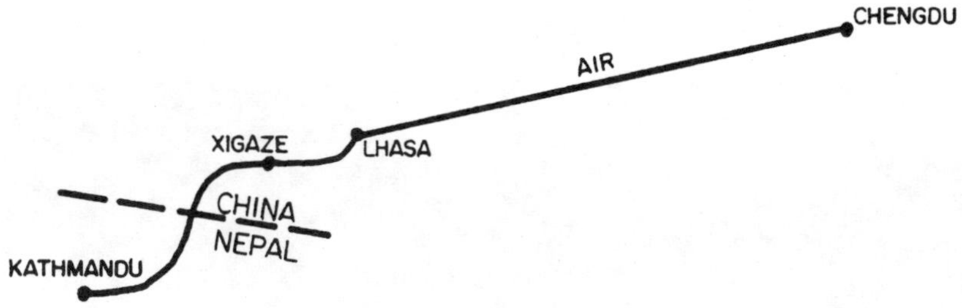

CHENGDU
AIR
XIGAZE   LHASA
CHINA
NEPAL
KATHMANDU

FROM XIAN(AND RETURN) — 20-30 DAYS

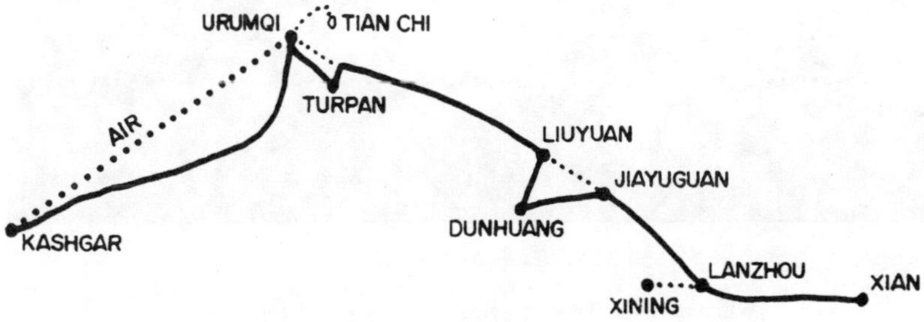

URUMQI   ○ TIAN CHI
AIR
TURPAN
LIUYUAN
JIAYUGUAN
KASHGAR
DUNHUANG
LANZHOU   XIAN
XINING

FROM BEIJING(AND RETURN) — 7 DAYS

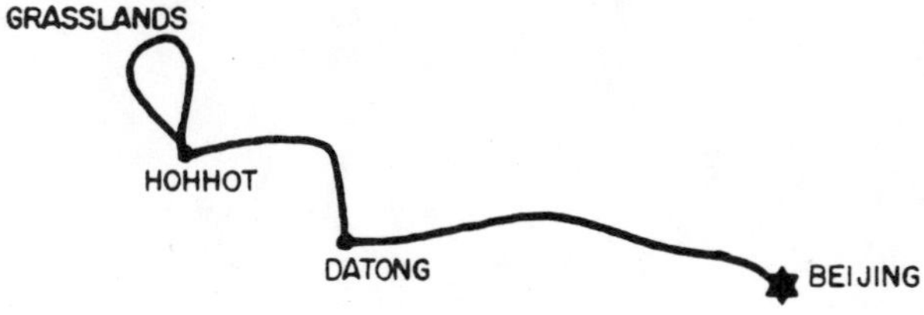

GRASSLANDS
HOHHOT
DATONG   BEIJING

Wudang Zhao: Tibetan style monastery near Baotou (K)

Add-on routes

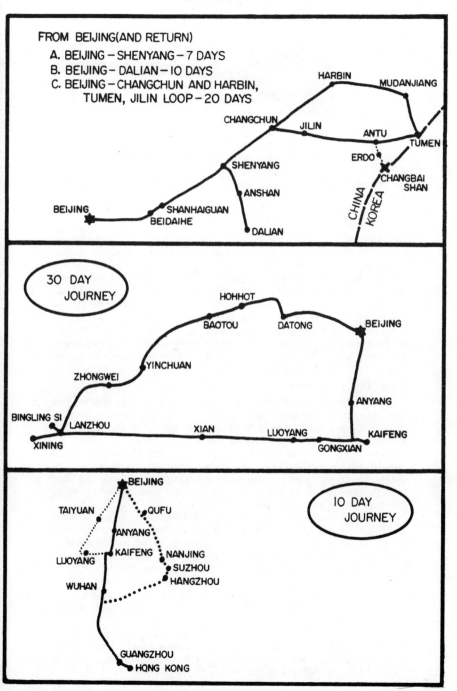

FROM BEIJING (AND RETURN)
- A. BEIJING – SHENYANG – 7 DAYS
- B. BEIJING – DALIAN – 10 DAYS
- C. BEIJING – CHANGCHUN AND HARBIN, TUMEN, JILIN LOOP – 20 DAYS

HARBIN
MUDANJIANG
CHANGCHUN
JILIN
ANTU
TUMEN
ERDO
CHANGBAI SHAN
SHENYANG
ANSHAN
CHINA
KOREA
BEIJING
SHANHAIGUAN
BEIDAIHE
DALIAN

30 DAY JOURNEY

HOHHOT
BAOTOU
DATONG
BEIJING
ZHONGWEI
YINCHUAN
ANYANG
BINGLING SI
LANZHOU
XIAN
LUOYANG
KAIFENG
XINING
GONGXIAN

BEIJING
TAIYUAN
QUFU
ANYANG
KAIFENG
NANJING
LUOYANG
SUZHOU
HANGZHOU
WUHAN
10 DAY JOURNEY
GUANGZHOU
HONG KONG

TRANS-SIBERIAN RAILWAY

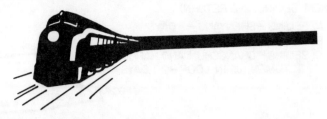

ARRIVING: Travellers arriving in Beijing from Europe by train across the USSR and Mongolia are given only a seven-day visa for China. Upon reaching Hong Kong some apply for a 30 day visa to return to China. Upon their return to China they extend their visa.

Some travellers arriving in Beijing (in 1985) bought their trans-Siberian tickets in Budapest for US$60, or US$42 with a Student Card.

DEPARTING: To travel to Europe by train reserve your seat at the Beijing office of CITS. The Russian train departs Beijing on Saturdays at 1940 hours. It travels via Manchuria. If you do not want to travel by train all the way to Moscow, disembark at Irkutsk and fly to Moscow. The Chinese train (apparently better) leaves Wednesday mornings at 0720. It travels via Ulan Bator (Mongolia) and takes five days to reach Moscow, seven to Berlin. The cost to Berlin is Y361.70 for 3rd class hard sleeper (bunks have mattresses). If ˙you travel through Mongolia, carry canned food or other rations as the food available is not of good quality. If you are a beer drinker, stock up before you leave China as the train's supplies run out quickly. If you wish to stop over on route, you must preplan and prepay for stopovers.

STOPPING IN USSR:

If you wish to make stops in the USSR you should allow two to three weeks to complete the arrangements in Beijing. The least expensive hotels in the USSR, for a single traveller, are US$33 per night. The cheapest double rooms are US$25 per person per night.

On the train, food is sold from trolleys wheeled along the aisles. Items sold include halcb (bread), kafir (yogurt), malaoo (milk) and occasionally, fruit. On the station platforms you can buy the same items and canned fish and fruit. As there is little variety on the train or in the cities you may consider carrying some of your own food.

If you are the independent type you can save US$20 at each stopover in the USSR by declining the hotel transfers. When you book your train ticket at the INTOURIST office at the Soviet Embassy in Beijing, ask the clerks to allow you to travel without paying for transfer charges. These charges are for an Intourist representative to meet you at the railway station and assist you to the hotel, and to return you when you depart. Each transfer costs US$10.

You can easily get to the hotel yourself. You will be carrying a travel voucher and hotel vouchers which you can show to local people; they will help.

In the cities you are free to wander without a guide. You can take public transport; guide books and maps in English are available. Hotels in the USSR provide breakfast which is included in the overnight charge. You can shop for food in the markets and in the streets.

A sample cost for a single traveller going from Beijing to Berlin with two nights in Irkutsk, three in Moscow, three in Lengingrad, two in Vilnius (Lithuania) and two in the Warsaw (Poland) is US$560.

Incidentally, some travellers have slept in the waiting hall in Moscow's Belaruski Station while waiting for an onward train connection. This applies more to those with transit visas.

VISAS FOR TRANS-SIBERIAN: Visas can be obtained in Beijing, in the following order:

POLAND: Open Monday, Wednesday, Friday 0900-1200.
2 photos. Y15. Issued while you wait.

USSR: Open Monday, Wednesday, Friday 0900-1200.
3 photos. Free.
A transit visa takes about five days, but three are possible. Allow two to three weeks for a tourist visa, required if you plan to stopover in the USSR.

MONGOLIA: Open Monday 1400-1500, Tuesday and Friday 0900-1200.
1 photo. $2.00 in U.S. bills or Swiss francs.
Same day service. Booth photos are acceptable for visas.

ROUND TRIP TO MONGOLIA AND USSR: You can take a train from Beijing via Ulan Bator (Mongolia) to Irkutsk, then fly to Beijing. (You cannot return by train).

From Irkutsk, another idea is to travel by train to Khabarovsk then fly to Beijing.

Visas for Mongolia and USSR can be obtained in Beijing.

Both the Chinese and Russian international train services have two berths in soft class and four in hard class.

All international trains have hot boiled water, available free. Train schedules are posted on the wall in each coach, including stopping time at each station. This allows you to get out and exercise at appropriate stations.

WHAT TO KNOW BEFORE YOU GO

ANTIQUES: If you buy an antique from a Friendship Store, make sure you are given a Customs Declaration form at the time of purchase. Check that the antique has a red wax seal.

BAGGAGE: Carrying a backpack is quite acceptable. In addition to tagging your baggage, write your name inside in case the tag gets torn off.

BLACK MARKET: The Friendship Stores sell merchandise for Foreign Exchange Certificates only. Many of the items sold are not available to the Chinese man-in-the-street unless, of course, he has Foreign Exchange Certificates (tourist money). You may be approached to exchange with them some of your "tourist money". You will be offered the equivalent amount in renminbi, plus 30 - 50%. This practice is, of course, against the law.

CAMERAS: As a tourist you can take in still cameras, 8mm movie cameras and video cameras, but not 16mm movie cameras.

If you wish to take photos at cultural performances in a theatre, plan on shooting with the available light. The stage is usually lit brightly enough to give good results with a fast film. See if you can crouch down at the front near the stage. Shooting a flash from the middle of the theatre disturbs the audience. Many flashes are only effective with subjects up to twenty feet away, so a flash inside a theatre may not give you a good picture.

CRIME: You have little to fear about physical abuse or theft. A Chinese would have a hard time explaining where he obtained an item of foreign manufacture. Bicycles, however, are subject to theft. If you hire one, use the lock and park it at a licensed bicycle stand where an attendant looks after it. Incidentally, it is illegal to "double" a person on the crossbar.

CULTURAL EVENTS: To learn of cultural events, check with China International Travel Service (CITS), ask members of tour groups or ask the hotel staff to check the local paper. If told the performance is sold out, go to the theatre anyway. Seats are reserved for dignitaries who arrive unexpectedly. You may get one of these if available, if you persist.

If you attend the opera, acrobats, classical dancing or any other theatrical performance there is no need to "dress up" for the occasion.

ELECTRICITY: Electric current is 220 volts, 50 cycles.

EQUALITY: Do not talk down to staff of trains, hotels or restaurants. The people in China are considered equal.

FACE, Loss Of: A Chinese does not want to appear unknowledgeable. You will encounter this type of vanity. If he makes a decision and it turns out to be wrong he does not want his mistake discussed. In other words, he does not want to "lose face."

MAIL: You can buy postage stamps in most tourist hotels. Mail your letters and any printed matter from there also. If you want to mail home film, you will have to go to the International Post Office (in the larger cities only). If you need a place to have mail sent, you can have people send it to Post Restante, General Post Office, Beijing, or to the main post office in any other city in China. You can also send it to Visitors Mail, Your Country's Embassy, Beijing. Another place mail can be sent is to American Express, Room 1527, Beijing Hotel, Beijing. But you must be a client to use this office.

MEALS: Meal times in China are approximately as follows:

Breakfast — 0700-0830
Lunch — 1130-1300
Dinner — 1700-1830

Meals start promptly. Be on time. Leave when you have finished. Chinese do not linger after eating. If you are a vegetarian, expect to have difficulties as many dishes have chopped meat.

PASSPORT: Memorise your passport number and date of issue to facilitate quicker replacement if lost. Also, as you have to write your passport number on the hotel registration forms it is more convenient for you to have the number memorised.

PHYSICAL CONTACT: Apart from hand shaking, physical contact is frowned upon. Comments of a sexual nature are considered offensive.

POLITICS: Do not make disparaging remarks or comical reference about Chinese politics or the system of Government. The majority of Chinese respect the Government and what it has achieved.

PUNCTUALITY: The Chinese expect you to be punctual for meetings and social functions. We learned this rule through experience. We and other individual travellers befriended a local teacher who agreed to arrange a multi-course dinner for ten of us at a local restaurant. He arranged it for 6 p.m. At 6:05 p.m. we arrived with our teacher friend and found that not only were tables set and chopsticks in place, but the food was already on the table!

SCHOOLS: Most children over the age of seven attend school. If you visit a school the students will clap as you arrive. You should reciprocate by clapping. The same principle applies when visiting a commune or a factory.

You will see some students between the ages of seven and fourteen wearing red kerchiefs. They are Young Pioneers, an organization roughly equivalent to the Boy Scouts or Girl Guides/Scouts found in most Western countries.

SIGHTSEEING: If seeking a particular tourist site, carry a postcard of it or a picture from a brochure and show it around. Pick up brochures in Hong Kong. Request a local person, say a hotel clerk, to write directions or destinations in Chinese.

Hotels that deal with foreign tourists will have information brochures in stock at the small store or sales counter. Usually these are in Chinese (Putonghua) and English.

When you arrive at a railway station, do not leave until you have purchased or tried to purchase a city map. Often these are in Chinese only, but they will always have bus routes and numbers which are indispensible. Later, you may be able to buy an English version of the same map at the hotel or CITS office. The city maps in most cases are very good, even though they are in Chinese. Buy one anyway, and compare it to the sketch maps in this book.

Also buy the China Railway Timetable which gives you the arrival and departure times of every train in China. This book is in English and Chinese, and is updated periodically.

We suggest that you also carry a second guide book to China if you want more detail about sights and history. Evelyn Garside's book, China Companion, and China Guidebook by Kaplan and de Keijzer are recommended.

TIME: The 24 hour clock is used in China. All times shown in this guide use the 24 hour clock. For example 1500 hours is 3 p.m.

TIPPING: Tipping is not an accepted practice. A smile and a word of thanks is sufficient. If you wish to give a token of appreciation, keep it small and of low value.

WATER: Do not drink the tap water in hotels. Vacuum flasks of hot water are made available for each room. Pour some into a glass to let it cool, or drink tea or coffee.

It is a good idea to carry a one litre water bottle, one that will not melt when boiling water is poured in. This will allow you to have cool water at all times, especially on trains. You can buy such a water bottle in Hong Kong.

TIME AROUND THE WORLD

The time of day in China is the same throughout the whole country except in Kashgar where the Uygurs use their own time. Theirs is two hours later than China Standard Time.

When China Standard Time is 12 noon (1200 hours) the time elsewhere is:

Calgary	2100*
Cape Town	0600
Chicago	2200*
Delhi	0930
Hong Kong	1200
Honolulu	1800*
London	0400
Manila	1200
Melbourne	1400
Montreal	2300*
New York	2300*
San Francisco	2000*
Sydney	1400
Tokyo	1300
Toronto	2300*
Vancouver	2000*
Washington D.C.	2300*
Wellington	1600
Zurich	0500

*means the previous day.

GOVERNMENT ORGANIZATIONS

公安局

PUBLIC SECURITY BUREAU *(GONG ANGHEE)* is the Government office that issues your Alien's Travel Permit. You present this Permit to hotels and ticket offices, upon request. These bureaus are found in all or most towns you will visit.

Each time you have more cities entered in your travel permit it will cost you Y1 and some time. It is recommended you have entered all the cities and counties you will have a chance of visiting. You can have as many names put in as you want, all for the same price of Y1. Ask if you can have a list of the cities and places open to foreign travellers.

中华民航大楼

CIVIL AVIATION ADMINISTRATION OF CHINA (CAAC) is the national airline. Flights can be booked at the airline offices or at a CITS office. Flights are often postponed due to inclement weather. In-flight service on the domestic routes usually consists of the handing out of soft drinks, candy and a key chain (or other knick-knack). Food is not served.

友宜商店

FRIENDSHIP STORES are Government department stores that sell imported goods and good quality Chinese arts and crafts, shoes, clothing, and fabrics. Foreign exchange certificates only are accepted. You can change travellers cheques at Friendship Stores.

中国国际旅行社

CHINA INTERNATIONAL TRAVEL SERVICE (CITS) is the Government tourist agency, called LUXINGSHE in Chinese. Invariably they are located in tourist hotels. They can arrange onward travel by plane or train, accommodation in other cities, local tours and theatre tickets. They charge a nominal fee. If CITS cannot confirm a transportation booking for when you want to go, you should go directly to the ticket office where tickets are sold to the general public.

BAGGAGE: WHAT TO TAKE

For carrying luggage, our personal preference leans toward a soft bag, be it a duffel bag with zipper and strap, or a backpack. We carry backpacks that have a built-in frame. The straps can be tucked away out of sight when a look of respectability is required, such as checking into a hotel. The backpack will then take the appearance of a soft suitcase. We carry our camera in a shoulder bag which we have lined with foam rubber to protect the camera against knocks. Some foam emits a chemical that is injurious to film; check with the dealer.

Never overpack. After packing, check again and remove 20% or more of the weight.

SUGGESTED LIST

Pair of tough shoes.

Leather sandals.

Rubber thongs (wear in communal bathrooms and in showers to prevent foot diseases).

2 pair trousers for men, 2 pair slacks for women, and a drip-dry skirt.

1 sweater.

1 jacket with plenty of pockets.

3 shirts for men, 3 blouses for women. (South China can be hot; cottons and loose fitting clothes are suggested).

3 changes of underwear.

3 pairs of socks.

3 handkerchiefs.

1 towel (not too heavy as it will take too long to dry).

Hat (soft).

Swim suit.

Gloves (for winter).

Sleeping sheet (that is, a sheet liner as used in sleeping bags).

Cord for clothesline (string it across your hotel room).

Water bottle (not essential, but handy. Fill it with the hotel's boiled water).

Chopsticks (restaurant chopsticks can spread disease).

Spoon (if you are not adept with chopsticks).

Knife and/or vegetable peeler (peel fruit before eating).

Combination can opener, bottle opener and corkscrew.

Small can of food (to be used as rations if restaurants are closed).

Reading matter. Paperbacks are sold at some tourist hotels but the variety of titles is small. Take your own; you can exchange with other travellers.

Radio/Cassette players. Short wave radios for news and cassette players for music can be bought in Hong Kong.

Soap in plastic container, toothbrush and paste, shampoo, razor blades, nail scissors, aspirins, cold remedies, sanitary napkins, mosquito repellent, adhesive plasters, ointment for bites, needle and thread, malaria tablets.

Matches (to light mosquito coils). Or maybe a cigarette lighter.

Small flashlight.

Lightweight travelling alarm clock.

Writing paper and envelopes.

Pen and note paper (keep them handy at all times).

Toilet paper (hard to find in China; some Friendship Stores sell it).

Plastic bags (to carry soiled clothes, wet clothes, or fruit bought at markets).

Sink plug (universal type to fit all wash basins, for washing clothes).

Tin cup with lid (for drinking tea on trains; buy in China).

Tea, coffee, sugar, cream substitute (for use on trains because only hot water is provided).

Camera, film, flash or strobe and extra batteries. (Take all your requirements. Pack your film in the middle of your luggage as protection against humidity and temperature changes). If you take a polaroid camera in addition to your 35mm camera, please restrict yourself with its use. If too many travellers give out polaroid pictures the local people will expect the same from every photographer, whether or not they carry a polaroid camera.

Used postage stamps. (These can be given as tokens of appreciation. Many Chinese are avid collectors).

Lapel pins with your country's flag (for gifts).

Map of China. Buy in Hong Kong or at hotel in Guangzhou.

Passport, travellers cheques, airline tickets.

BAGGAGE: WHAT TO EXCLUDE

Tent and sleeping bag unless you plan to hike and camp.

Because food is cheap and nutritious, carrying a portable stove is not necessary.

A large backpack is cumbersome on trains and buses. Most buses in "China Proper" have little or no storage space. Buses in Xinjiang (the desert area) have much more.

FOOTNOTE: Halter tops and shorts for women are frowned upon in China. For men a tie is rarely, if ever, needed. In Hong Kong you can buy a folding umbrella if necessary. Take clothing that you can put on in layers. As the day warms you can "peel off."

HEALTH

No injections are mandatory unless coming from an infected area. You should take malaria tablets only if you are planning to be in rural areas. However, few travellers reach those places. If you plan to, start taking malaria tablets (eg. chloroquin) before entering China. As mosquitos in South China are resistant to quinine based malaria tablets you must buy FANSIDAR malaria tablets in Hong Kong. They are available without a prescription.

MONEY

You will handle two types, Foreign Exchange Certificates (FEC) and Renminbi (People's Money), written as RMB.

The Foreign Exchange Certificates will be given in exchange for your travellers cheques. Save your bank receipts so you can change excess Foreign Exchange Certificates into Hong Kong dollars upon your departure. You will call these certificates "Tourist Money" or F.E.C.s.

Renminbi will sometimes be received in change when making purchases. You cannot change any excess into Hong Kong dollars upon departure. And you cannot take it out of the country.

With both types the main unit is the YUAN.

1 YUAN = 100 fen
1 YUAN = 10 jiao

In some places in the south of China you may hear the *yuan* being called a yen, but the universal slang word for yuan is *kuai*. You can use this word all over China and you will be understood. Also in the south some people use the term *jiao* for the 10 fen notes but most people called the 10 fen notes a *mao*. In the north, northwest and west, every one uses the terms kuai, mao and fen (fen is called fen everywhere).

Major travellers cheques are acceptable. You can only exchange travellers cheques at the bank or at a branch office in a tourist hotel or at a Friendship Store. The use of credit cards is limited to Guangzhou and to some Friendship Stores elsewhere in China. VISA is the acknowledged credit card.

In September, 1985, Y1 = US$0.50 approximately.
Approximately HK$7.35 = US$1

FOOD

In the north most dishes are wheat based (for example, noodles) while southern foods are rice based. The cultivation of rice dominates farm life south of the Yangtze River (or Chang Jiang). Marco Polo, who was in China in the thirteenth century, is said to have introduced noodles to Europe where the dish, in Italy, became known as spaghetti.

Some tourist hotels in the major cities serve a Western style breakfast of toast, eggs, tea or coffee. You could request a Chinese breakfast which usually consists of rice porridge, steamed buns and green tea.

Many large hotels have two restaurants, one serving Western food and one serving less expensive Chinese food. Sometimes we can only eat in the more expensive one.

For information about Beijing (or Peking) Duck, see under "Beijing".

Our eating places ranged from roadside stalls to good hotel restaurants and not once did we suffer ill effects. However, if you buy fruit make sure you peel it before eating.

You are bound to make mistakes when ordering food because of the language problem.

Three of us ordered dinners of chicken and rice, expecting steamed rice topped with chopped chicken. When the food arrived we were given bowls of rice and a whole chicken! Another time we wanted a small meal consisting of dumplings, noodles and soup. When the food came we found we each had three main dinners to contend with: a dumpling dinner, a noodle dinner and a soup dinner!

In a hotel restaurant at an adjoining table sat a group of six travellers. For one of their courses they ordered soup, expecting a small bowl for each. When the kitchen door opened, out came six large communal bowls of soup, each with a ladle! Although one bowl would have been sufficient for the entire group, three of them vowed to drink all their soup, and they did!

WHERE TO EAT ON A BUDGET

Try the *restaurants for the masses*. These are noisy, busy ground floor restaurants. Look to see what others are eating or go into the kitchen and point. At the table, before ordering, show the waiter how much you want to spend. For two people, order three dishes plus rice. Rice is not counted as, or called, a dish. In South China you will be served tea. In the north we found it almost impossible to get tea in these cheap restaurants; only beer was available.

Some *restaurants for the masses* display their dishes behind a glass counter, complete with prices. You point, they give; you pay, you eat.

The waiter or manager may indicate you go into one of their private dining rooms. We feel that he does this in the belief that a) solitude is what you prefer or b) by "hiding" you, he is stopping his dining room from being disrupted. We found that diners would ignore their food to watch us with curiosity.

In busy restaurants it is not uncommon to share your table with Chinese diners.

If you are given a bill, the words will be in Chinese but the numbers will be like ours. Quite often you pay when you order, sometimes before the food. You could try going to the kitchen to point and, in the process, cause a small riot!

Remember that you will have a greater variety of dishes if you have more people dining. Consider getting other travellers from the hotel to join you. You could celebrate with mao tai, a potent drink made from sorghum and wheat yeast.

If you attend a banquet, ask how many dishes there are so you can mentally gauge how much of each dish to eat.

Apart from restaurants, do not overlook the little noodle shops and the steamed bun shops. The buns sometimes have a sweet bean curd mixture inside.

If you have an upset stomach, consider rice congee, a sort of rice porridge. It is easy on the stomach. Stay away from spicy dishes and fatty dishes. As human and animal waste are used as fertilizer, avoid watermelon and other fruit that contain a lot of ground water.

When eating rice from a bowl you can raise the bowl toward your mouth and push the rice in with your chopsticks.

To signify to a waitress or waiter that you need your teapot refilled, upturn the lid on the teapot.

SHOPPING

WHERE TO BUY:

Friendship stores offer a wide selection of goods from imported food products to clothes and crafts. You must pay for purchases with Foreign Exchange Certificates.

Local Department stores carry locally made crafts as well as clothes and household products made in China. These stores are usually over-crowded with not many people appearing to be buying anything.

Prices in stores are fixed and bargaining is considered bad manners. Stores are open from 8:30 a.m. to 8:30 p.m.; some close for lunch.

When you see something you would like to purchase, buy it. Do not wait to buy it near the end of your trip; you may never see the same thing again. Some articles are produced in only one area and not sold in any other part of China.

THINGS TO BUY:

Silk, brocades, embroidery, carpets, weavings, down blankets/jackets, block prints.

Paper cuts, paintings, kites, clay figurines, pottery, wood carvings, cloisonne vases and jewellery.

Stone rubbings, antiques.

Clay figurine

TRAVEL NOTES

BOXERS: Known in China as Yi He Tuan, the "Society of Religious Fists." They were a group who originally hated their rulers and landlords. In 1899 and 1900 they turned their hatred toward foreigners, running amok in the countryside killing Chinese Christians, missionaries and other foreigners.

The Buddha, c. 500BC

BUDDHISM: Buddhism came to China by way of the Silk Road in the 1st Century AD. It came along the trading route from India to western and northern China where it gained acceptance by the non-Chinese. After the 4th century it spread to the Chinese population and became more widely known; by the 7th century it had established itself as a major religion in China.

As you travel throughout China you will notice that caves and temples are being restored after the neglect and damage caused by the cultural revolution, 1965-1976.

CATHAY: Medieval Europe called the country Cathay, probably from the name Khitai. Khitai is a form of Khitan, the northern tribe that established a dynasty from 907 to 1125 AD.

CHILDREN: To reduce the birthrate, the Government has dictated that urban parents should have only one child. A second child would not receive the privileges that an only child would receive, such as better schooling. Rural families are allowed two children, as are National Minority parents. Concern is now spreading throughout China about the one-child families, particularly those having baby girls. Parents permitted only one child prefer a boy to assure them of a more comfortable life in their old age.

CHOP: A seal. This rectangular block, sometimes about ten centimetres long, has an engraving at the end which is used as a signature. The inked end is imprinted onto paper or onto a painting.

CHRISTIANTITY: Introduced into China in the 7th century; it failed to gain ground. In the 16th century, missionaries returned and gained some success. However, it is thought that over subsequent years lack of major successes was due to the superior attitude of the Chinese (they regarded Europeans as incapable), the profusion of Christian sects, the anti-European feeling that grew because of the West's economic exploitation and the non-tolerance of some Chinese customs such as foot-binding.

A Typical Buddhist Temple

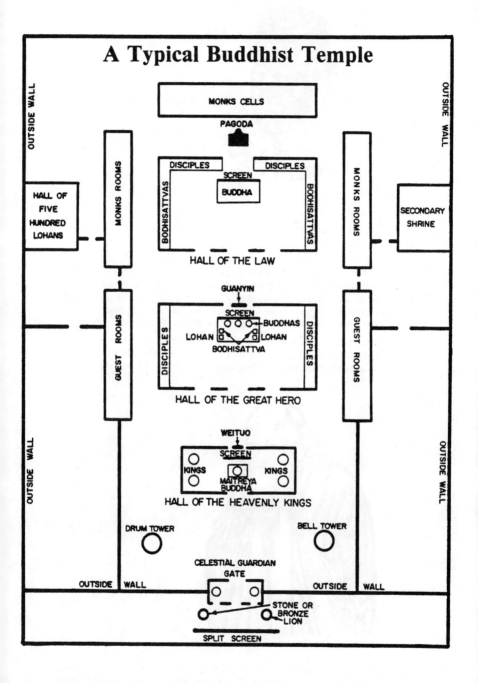

MONKS CELLS

PAGODA

DISCIPLES · DISCIPLES

SCREEN

BODHISATTVAS · BUDDHA · BODHISATTVAS

HALL OF THE LAW

OUTSIDE WALL

MONKS ROOMS

HALL OF FIVE HUNDRED LOHANS

MONKS ROOMS

SECONDARY SHRINE

GUANYIN

SCREEN

DISCIPLES · BUDDHAS · DISCIPLES

LOHAN · LOHAN

BODHISATTVA

HALL OF THE GREAT HERO

GUEST ROOMS

GUEST ROOMS

WEITUO

SCREEN

KINGS · KINGS

MAITREYA BUDDHA

HALL OF THE HEAVENLY KINGS

DRUM TOWER

BELL TOWER

CELESTIAL GUARDIAN GATE

STONE OR BRONZE LION

OUTSIDE WALL

SPLIT SCREEN

Confucius, 551-479BC, Philosopher

CONFUCIANISM: Confucius lived in the sixth to the fifth centuries B.C. He taught benevolence and a system of social relations. It was more a code of ethics than a religion.

COURTING: In the parks you will encounter young courting couples. There are few other places it seems, to court. Unmarried people live in dormitories for unmarrieds, or with their parents. Although communist policy does not favour arranged marriages because of its feudal overtones, the practice still exists in some traditional towns and villages. In the cities the practice is fast dying out. Boys going in search of girls is colloquially termed "fishing".

DAGOBA: A Buddhist monument consisting of a solid mass of earth and stone in the shape of an inverted bell. Encased in a casket embedded in the middle of a dagoba are sacred relics, quite often bones of a saintly person.

Lao Zi (Lao-Tzu), c.604-531BC.

Founder of Daoism

DAOISM (pronounced Dow-ism): Its popularity spread during the 1st Century, particularly among the Han Chinese. Lao-tzu, the founder of DAOISM was a contemporary of Buddha.

FO: Chinese name for Buddha.

FREE MARKETS: Towns throughout China have their street markets where privately grown produce is sold for private profit.

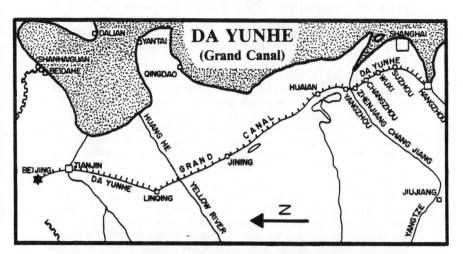

GRAND CANAL: The Grand Canal was begun 2,400 years ago during the Warring States Period (476 - 221 BC). Construction continued under the Sui dynasty (581 - 618 AD), under the Tang (618 - 907 AD) and was completed under the Mongolian Yuan dynasty (1280 - 1368).

HAN CHINESE: This group of people comprise the bulk of China's population, about 94%. The term comes from the Han dynasty (206 BC-AD 221). Leaders in government are Han Chinese. To establish border security in traditionally non-Han areas, Han Chinese are being settled there. The non-Han population consists of 55 ethnic groups known as National Minorities. See "National Minorities".

ISLAM: Traders from Arabia and Persia introduced Islam into China in the mid-7th century AD. It gained strength in the 13th century.

LAMAISM: This religion takes its teachings from Buddha but is mixed with other beliefs. It is popular with Mongolians and Tibetans.

LANGUAGE: Although there are dozens of languages spoken, the writing is the same. There are about 6,000 characters in fairly common use although newspapers restrict their usage to about 3,000. At the end of this book is a Chinese language supplement.

Chinese is a tonal language. Although you think you are pronouncing a word correctly, the Chinese may not understand you because you are using the wrong tone.

Learn how to say yes, no, thank you and hello in Cantonese and Mandarin.

LONG MARCH: 1934/35. The Guomindang (Nationalist) forces under Chiang Kaishek and the Communist forces were at war. The former force was starving out the Communists in their mountain strongholds. The Communists broke out and began a long march of 10,000 kms to Yanan. 100,000 started; 20,000 finished, we are told. Under Mao Zedong, a government was convened in caves in Yanan.

NATIONAL MINORITIES: There are 55 ethnic groups that make up 6% of the population. Some of these are Mongolian, Hui (Moslem), Tibetan, Korean, Manchu, Kazak, Tatar, Yi.

PEOPLE'S LIBERATION ARMY (P.L.A.): Everywhere you travel in China you will see green-uniformed army personnel visiting the tourist sights in groups. They are unarmed, friendly conscripts who are in the army for three or more years. The men dressed in the blue uniforms are naval personnel.

RATION TICKETS: Some staple foods are rationed such as wheat flour, rice, sugar, pork and cotton cloth. All Chinese people have these small tickets which look like the smallest money notes. Often you will be asked for this "piao" (ticket) when paying for a restaurant meal or if you buy some food in a store. Sometimes they ignore the fact you do not have one, and other times you may have to pay 5% to 10% more for the meal or item. Remember the name "piao". With economic reforms that have taken place recently, ration tickets may become a thing of the past.

SCHOOL GRADUATES: As schooling is provided by the Government, the Government can decide where to send a graduate to practise his profession. If it is to another city it could break up a husband and wife for a number of years because the spouse cannot automatically follow. However, a transfer can be arranged but it is not easy. If, say, a teacher in Harbin wants to transfer to Nanjing he must write to the Nanjing school to see if a teacher there wants to transfer to Harbin. He also must ask if the Nanjing school would accept his transfer from Harbin. He must get permission to quit his Harbin post. The Nanjing teacher must go through similar channels to apply for his transfer.

When couples live apart they are able to see each other for about twelve days per year during their holidays.

SILK ROAD: The trade route extended from present-day Xian (formerly called Chang'an) to the shores of the eastern Mediterranean. An important port there was present-day Antakya (formerly called Antioch). China exported silk embroideries, brocades, jade and tea. They imported long-staple cotton, peaches, pomegranates and raisins.

The trade route became active during the Han dynasty (206 BC to AD 220) when trade was established with centres in central and western Asia, including outposts of the Roman Empire and even Rome itself.

The Roman Empire collapsed. The Han dynasty collapsed. Trade along the Silk Road petered out. Without government controls, tribal skirmishes occurred along the route, rendering it unsafe. China did not have a strong unifying government for more than 300 years. Then the Tang Dynasty (618 - 907 AD) established itself and encouraged trade. Many Muslim merchants settled in Xian (then called Chang'an) at this time.

Corruption in the court, peasant unrest and army disenchantment toppled the Tang dynasty. As before, the Silk Road closed.

It was reopened by the Mongols who established the Yuan dynasty (1280 - 1368). It was during this time that Marco Polo visited China.

The importance of the Silk Road declined when sea routes were established during the 14th century.

SPITTING: At any time of the day or night, you will hear a throaty roar of someone about to spit. Spitting occurs on sidewalks, on boats, in buses, in trains and even in airplanes. We took a domestic flight and suffered while other passengers spat between their feet and in the aisle.

Westerners will be pleased to hear that the Government is discouraging spitting.

Some older people wear red armbands, particularly at train stations. In addition to making people stand in orderly lines at ticket windows they are supposed to chastise spitters.

TAIWAN: When in China, refer to the country as the People's Republic of China, not Red China. Refer to Taiwan as a province of the People's Republic of China. If you have a visa for Taiwan in your passport it will not prevent you from visiting the People's Republic. Conversely a P.R.C. visa in your passport will not preclude you from entering Taiwan.

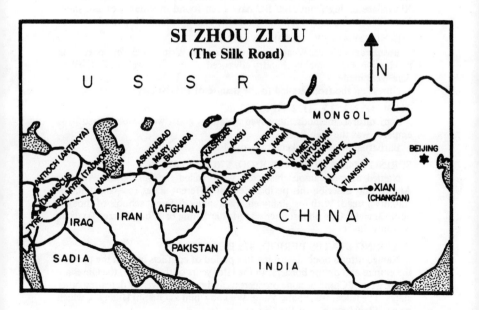

THE CHINESE DYNASTIES

XIA	2205 BC - 1766 BC
SHANG	1766 BC - 1122 BC
ZHOU	1122 BC - 770 BC
SPRING AND AUTUMN PERIOD	770 BC - 476 BC
WARRING STATES	476 BC - 221 BC
QIN	221 BC - 206 BC
HAN	206 BC - AD 220
THREE KINGDOMS	AD 220 - 265
JIN	AD 265 - 420
SOUTHERN AND NORTHERN	AD 420 - 589
SUI	AD 589 - 618
TANG	AD 618 - 907
FIVE DYNASTIES AND TEN KINGDOMS	AD 907 - 960
SONG	AD 960 - 1280
YUAN	AD 1280 - 1368
MING	AD 1368 - 1644
QING	AD 1644 - 1911

CHINESE HISTORY IN A CAPSULE
4,000 Years in 4 Minutes.

NEOLITHIC CIVILIZATION. Flourished in China before 2000 BC. The Ban Po Village at Xian is an example (see Xian).

XIA DYNASTY. 2205 BC to 1766 BC. China's first dynasty. The first leader was Yu the Great; he began canal construction projects. The remains of a Xia palace dating from 2100 BC have been found in suburbs of Luoyang. The silk industry and a system of writing began during this period.

SHANG DYNASTY. 1766 BC to 1122 BC
Bronze age culture. Weapons were improved. Writing was developed. Silk production and animal husbandry advanced. Astronomy was studied, calendars were made.
Unrest on the frontiers led to the demise of the dynasty.

ZHOU DYNASTY. 1122 BC to 770 BC
Agricultural methods improved. Nature gods were worshipped; the emperor was the high priest.
Barbarian attacks weakened the dynasty.

SPRING AND AUTUMN PERIOD. 770 BC to 476 BC
Named after a famous historical work called the Spring and Autumn Annals that describe this period. Several different states rose and fell. Instability spread. With instability emerged many different schools of thought about society. One philosopher was Master K'ung or K'ung-fu-tze. To us he is Confucius.

WARRING STATES PERIOD. 476 BC to 221 BC
Named after a book describing this period of conflicts in both the heart of the empire and on the borders. In the later years of this period, the Qin State in the west of China became prosperous and rose to power by defeating other states. The leader was Shang Yang. We know him as Qin Shi Huangdi, which means First Emperor of the Qin.

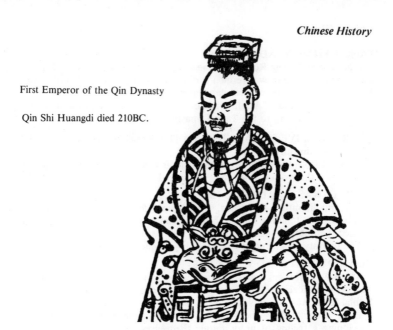

First Emperor of the Qin Dynasty

Qin Shi Huangdi died 210BC.

QIN DYNASTY. 221 BC to 206 BC

China was unified by Qin Shi Huangdi. Coinage and weights and measures were standardised, written language was reformed, length of carriage axles was fixed at a uniform length, walls were linked to form the Great Wall. The terra cotta soldiers to be seen at Xian are part of his burial complex.

His capital was overrun by rebels whose leader established the Han Dynasty.

HAN DYNASTY. 206 BC to AD 220

Unity had already been created by the Qin. The Han strengthened the unity to the extent that today modern Chinese refer to themselves as the Sons of Han or Han Chinese to distinguish themselves from the national minorities.

By establishing the Silk Road the Han developed links with the Roman Empire.

Peasant unrest, high taxes and corruption in the court brought down the empire.

THE SIX DYNASTIES PERIOD. AD 220 - AD 589

This period includes Three Kingdoms period, AD 220 to 265; Jin, AD 265 to 420; and Southern and Northern Dynasties, AD 420 to 589.

There was an attempt at law and order and land reform but unity broke down. Uncertainties and anxieties grew. Northern tribes invaded. The country opened, allowing a greater spread of Buddhism.

SUI DYNASTY. AD 589 to 618

The Grand Canal was built and the Great Wall restored.

Diastrous war campaigns, disenchanted soldiers and peasant revolts caused by poor harvests drove the Sui from power.

TANG DYNASTY. AD 618 to 907

Trade along the Silk Road flourished. Religious tolerance existed. Printing was invented. Culture was refined through its poets, craftsmen and artists. Try to see some Tang classical dancing if you visit Xian.

Unevenly distributed land, rebellious governors and corruption in the court brought an end to the Tang Dynasty.

PERIOD OF FIVE DYNASTIES AND TEN KINGDOMS. AD 907 to 960

Period of disunity.

Invasion from the north occurred, including that of the Khitan (or Khitai) from which the word Cathay may be derived.

SONG DYNASTY. AD 960 to 1280

Art and literature flourished. Science and technology advanced. New techniques of building boats, bridges, drainage canals and locks were devised. Gunpowder was invented.

The dynasty was brought to a close by conquest by the Mongols.

YUAN DYNASTY. AD 1280 to 1368

This was a Mongol dynasty. Trade was encouraged. The Mongol policy was to recruit foreigners. Marco Polo was one of these. The famous emperor Kublai Khan was his employer.

Being dominated by the Mongols resulted in the disenchanted Chinese developing a feeling of unity among themselves. A revolt broke out, the Mongol administration disintegrated and the emperor fled.

MING DYNASTY. AD 1368 to 1644

This was a native Chinese dynasty. Ming means brilliant. Social stability was established. Agricultural productivity expanded. In Beijing, the Ming capital, Imperial palaces were built on terraces of white marble.

The Ming dynasty started to falter. The Japanese were threatening. The Mongols were attacking. The Manchus, a Mongolian people, seizing three provinces north of Beijing. Peasants gradually were being deprived of land by the court. Peasants revolted. Rebel forces attacked Beijing. The last Ming emperor fled to the artificial hill, Jingshan (Coal Hill), and hanged himself. You can also climb the hill. (See map of Beijing).

A Ming general asked the Manchus to help save the empire. The Manchus agreed and came through the Great Wall. They took over the government and established their own dynasty.

QING DYNASTY. AD 1644 to 1911

This foreign dynasty was established by the Manchus from the north. They integrated their method of government with the Ming system; they worked side by side with the Chinese officials but always retained their privileged position. Prosperity rose and fell. European countries forced their way into China to trade.

In the 1840's, peasant unrest grew into the Tai'ping Rebellion which tried, unsuccessfully, to dislodge the Manchus.

Japan attacked and defeated China in 1894 - 95. At the turn of the century the anti-foreigner Boxer Rebellion fomented but was contained.

In 1911 a revolt that erupted in the Yangtze Valley spread quickly and toppled the Manchu dynasty. The hero was Sun Yatsen who became provisional president of the new Chinese Republic.

THE REPUBLIC OF CHINA, 1911 to 1949

A state of confusion reigned in the early years. Internal hostilities occurred between warlords trying to rule their own territories. Trade decreased.

In Russia, Lenin denounced imperialism and encouraged world revolution. His voice was heard in China where, in 1921, the Communist Party of China was formed. Mao Zedong was a founding member. Also in 1921, Sun Yatsen was elected president of the independent Nationalist government which intended to create national unity. A programme of modernisation and education for self-government was to be carried out by the National People's Party, the Guomindang (Kuomintang). The Chinese Communist Party joined it in 1924.

In 1925, Sun Yatsen died of cancer. You can visit his mausoleum in the Purple Mountains near Nanjing.

Chiang Kaishek led the Guomindang, broke with the Communists and expelled them from the Party. Military clashes ensued. The Long March by the Communists started in 1934.

In 1936, when the Japanese were attacking, Chiang Kaishek was captured at Xian and released after agreeing to commit his forces alongside the Communists against the Japanese. (See under Xian; Hua Qing Hot Springs Park).

The Chinese forces did not have much success. World War Two broke out. In 1945 Japan was defeated and its troops in China were pulled out. Both the Guomindang and the Communists wanted to govern; civil war broke out in 1946. The Communists promised land reforms and prosperity during a time when the Nationalists had a record of corruption, disillusioned peasants and inflation. By 1949 the Communists had routed the Nationalists. The Nationalists under Chiang Kaishek fled to Taiwan.

THE PEOPLE'S REPUBLIC OF CHINA

The new republic was declared by Mao Zedong on 1st October 1949 at Beijing's Tiananmen Square. Today, Mao's portrait overlooks the square. It has been placed over the archway of the Tiananmen Gate, the entrance to the Imperial City.

Under the new government land was confiscated from landlords who were executed if the need arose. The land became state-owned.

In 1965 the Cultural Revolution started. The young Red Guards were organized to do away with the old culture. Temples and religious caves were defaced. (Today you will see evidence of the damage being repaired). A little red book on the thoughts of Chairman Mao became required reading. After ten years the revolution wound down. Mao died in September 1976. (In Tiananmen Square you can visit the mausoleum and view his body lying in state).

His wife and three of her cohorts, dubbed "The Gang of Four", and other members of the government were arrested for misdeeds during Mao's administration. Mao's wife, Jiang Qing, has been given a life sentence.

The cult surrounding Mao has declined. The large portraits of Mao that once adorned the city walls have mostly been removed.

BUDDHIST CAVES IN GANSU AND NINGXIA

There are dozens of cave temples or Buddhist caves in China, mostly in the drier areas in the north-central and western regions of the country. The sculpturing of these caves was apparently begun in 366 AD during the Sixteen Kingdoms Period of the Jin Dynasty (265 - 420 AD). The work continued until about the years 841 - 845 AD in the late Tang Dynasty (618 - 907 AD). At that time there was a change of government that resulted in Buddhists being relegated to a lower social status.

China between 1280 and 1368 AD was governed by foreigners, the Mongolians, who established the Yuan Dynasty. As favourable treatment was extended by them to Buddhists, construction of the cave temples continued. The Yuan Dynasty collapsed in 1644 and the Ming Dynasty, one comprising Chinese people, began. Under the Ming Emperor Jia Jing (1522 - 67 AD), China again became intolerant of Buddhist ways and social dominance; this attitude put an end to the Buddhist caves art.

Many of these ancient caves are in the provinces of Gansu and Ningxia, as we see on the map. Most of these have been destroyed by weathering and by man, many of whom were Muslim fanatics. Most of them are being restored or are under the guard of the PLA (People's Liberation Army). Two that are open to foreign travellers include Bingling Si near Lanzhou and the Mogao Grottoes near Dunhuang. Another one which should be open by now is Maijishan, south of Tianshui. This one is ready for tourists but apparently there has not been a hotel of good quality in the vicinity.

The Xumi Shan caves near the town of Guyuan in southern Ningxia has one cave with a statue 19 metres high. Near Zhangye are the Matisi (Horseshoe Temple), and the Qingyang caves near the junction of the Ru and Pu Rivers. The Wenwushan caves are near Juiquan and the Changma caves near Yumen. To the northwest, in the Mogao Group, are the Yulinsi and Anxi caves. The last in the area is the Qianfoya (Thousand Buddha Cave) near South Lake.

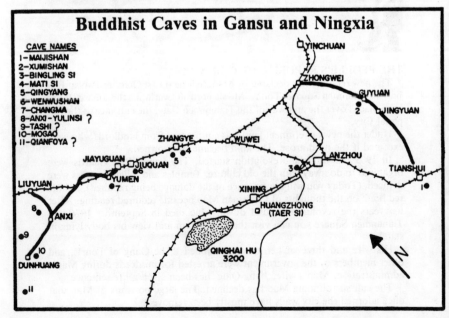

Buddhist Caves in Gansu and Ningxia

CAVE NAMES
1—MAIJISHAN
2—XUMISHAN
3—BINGLING SI
4—MATI SI
5—QINGYANG
6—WENWUSHAN
7—CHANGMA
8—ANXI - YULINSI ?
9—TASHI ?
10—MOGAO
11—QIANFOYA ?

YINCHUAN
ZHONGWEI
GUYUAN
2   JINGYUAN
ZHANGYE   WUWEI
JIAYUGUAN
JIUQUAN 5   LANZHOU
YUMEN   3   TIANSHUI
7   1
LIUYUAN   XINING
8   HUANGZHONG
ANXI   (TAER SI)
9
10   QINGHAI HU
DUNHUANG   3200
11

BUDDHIST CAVES IN XINJIANG

Baijikalika or Thousand Buddha Caves are near Turpan. This site is visited by many tourists who go there by tour bus from Turpan. Included in the same half-day tour are the ruins of Gaochang in the same general area, 30 kms east of Turpan. If there are no other groups going you can form a group of your own at the Turpan Hotel. There are often other travellers around.

Other caves open to the public are the Sanxian Buddhist caves just north of Kashgar. There are only three caves here. One has to be taken there by a guide in a four wheel drive vehicle. A long ladder must be available to reach the caves on the face of a cliff.

Some Buddhist caves in Xinjiang which may open to the public in the future include the Kizil Caves, about 60 kms west of Baicheng. Consisting of 236 caves, they are apparently near a commune named Baicheng. Many of the following caves have wall paintings and are now under government protection: The Toksu caves, near the town of Xinhe or Toksu; the Kumtula caves, numbering about 70, about 30 kms northwest of Kuqa; the 52 caves, part of the Simsim grottos, located 40 kms northeast of Kuqa; the Yanqi caves, near Bosten Hu (Lake); and finally, some caves near the town of Shanshan, east of Turpan.

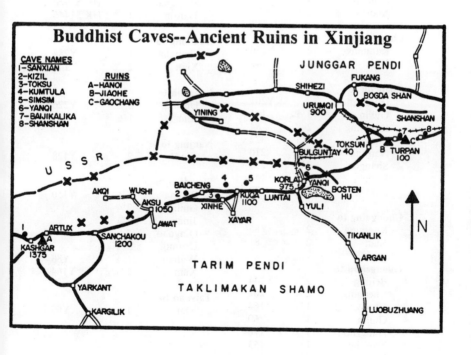

47

TRANSPORTATION

AIR (Duration and fares)

Beijing to

Changsha	2	Y179
Chengdu	2¼	200
Guilin	2½	232
Hangzhou	2	150
Hohhot	1½	55
Jinan	1	52
Kunming	3	361
Nanjing	1½	123
Shanghai	2	150
Tianjin	¾	
Urumqi	4	
Xian	2	

Changsha to

Kunming	2	Y150
Xian	2	145

Chengdu to

Guangzhou	3	Y201
Guilin	3½	141
Kunming	2	84
Lhasa	2¼	322
Nanjing	7½	210
Shanghai	3½	250
Wuhan	2¼	147
Xian	2	79

Chongqing to

Kunming	2½	Y86
Xian	2	81

Guangzhou to

Beijing	2¾	Y244
Chengdu	2¼	201
Chongqing	1¾	164
Guilin	1	60
Hangzhou	1¾	176
Nanjing	1¾	153
Kunming	3¾	163
Shanghai	2	155
Wuhan	1½	106
Xian	4¼	221

Guilin to

Beijing	2¾	Y232
Chengdu	3½	141
Hangzhou	1¾	
Kunming	1½	

Hong Kong to

Beijing	3	HK $1446
Guangzhou	½	HK $ 297
Hangzhou	1½	HK $ 925
Kunming	3	HK $ 976
Shanghai	2	HK $ 960
Tianjin	3	HK $1446

Kunming to

Shanghai	4	Y284
Xian	2	149

Lanzhou to

Urumqi	3	Y226
Xian	1½	63

Nanjing to

Xian	2	Y128

Shanghai to

Beijing	1¾	Y150
Guilin	2¼	
Jinan	3¼	
Qingdao	2	
Urumqi	5½	
Wuhan	1½	Y88
Xian	2¾	Y164

Taiyuan to

Xian	1½	Y69

BICYCLES

You can cycle independently without restriction in areas open to foreigners, not only within cities, but between cities.

TAKING YOUR OWN BICYCLE: You can take your own bicycle into China without having to pay a tax. Your problem will be obtaining spare parts, if the need arises.

RENTING A BICYCLE: You can rent a bicycle to pedal around a city or you can rent for a longer period to cycle between cities. However, you must return the bicycle to the city in which you rented it. The cost of rent for, say, two months, could equal the cost of outright purchase.

BUYING A BICYCLE: In Hong Kong you could buy a bicycle for between HK $500 and $600. You can buy a new bicycle in China for Y160 to Y230, depending on the equipment it has. Then just get out on the road and go. If you get tired, ride to a train station and take a train. If you are considering cycling, plan ahead and bring from home special packs or saddle bags for carrying luggage on bicycles. Pack sacks which fit 10 speed bikes should also fit Chinese bikes. Consider also taking a sleeping bag and tent.

BICYCLE TOURS

Travelling on a pre-arranged bicycle tour is becoming more popular. You can take your own bicycle or rent one in China. We suggest renting one. After cycling in one area, the group will fly or travel by train to another area for more cycling. Those who have rented bicycles do not have to take the bicycles with them; they will be given new ones at the new destination. Those who have taken their own will have to box them when they fly.

Common sense dictates that you should be reasonably fit as you will ride about 35km a day. A bus travels with the group in case you get tired. Luggage is carried on the bus. Hotel accommodation is used. If rain disrupts the itinerary, sightseeing will be done by bus and outdoor activities will be substituted by indoor tours.

The bicycle tours vary from 13 days to 22 days; daily costs average about US$90. They are arranged through the All-China Sports Federation by China Passage, Inc., 302 Fifth Avenue, New York, N.Y. 10001, USA. (Telephone 212-564-4099). The Hong Kong office is China Passage Ltd. 43-55 Wyndham Street, Room 103, Hong Kong. (Telephone 5-250964). From China Passage you can find out who their General Sales Agent is in your country. However, some addresses are:

CANADA: WestCan Treks Ltd., 10918 - 88th Ave., Edmonton, Alberta, T6G 0Z1, Tel: (403) 439-0024, Also at WestCan Treks Ltd., Vancouver, Calgary, Toronto

GREAT BRITAIN: Exodus Expeditions, All Saints Passage, 100 Wandsworth High St., London, SW18 4LE. Tel: 01-870-0151

AUSTRALIA: Peregrine Expeditions, Suite 710, 343 Little Collins St., Melbourne, Victoria 3000. Tel: (03) 60 1121

BOATS

Chongqing - Wuhan	3 days, 2 nights (58 hours). Through the Yangtse River Gorges. Leaves 0700 daily. Second Class Y101.50 Third Class Y37.20 Fourth Class Y25.80
Dalian - Yantai	Daily boats.
Guangzhou - Wuzhou	20 hours on the Pearl River - Y4.80, includes sleeping accommodation. Because you travel during daylight hours you will see the river and riverside life.
Guilin - Yangshuo	6 hours, Li River. Tourist trip, Y60. Trip on Chinese tour, Y25. Both include lunch and return by bus.
Hong Kong - Guangzhou	3 hours by hydrofoil.
Hong Kong - Macao	1 hour by hydrofoil.
Hong Kong - Wuzhou	10 hours (bypass Guangzhou).
Hong Kong - Xiamen	22 hours.
Ningbo - Putuo Shan	5 hours. Y3.80. This boat leaves Ningbo at 0700 daily, arrives at 1200 on Putuo Shan Island. (Putuo Shan is one of the nine sacred mountains in China).
Shanghai - Dalian	2nd class, Y39; 3rd class, Y15.
Shanghai - Fuzhou	16 hours. 3rd class Y27; 5th class Y15 (similar to hard class on trains).
Shanghai - Hong Kong	3 day trip, Y90.
Shanghai - Putuo Shan	Overnight, daily.
Suzhou - Hangzhou	13½ hours. Y2.05 for a seat; Y4.10 for a bunk in a quad room. Boat travels man-made Grand Canal. Overnight trip. Departs 1730, arrives 0700 next day.
Wuxi - Suzhou	3½ hours.

BUSES

DURATION OF JOURNEY (In Hours)

Antu - Erdao	5 hours (near North Korea).
Beijing - Great Wall	1½ hours.
Dunhuang - Liuyuan	2½ hours.
Guangzhou - Foshan	1 hour.
Guangzhou - Guilin	40 hours (includes overnight in Wuzhou).
Guangzhou - Seven Star Crags	3½ hours.
Jiuquan - Dunhuang	10 hours.
Kashgar (Kashi) - Urumqi	3 days, 2 nights. Nights are usually at Karazolgun and Kuqa.
Kunming - Dali	2 days, with an overnight stop.
Kunming - Shilin	3 hours.
Luoyang - Dengfeng	2½ hours.
Macau - Zhongshan	1½ hours.
Seven Star Crags - Foshan	2½ hours.
Turpan - Urumqi	5 hours.
Urumqi - Kashgar	3½ days, 3 nights spent enroute, usually at Yanqi, Xinhe, and Sanchakou.
Urumqi - Tian Chi	3 - 3½ hours.
Wuzhou - Yangshuo	8 hours (near Guilin).
Xian - Yan'an	2 days with an overnight stop at Huangling.
Yangshuo - Guilin	1½ hours.
Zhongshan - Foshan	5 hours.
Zhongshan - Seven Star Crags	4½ hours.

NOTE: On bus rides of only a few hours duration, luggage space is limited. Sometimes you may have to carry your pack on your knees. If that is a problem, there may be space near the driver. Buses going on very long trips, such as those from Urumqi to Kashgar, have luggage racks on top. But in this case, the up-top luggage stays on top for the duration (3 or 4 days!), safely tied down, day and night. On the Urumqi-Kashgar trip, carry a small second pack or bag with items you need for the duration of the bus ride.

TRAINS

Travelling by train is the most economical way of seeing China. There are two train fares in China, one for the Chinese and one for foreign visitors which is 70% higher. As Chinese workers contribute to the economy of their socialist state the Government subsidizes fares for them. Some travellers ask local Chinese to buy their tickets and so pay the lower price. Be warned that a conscientious conductor on the train can demand from you the extra money due. Chinese officials stress that they do not want individual travellers to flaunt the system. It could jeopardize future travel for individuals.

Types of Trains

Trains are numbered.

1 to 100 — Express trains.

101 to 400 — Normal express (slower).

401 and up — Slow.

Chinese trains leave on time.

Class of Service

Soft Seat — Comfortable seat in a first-class carriage.

Soft Sleeper — A bunk in a four-berth compartment. The compartment door can be closed.

Hard Seat — Travel with the proletariat.

Hard Sleeper — A bunk in a six-berth compartment. The bunks are open to passers-by in the passage, hence no privacy. We always travelled hard class. A sleeper is charged by the distance you have it for. An overnight trip would cost about Y10 in addition to the basic seat fare. Warm quilts are provided.

China Railway Timetable

This small booklet at Y0.50 is invaluable. Written in Chinese and English, it contains all the country's schedules, is easy to read and is updated periodically. It precludes you from having to ask help from CITS or from someone else who speaks English.

Booking A Train

Either your hotel will book it, CITS will book it or you will book it yourself at the train station. When booking through CITS you pay in FEC notes and a fee of Y2. All tickets sold at stations where the train begins its journey will have the train number, the coach number, seat number, date of departure and destination.

Do not discard your train ticket during your journey; you must show it when you leave the station.

You can only buy train tickets to take you to your next destination. Onward transportation from there cannot be pre-booked.

You can save time by taking night trains.

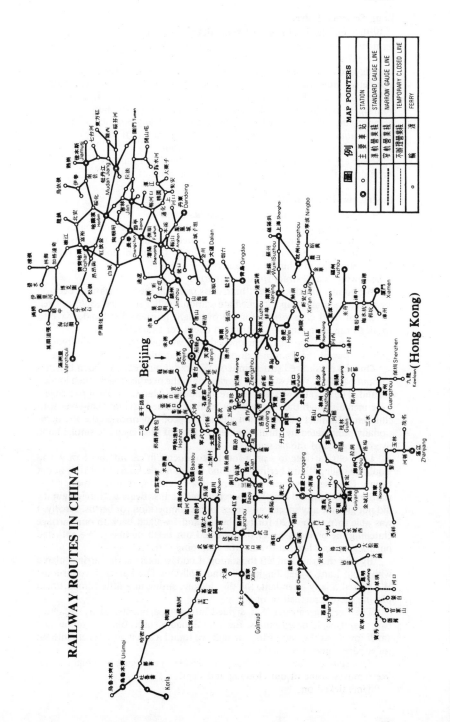

RAILWAY ROUTES IN CHINA

Long Distance Travel

With your "point to point" train ticket you can disembark at any intermediate station then board the next train, say, 24 hours later. For a journey that would normally take 24 hours non-stop, you are allowed about four days to cover the distance. The longer the journey, the less the fare is per kilometre. However, when you disembark you lose your seat reservation. When you board the next train you can only hope for a seat. It is easier on yourself to buy your original ticket on an express train (numbered 1 - 100) because you will be entitled to reboard a train of any number. If you buy your original ticket for a slow, high numbered train (401 and up) you will have to pay surcharges to travel on a faster train.

Before approaching the ticket window use the China Railway Timetable to write down the destination, train number and class of seat.

Buying Hard Class Berths

The following information applies to hard class.

You cannot always be issued a hard sleeper number before boarding the train. You must arrange this with the conductor on the train who has a desk usually in Car No. 9, but sometimes Car No. 8. To find his location, refer to our question list in Chinese characters.

Following is an extract from our journal.

"We bought our tickets for "hard class *seats*" at the train station. Because we were boarding at an intermediate station the ticket office could not sell tickets for hard class *berths* for the overnight journey. We would have to speak to the attendant on the train to check for availability.

"The gates to the platform opened and we coverged with hundreds of Chinese toward the train in a disorganized scramble.

"Our tickets showed seat numbers. We found our seats, wooden benches without padding. We tossed our luggage onto the overhead racks then looked around. The carriage was a sea of green and blue Mao suits. Most passengers were men although there were a few women, some busying themselves with children. Murmurs of more than a hundred people permeated the air, occasionally punctuated by shrill laughter. A haze of blue cigarette smoke hung over the heads of the passengers.

"I left our carriage to search for the conductor in car number 8 or 9 who would be selling "hard berths". I found him at his desk surrounded by about twenty Chinese passengers clamouring for attention, thrusting money forward in an attempt to buy the few remaining berths. Being a "foreign guest" did not give me any special privileges in this competition for berths. Finally, I was able to pay the Y20 for two berths and I walked back to our carriage clutching the precious paper that showed our berth numbers. We gathered our luggage and headed toward the "sleeping carriage".

"By now the train had left the station. Loud speakers in the carriage blared with Auld Lang Syne, Jingle Bells and Roll Out The Barrel. Incongruous! We passed a lady attendant, the disc jockey, sitting in a little compartment playing these scratched records.

"The sleeping carriage was divided into compartments, each containing two sets of triple-tiered bunks. Each bunk had a sheet, blanket, pillow and small towel. At the end of the carriage we found a squat-type toilet (without toilet paper) and wash basins.

"This style of travel is not really conducive to changing into night attire. We removed some of our clothing and slept.

"Time ticked on.

"At lunch time the next day an attendant came through the carriage selling meal tickets for 50 fen. Along with almost everyone else we bought tickets. Half an hour later lunch boxes were handed out consisting of rice, vegetables and slices of pork fat. It was hot and tasty. We ate the lunch sitting on our bunks.

"During our exploration of the train we discovered a dining car. For our evening meal we dined there with a bottle of local wine.

"During the journey the carriage attendant swept the compartment floors and refilled vacuum flasks with hot water.

"As we neared our destination the attendant advised us, giving about half an hour's advance warning."

Footnote: When trying to buy a hard berth be persistent, even after the attendant says all have been sold. Persistence pays off with success.

TRAINS (in hours)

Beijing to

Datong	8
Guilin	40
Hohhot	14
Nanjing	19
Shanghai	21
Tianjin	1½
Xian	21

Chengdu to

Chongqing	12
Kunming	23
Xian	20

Datong to

Hohhot	5
Taiyuan	7

Guangzhou to

Beijing	34
Guilin	21
Hangzhou	29
Hong Kong	3
Shanghai	33

Guilin to

Hangzhou	27
Kunming	31
Nanning	7
Shanghai	30
Wuhan	18

Hangzhou to

Nanjing	8
Suzhou	5
Wuxi	5½

Kaifeng to

Nanjing	11
Zhenzhou	1¼

Nanjing

Luoyang	14
Shanghai	5
Suzhou	3
Wuxi	3

Luoyang to

Zhenzhou	2
Xian	7

Shanghai to

Hangzhou	3½
Suzhou	1½
Wuxi	2¼

Suzhou to

Wuxi	¾

Taiyuan to

Xian	12

HOTELS

You must stay in tourist hotels or in hotels designated for Overseas Chinese.

The staff at a hotel not accepting foreigners will direct you to one that will. A clerk may even phone ahead to insure you will have a bed. Hotels for foreigners usually will have an English speaking employee, a CITS office, post office facilities and a money exchange.

Checking into a hotel

Request a dormitory or share a room. A dormitory may be a room with three, four or ten beds with each bed costing about Y6. Sometimes there are separate dorms for men and women; sometimes the same dorm is shared. The shared bathroom is usually squat-style (with a hole in the floor). If a hotel does not have shower facilities it will have a wash room with water and buckets. Fill the bucket, take it into a toilet stall and wash down.

If the reception desk staff tells you the hotel is full, don't go away. Insist, be patient and wait. Tell them that you are prepared to sleep on the floor if need be. They will find a place for you, be it on a mattress in a conference room or in a hallway. Carry your sleeping sheet for such an eventuality.

Most hotels have rooms of different grades. You can choose a twin or double room with facilities for Y14 to Y20 per person per night. Soap and toilet paper are provided. The toilet is a Western style "sitter".

Tea And Coffee

Vacuum flasks of hot water are always available in hotels. Chinese green tea can be bought in shops; black tea as known in the West is virtually unobtainable. Carry your own green or black tea, or coffee.

Some large hotels in major cities will serve a Western style breakfast of eggs, toast, tea/coffee.

Booking trains

Some hotels will book your train ticket.

Renmin hotel in Xian, an example of Russian architecture (J)

HOTELS

City	Hotel (Binguan)	Cost Per Person	How To Get There
A			
Anshan	Anshan	Y15-Y20	Any trolley going east; 1 km.
Antu	Di Er	Y5-Y10	Walk 2 kms east, then north.
Anyang	Anyang	Y15-Y20	
B			
Baotou	Dong Li	Y6	Bus 5 from the train station.
Beidaihe	Several hotels; various prices		
Beijing	Qiao Yuan	Y8	Bus 20 from train station; or bus 106 from the Chongwenmen Hotel, then walk west for 1 km
Beijing	Guang Hua	Y10	Bus 9 from train station.
C			
Changchun	Chun Yi	Y20	Across the square from train station.
Changsha	Xiang Jiang	Y5	Bus 1 from the train station.
Chengde	Chengde	Y20	Bus 5 or 7 from train station.
Chengdu	Jin Jiang	Y9	Bus 16 from train station.
Chongqing	Renmin	Y4	Walk up hill from train station, then bus 15, then walk 1 km.
Chongqing	Chongqing	Y6-Y8	Walk up hill from train station, then bus 1.
D			
Dalian	Dung Feng	Y5-Y15	Walk from train station.
Daqing	Daqing Dong Feng	Y15-Y20	Bus 5 from train station.
Datong	You Yi	Y6	Bus 15 from train station.
Dazu		Y6	
Dengfeng	Song Shan	Y18	Walk 1 km east from bus station. (Cheaper rooms should be available).
Dunhuang	Dunhuang	Y5	Walk 1 km east from the bus stop or the bus station.
Dunhuang	Zhou de Soa	Y4	Walk south from the bus stop; but walk north from bus station.
E			
Emei	Emei	Y3	Bus from train station, then stop in town centre.
Erdao	Ba Ho Ge	Y7	Walk 2 kms south of the bus station or 4 kms south of the train station.
Erdao	Man Y	Y4	300 metres south of railway station. No showers. Toilet is outside.
F			
Foshan	One hotel		
Fushun			
Fuzhou	Hua Zhou	Y8	Bus 2 from bus or train station.

Hotels

G

Gongxian	Gongxian	Y12	Walk south 2 kms from train station.
Guangzhou	Liu Hua	Y8	Opposite Guangzhou train station.
Guangzhou	Railway Station Hotel		Beside the Liu Hua.
Guangzhou	Na Fang Mansion		49 Yanjiang Rd.
Guangzhou	Shengli		54 Shamian St.
Guangzhou	Dongfang		Xicun Highway
Guangzhou	Renmin Daxia		207 Changdi Road
Guangzhou	Huanqiao Daxia (Overseas Chinese Mansion)		Haizhu Square
Guangzhou	Shamian Guest House		52 South Shamian Avenue
Guangzhou	Baiyun Guesthouse		Huashi Rd. E.
Guilin	Osmanthus	Y5	Bus 11 or 3 north from train station.
Guilin	Hidden Hill	Y7	Walk north 3 or 4 minutes from train station.
Guilin	Guilin		Bus 11 or 3 north from train station.
Guilin	Lijiang		Bus 11 or 3 northwards from train station. Get off at Fir Lake and walk to hotel, 1 km.

H

Haikou	Hua Zhou	Y4-Y8	
Handan	Handan	Y8	Take motor rickshaw.
Hangzhou	Hangzhou	Y5	Bus 7 from the train station.
Hangzhou	Huagang	Y4-Y6	Bus 7 from train station, then bus 4.
Harbin	Guo Ji	Y20	Take any trolley south from train station.
Harbin	Hua Zhou	Y18	Take any trolley south from train station, or walk to either of the above hotels.
Hohhot	Xin Xi	Y3	Walk 25 minutes from train station, or possibly find a taxi.
Hohhot	Hohhot	Y8	From train station walk two blocks east, then two blocks south.
Huang Zhong	Huang Zhong	Y4	Across the street from the bus stop.
Huang Zhong	Taer Si	Y7	Walk south up the hill from the bus stop to the Taer Si (temple).

J

Jiamusi	Jiamusi	Y18	Walk 1 km northwest from the train station.
Jiayuguan	Jiayuguan	Y5	Bus from train station to city centre.
Jilin	Xiguan	Y8	Bus 1 from train station, then walk 1 km south.
Jiuquan	Jiuquan	Y3-Y8	Bus from train station to city centre.

K

Kaifeng	Kaifeng	Y20	Bus 5 from train station.
Kaifeng	Bian Jing	Y4-Y6	Bus 3 from train station.
Kashgar	Xin Binguan	Y4	Walk 30 minutes from bus station, or take donkey cart.

HOTELS

City	Hotel (Binguan)	Cost Per Person	How To Get There
Kunming	Kun Hu	Y3.50	Bus 2 or 23 from train station, or walk north for 5 to 10 minutes.
Kunming	Kunming	Y12	Bus 2 or 23 north from train station, then walk east 5 minutes.
L			
Lanzhou	You Yi	Y6	Bus 1 from the train station.
Leshan	3 hotels	Y3-Y9	Just west of bus station, near DA FU.
Lhasa	Di Er	Y5	In the old part of Lhasa. Take CITS bus from airport.
Lhasa	Di San	Y200	In the new part of Lhasa. Take CITS bus from airport.
Luoyang	You Yi	Y4-Y6	Bus 2 from train station.
M			
Mudanjiang	Mudanjiang	Y21	From train station, turn left (north) and walk 10 minutes.
N			
Nanjing	Shengli	Y6	Bus 1 or 33 from train station.
Nanjing	Ding Shan	Y8	Bus 1 or 33 from train station, then bus 16, then walk 1 km.
Nanjing	Nanjing	Y15-Y20	Bus 33 from the train station, then bus 16.
Nanning	Yong Jiang	Y7	Bus 5 from the train station.
Ningbo	Hua Qiao	Y15	Walk half a km (5 minutes) from the train station.
Q			
Qingdao	Zhanqiao (Hua Zho)	Y12	Walk 5 minutes east from the train station.
Qingdao	Huiquan		Bus 6 from the train station.
Qiqihar	One hotel		
Qufu	Kong Family Residence	Y15	Bus from Yanzhou, but get off one stop after the Qufu bus station.
S			
Sanmenxia	One hotel		
Shanghai	Pu Jiang	Y6	Bus 65 from the train station.
Shanghai	Jin Jiang	Y6	Bus 41 from the train station.
Shanhaiguan	Shanhaiguan	Y4-Y6	Walk northwest along the city's main street for 1 km to the southeast gate of the city.
Shaoxing	Shaoxing	Y5	Walk from the train station.
Shenyang	Liaoning	Y15-Y18	Trolley bus 6 from the train station.
Shihezi	Shihezi		
Shijiazhuang	Shijiazhuang	Y18	Bus 6 from the train station.
Shilin	Shilin	Y4	Walk 200 metres from the bus stop.
Suzhou	Suzhou	Y5	Bus 2 from train station, then transfer to bus 4.
Suzhou	Nanlin	Y8	Bus 2 from train station, then walk or transfer to bus 4.
Suzhou	Lexiang	Y8	Bus 1 from train station.

Hotels

T

Taiyuan	Yingze	Y15-Y18	Take any bus going west from the train station along the main street. Or walk 10 minutes.
Taiyuan	Bingzhou		Walk west from the train station, then turn south, or left.
Tianjin	Tianjin		Take trolley 96 or bus 13 from train station.
Tianjin	Di Yi		Trolley 96 or bus 13 from train station.
Tianshui	New hotel		
Turpan	Turpan	Y4	Walk east, then south - about 10 minutes.

U

Urumqi	Bei Hua Zhun	Y4.50	Bus 8 from train station.
Urumqi	Hua Zhou	Y4	Bus 10 from the train station, then bus 7, or walk south.

W

Wuhan	Jianghan	Y6	Walk south from the train station or bus 30 from boat docks.
Wuhan	Aiguo	Y7	Bus 30 from boat docks or walk from train station.
Wuhan	Shengli	Y6	Bus 30 from the boat docks or walk from train station.
Wuxi	CITS	Y6	Walk from train station.
Wuxi	Taihu	Y6	Bus 2 from the train station.
Wuxi	Liyuan		Bus 2 from the train station.
Wuzhou	Wuzhou	Y2.50	Walk 30 minutes from the boat dock or the bus station.

X

Xiamen	Hua Zhou	Y5	Bus 1 from the train station. Or walk from the bus station. Or walk from the ferry terminal.
Xian	Jiefang	Y6-Y8	Southeast of the train station, 100 metres.
Xian	Renmin	Y14	Bus 3 from the train station.
Xian	Bell Tower		Bus 3 from the train station
Xilinhot	Xilinhot	Y10	
Xining	Xining	Y6	Bus 9, or hotel bus, from the train station.

Y

Yan'an	One hotel		
Yangshuo	Yangshuo	Y5	Walk 3 minutes from bus stop.
Yangzhou	Liuyang	Y9	Near city centre.
Yantai	Yantaishan		
Yantai	Zhifu		
Yichun	One hotel.		
Yinchuan	Yi Soua	Y6	Bus 1 from the train station.

Z

Zhangzhou	Zhangzhou	Y6	Walk south a km from the train station.
Zhengzhou	Er Yue Che	Y5	Bus 2 from the train station, or walk the km to the hotel.
Zhongwei	Zhongwei	Y7	Walk the one km south from the train station.

ANSHAN 鞍山

The city of Anshan, famous for its iron and steel production, is located in the southeast part of Liaoning Province on the main rail line between Shenyang and Dalian. The population of Anshan is over one million. The steel complex is one of the biggest in China. Anshan's (Saddle Mountain) iron resources have been exploited since the Western Han Dynasty (206 BC - 220 AD). There is one hotel in Anshan. Get there from the station by taking any trolley bus going in an easterly direction. Alight after about three stops, or near the large traffic circle. There are no cheap rooms in this hotel so plan to pay Y18 or Y20 a night for a bed.

East of Anshan are the QIAN SHAN with many canyons and peaks, streams and temples. There is also the Thousand Hills Sanatorium, built in 1949. In front of the train station look for Bus 8 which leaves every half hour or so; it takes about 45 minutes to reach the mountains' base. You walk into the mountains from the bus stop. See the hiking section and the Qian Shan map for more details.

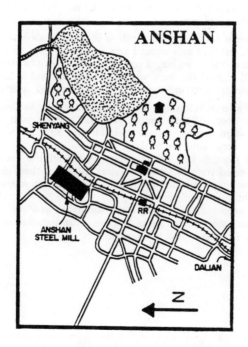

ANTU 安圖

LOCATION AND TRANSPORTATION: Antu is a small town in the eastern part of the province of Jilin, which is in the northeast of China. Many of us in the west know this region as Manchuria but the Chinese call it the Dong Bei, or North East. You will need permission to go to Antu; permission is given to Antu County which includes all of eastern Jilin Province. The places you will want to visit are Antu town and Changbai Shan and Tumen, both on the North Korean border. See the hiking section in this book for details on how to reach and climb Changbai Shan, an enormous volcanic crater.

Getting to Antu (on some maps it is referred to as Mingyuegou) is by train only. It is on the rail line running between Jilin and Tumen. Train 433 arrives at Antu at 0458 while Train 431, also from Jilin, arrives at 1622. Both of these trains go on to the North Korean border town of Tumen where you can walk to the border and view the river separating the two countries. To return to Jilin, leave Antu at 0934 or 2022 on Trains 432 or 434.

If you are heading for Changbai Shan there are several buses each morning leaving Antu, bound for Erdo (pronounced Ardo). There are about five buses daily, all of which leave before noon. Buy your ticket at the bus station the day before if you can.

HOTEL: The one hotel in town is the Di Ar Binguan. Walk out of the station and turn east, left, and walk about 2 kms as shown on the map. The cost is Y5 a bed in a double room but, if you want to be sure to be alone the room will cost Y10. In 1985 the toilet was outside and you had to take a bucket bath in the laundry room (no showers). The hotel is clean, quiet and restful.

SIGHTS: Of interest in this town are the Korean people. As Koreans sit and sleep on the floors of their homes, you must remove your shoes when entering. In warm weather you can see inside the homes as you wander the streets. Also conspicuous are the large chimneys in front of the homes. In cold weather Koreans light fires in pit stoves beneath the floors, thus the rooms are heated from beneath the floors. Many of these chimneys are simply hollowed out logs which rise to about seven or eight metres, and are a common sight.

Korean women usually have different hair styles, wear different clothes and carry their babies in chest packs. It is one of the more interesting parts of China if you are interested in minority peoples.

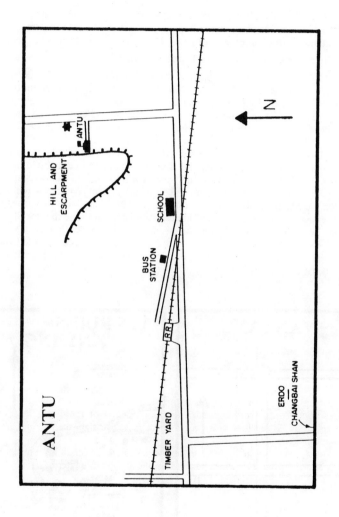

ANYANG 安阳

LOCATION AND TRANSPORTATION: Anyang is located in the extreme north of Henan Province, on the Beijing-Quangzhou railway line. It is about two hours north of Zhengzhou by rail. Many trains pass each day.

HOTEL: The hotel is called the Taihang Binguan.

SIGHTS: Anyang was the capital of the Middle Kingdom (Zhong Gua) or China, during the Shang Dynasty (1766 - 1122 BC) roughly between the dates 1300 to 1066 BC. Its name at that time was Yin but, when this city was destroyed at the beginning of the Zhou Dynasty (1122 - 770 BC), it was rebuilt at a slightly different location. At a later date it was named Anyang.

The WENFENG DA SI is an interesting pagoda-shaped structure built in 952 AD in the Five Dynasties Period (907 - 960 AD). This temple, octagonal in shape, stands 38 metres high and is one of the more unique buildings in China. The Wenfeng Da Si is within walking distance of the railway station, as shown. The Yin ruins found northwest of the present city are the remains of the old Shang capital from the 13th century BC. They were unearthed in this century. From excavations of imperial tombs it was found that the Shang rulers were buried along with slaves, dogs and horses. In recent years fourteen imperial tombs have been found as well as remains of the old living quarters and an industrial area of that time. Today there is a museum in the middle of this historic site.

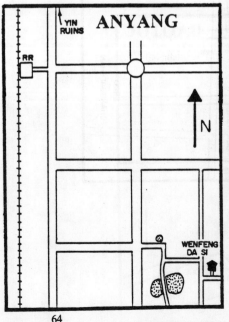

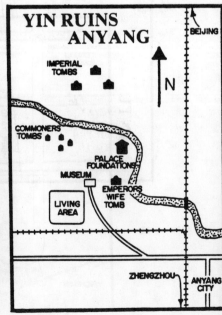

BAOTOU 包 头

LOCATION AND TRANSPORTATION: Baotou is located in the Nei Mongol (Inner Mongolia) Autonomous Region and is about 4 hours by train west of Hohhot, and about 17 hours from Beijing. Going West, it is about a 10 hour train ride to Yinchuan in Ningxia. Be sure and get off the train at the BAOTOU DONG ZHAN (Baotou East Station).

HOTEL: The only hotel in town is the Dong Li Binguan. To get there from the train station take bus 5, or walk. The distance is not that great. There are triple rooms for Y6 a bed.

SIGHTS: Baotou is a large industrial city in Nei Mongol. It is the largest city in the province and one of the most important steel manufacturing centres in all of China. The Chinese often refer to it as the "steel city on the prairie". Tours of the steel mills and nearby coal mines could be arranged by CITS at the Dong Li Hotel, if this is your interest.

The main reason most tourists stop at Baotou is to see the Tibetan-style monastery of WUDANGZHAO. This monastery was built in 1749 during the Qing Dynasty (1644 - 1911 AD) and is today an active Buddhist lamasery with many monks. To get there take the daily 0700 bus from the bus station, located just in front of the East Baotou Station. This ride takes about 2½ hours. The bus actually stops at a small village about 1 km south of the monastery, then you walk. The same bus that takes you there returns in the late afternoon but, if you are in a hurry, you can get a ride back to Baotou on other vehicles. One can also look into the possibility of getting onto a round-trip tour bus to Wudangzhao by CITS at the hotel. It is also a possibility that you might stay overnight at the monastery, especially if you can communicate in Putonghua or Chinese (Putonghua actually means common language).

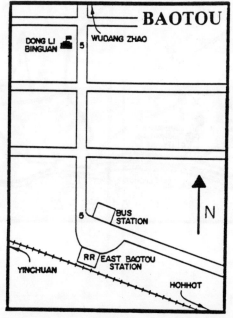

BEIDAIHE　北戴河

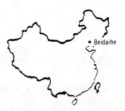

Beidaihe is a beach resort town located on the Bo Hai (Bo Sea) directly east of Beijing. It takes about 6 hours by fast train from Beijing to Beidaihe. Since it is on the main rail line connecting Beijing with the northeast of China, you can also stop here if you are coming from the northeast or Manchuria.

The three-city complex of Beidaihe-Qinhuangdao-Shanhaiguan, along a 90 km stretch of ocean is usually included as one area. Beidaihe boasts 10 kms of beaches and an assortment of hotels. As there are buses connecting the three-city complex it is easy to get around the area. Beidaihe is a popular weekend resort for both Chinese and foreign diplomats residing in Beijing. While there, remember that the eastern end of the Great Wall of China is at Shanhaiguan, just to the northeast of this town.

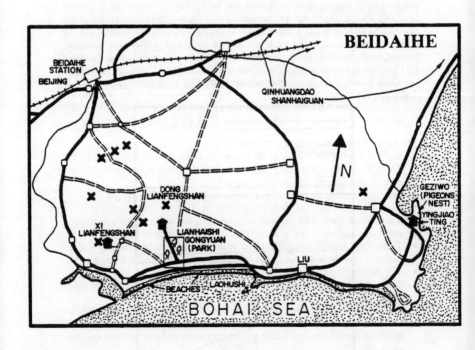

BEIJING 北京

LOCATION AND TRANSPORTATION: Beijing of course is the capital of The Peoples Republic of China or, as they say, Zhong Gua (Middle Kingdom). This city is located in the north of China. It is one of three city-states in China, the others being Tianjin and Shanghai. Each of these three has the same status as a province, but are under the control of the central government. Beijing has the busiest railway station in China. Foreigners have to buy their tickets in the special ticket office set aside for them. In this station you always pay in FEC notes and never have a chance to buy tickets at the people's price.

HOTEL: The cheapest hotel in Beijing is now the QIAO YUAN, located near the south railway station. It has a small CITS office, bank, and restaurant. It has large dorm rooms; each bed costs Y8 a night. Triple rooms are Y27, or Y9 each. To reach the Qiao Yuan, take bus 20 from the main railway station then walk west for half a km. However, if it is your first trip to Beijing, first go to the Chongwenmen Hotel near the main railway station. Ask for a room reservation for your chosen hotel from the CITS office located in the southern part of the hotel. Otherwise, you may be sent back to this office to make a reservation. It if is late, and the main CITS office is closed (open from 0900 to 1200, 1330 to 1700), go straight to the Qiao Yuan. If it is your second time to Beijing go straight to your hotel. Take bus 106 from the Chongwenmen to the Qiao Yuan. You can also try the Guanghua or Jiangua Hotels in the eastern part of town. Take bus 4 from near the station.

SIGHTSEEING IN BRIEF

* See the *Forbidden City* and *Jingshan*. Outside the northern gate of the Forbidden City is the man-made hill called *Jingshan* (Coal Hill). The top affords viewing of sunrises and sunsets.
* See the *Summer Palace,* 11 km north of the city. (颐和园)
* Visit Tiantan Park for *Temple Of Heaven* (Bus No. 39, southward).
* Visit *Beihei Park* with its lake, temples and the white dagoba erected in commemoration of the visit of the fifth Dalai Lama in 1652.
* To visit the *Mao Zedong Memorial Hall* and the *underground city* (escape tunnels) you must go on a tour. Contact CITS, Y5 and Y3 respectively.
* The Beijing Zoo has pandas.
* Take a tour to the *Great Wall* and *Ming Tombs,* 65 km and 50 km north of Beijing respectively.
* Opera, ballet and acrobats tickets are available from CITS, Y2. If they are sold out go to the theatre and try your luck. Some seats, we understand, are held for unexpected visits by dignitaries. You may get one of these seats.
* Bicycles can be hired over the road from the Friendship Store. You may have to leave your passport as security.
  You cannot cycle across Tian'anmen Square. (天安门)

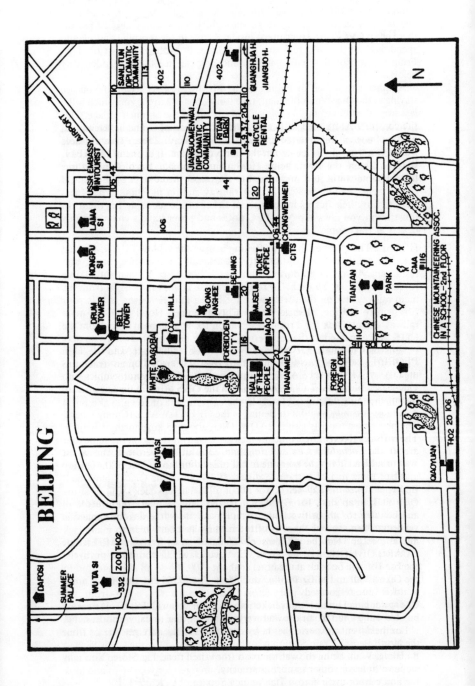

SIGHTS: A popular place to visit in Beijing is the FORBIDDEN CITY. The buildings are mostly 18th and 19th century restorations. This place is huge and takes at least half a day to go through. Do not worry about lunch as there are places where you can eat inside. Arrive in the morning and plan to spend most of the day. Just outside the city walls to the north is Coal Hill. From the top of this man-made mound one can see the Forbidden City below.

Another site to see in Beijing is the SUMMER PALACE. If you are staying at the Qiao Yuan Binguan, take trolley bus 102 to the zoo which is the last stop, then board bus 332 which ends its run at the Summer Palace. This site consists of a number of temples and other buildings. The best temple is on top of a small hill, overlooking a man-made lake. Inside are several places where you can buy lunch or snacks. An impressive sight is the MARBLE BOAT. It does not float, but is great for photos. Because of the long bus rides, plan an early start and expect to stay most of the day.

天坛

Temple of Heaven, Tiantan Park

Other sites include TIANANMEN SQUARE and the HALL OF THE PEOPLE located adjacent to each other. Bus 20 is a good one to reach this area. Also, TIANTAN PARK is worth the visit. It has several temples with blue-glazed tile roofs. Talk to the people in the CITS office in the Qiao Yuan, one of the most helpful offices in China.

A must for most visitors to Beijing is the GREAT WALL (Chong Chen). The place most tourists visit is BADALING, about 65 kms north of Beijing. The MING LING (Ming Tombs) which are usually included in the same tour are 50 kms away. When considering time, costs and convenience, the easiest way to see Badaling is to take one of the many tour buses. One of the easiest and best tours to join is the one run by CITS out of the Qiao Yuan Hotel. Buy your ticket the day before for about Y11. The bus picks you up at the Qiao Yuan at about 0730 or 0800. You will go to Badaling for the Great Wall and be there for about two hours. You can buy food there from numerous vendors. Then the bus takes you to the Ming Tombs, which to many lack interest, except for the columns of animals known as the "IMPERIAL GUARD OF HONOR", or "Spirit Way", which will be your first stop at the tombs. You will be back at the hotel at about 1700. To do an alternate tour to the Great Wall and Ming Tombs which costs about Y9, buy your ticket from a ticket booth located just across the street to the north from the Chongwenmen Hotel. However, to join this tour you will first have to take a bus from the Qiao Yuan or wherever you are staying to catch this bus.

For the adventurous traveller here is an idea. Take an afternoon train from the North Beijing Train Station (or a bus, or hitch hike) to the Great Wall at Badaling. Walk along the wall to one of the watch towers and sleep the night alone without any other tourists. In the morning, retrace your steps and look for a ride back to Beijing. Hitching in China can be great.

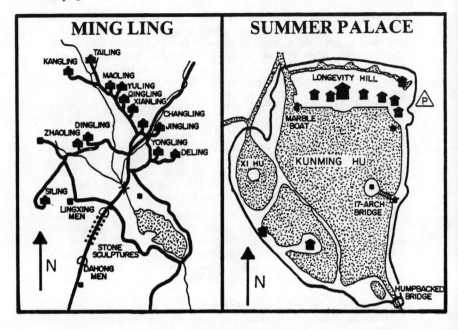

THE MAO ZEDONG MEMORIAL HALL

This hall stands on Tian'anmen Square. To enter you should be conservatively dressed. Shorts, thongs and bright colours are frowned upon. In the entrance hall you will see a statue of Mao seated, sculptured from white marble. You will then file past the crystal sarcophagus to view the body of Mao.

THE UNDERGROUND CITY

Below many streets of Beijing are tunnels into which the populace can descend in case of attack. Mao ordered the tunnels dug when there was fear of a Russian attack during the late sixties and in the seventies. With a CITS guide we entered a clothing shop and stood by the floor behind one of the counters. When a button was pushed a section of the floor slid away to reveal a descending staircase. We went down into a world of interconnecting tunnels and rooms. We visited a telecommunications room, a room with machinery to provide airconditioning, some shops, warehouses, a bakery and even a hotel. You can stay in this "underground city" hotel for Y2 a night. Contact CITS for bookings.

The tunnels we walked through were 2½ metres high, 1½ metres wide, had tiled walls and electric light bulbs. Escaping workers could enter the tunnels through numerous shops and follow the tunnels to the residential areas outside the city.

Many other cities also have their underground cities. You may find the tunnels and rooms being used as restaurants and "penny arcades".

THE GREAT WALL　万里长城

Parts of the wall date back to the 6th century BC when rival states constructed walls to protect themselves from each other. Qin Shi Huang Di, the 3rd century BC emperor who unified China, ordered the linking of the walls to maintain the Mongols and Manchus to the north. Subsequent dynasties either maintained the wall or let it fall into disrepair. An early Ming emperor in the 14th century AD initiated repairs to the wall.

THE MING TOMBS　十三陵

If you returned by train you would miss the Ming Tombs. On the bus tour two hours are spent at the Ding Ling tomb (time is given for buying lunch) and half an hour at the Chang Ling Tomb.

The Ming dynasty which lasted from 1368 - 1644 AD was a native Chinese dynasty. (Some other dynasties were of foreign import such as the Mongol's Yuan dynasty, 1280 - 1368 AD, and the Manchu's Qing dynasty, 1644 - 1911).

You can enter the well preserved Ding Ling, the tomb of Wan Li. The tomb has an underground palace. This Ming emperor ruled from 1573 to 1620 AD.

You may then drive around to Chang Ling, the tomb of Yong Lee who ruled from 1403 to 1425 AD.

SHOPPING

A good street for shopping is Wangfiejing Dajie which has department stores, calligraphy shops, book stores with English titles, camera stores and shops selling quick snacks such as dumplings, cakes and tasty yoghurt.

Souvenirs: Some of the main handicrafts you will see have been done in *cloisonné*. There are vases, jewellery pieces and tableware for sale. They consist of metal and coloured enamel. Fine, narrow strips of copper are bent into designs and soldered to the metal base. The spaces between the copper strips are filled in with pulverized enamel of different colours, then the item is baked.

The Beijing Friendship Store sells Kodak film, camera batteries, imported food, arts and crafts.

PEKING (OR BEIJING) DUCK　北京烧鸭

While you are in Beijing you may want to try Peking, or Beijing Duck. Possibly invite a group from the hotel and telephone a restaurant to make a reservation (somebody there most probably speaks a little English).

The duck will be brought from the kitchen on platters, already chopped into small pieces. The duck will have undergone boiling, a coating of molasses, drying and roasting over a fire until it browns. The skin will be shiny. You also will be served with small wafer-thin wheat pancakes, green onions and a bean sauce. To eat the duck you dip the morsel into the bean sauce, add some green onions, wrap the lot in a pancake and pop it into your mouth.

A popular Beijing dessert that we ordered was egg whites encased in a molten toffee. These balls of toffee are brought to the table hot; you dip them into bowls of water to solidify them.

71

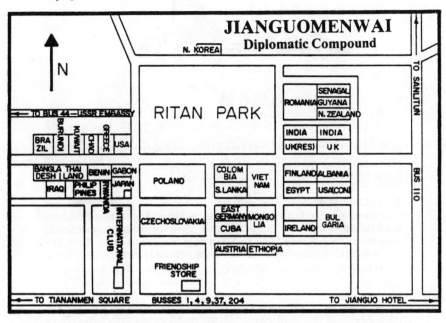

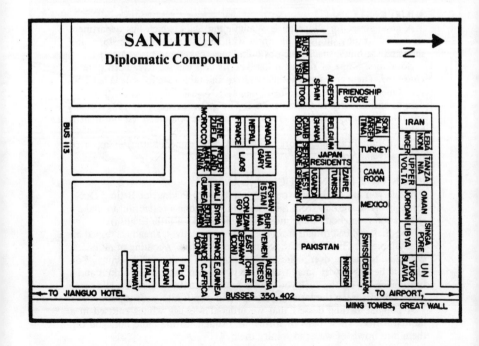

CHANGCHUN 长春

LOCATION AND TRANSPORTATION: Changchun is located in China's Dong Bei, or North East, on the main rail line connecting Beijing with Shenyang and Harbin. Changchun is the capital of Jilin Province, and is the largest city of the province.

HOTEL: There are several hotels from which to choose in Changchun, but the best is probably the CHUNYI BINGUAN, located just across the square from the railway station. This hotel has no cheap dorm rooms, so you will have to pay the full price of about Y20 a night in a double room. The CITS office is in this hotel as well; the staff is friendly and helpful.

SIGHTS: Changchun is not a tourist town but an industrial city a little over a hundred years old. Changchun is one the country's leading industrial cities with factories that produce tractors, railway carriages, autos and trucks. It is the most important motor vehicle manufacturing city in China. It also has the most famous film studio in the country. Contact CITS for a possible tour of any of these places.

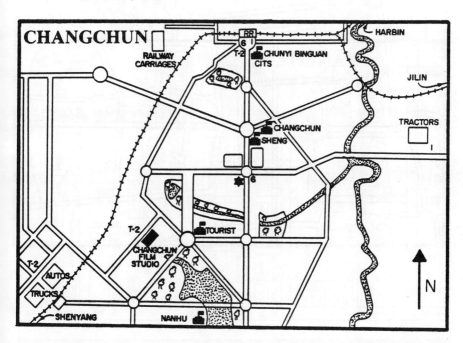

CHANGSHA 长沙

Changsha is located in northern Hunan Province and is the provincial capital. It is on the main rail line connecting Beijing and Guangzhou. By rail it is about 22 hours to Beijing and about 13 hours to Guangzhou. The hotel normally used by tourists is the XIANG JIANG BINGUAN. You can sleep here for Y8 for one bed in a triple room, or Y14 per bed in a double room. Take Bus 1 from the railway station to this hotel. The CITS office is found at the Furong Binguan.

Changsha was the boyhood home of Mao, the "Great Helmsman". There is a museum in town with a 2000 year old mummy which was removed from a nearby tomb.

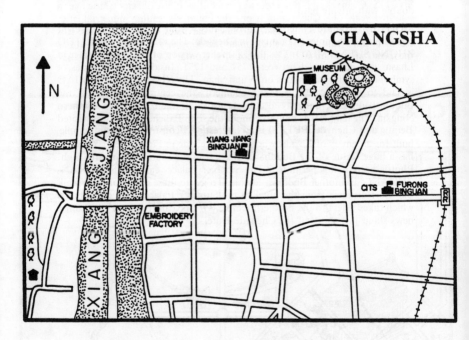

CHENGDE 承德

Chengde

LOCATION AND TRANSPORTATION: Chengde is located northeast of Beijing in Hebei Province. Almost all tourists visiting Chengde arrive by way of Beijing. There are several trains daily from Beijing; the most used is Train 325, leaving Beijing at 0720. It arrives about noon, giving you time to get to the hotel and visit about half the temples on the first day. The number 326 train leaves Chengde at 1416 daily for Beijing. This means you have an afternoon and a morning to see the sights which for most people is enough time, but others may want to spend two nights or more in Chengde.

HOTEL: From the railway station take bus 5 or 7 and get off near the CHENGDE BINGUAN. The price of a bed for each person is Y20 in a double with private bath.

SIGHTS: If you are a "temple tourist", this is your place. There are eight big, impressive temples (si or miao) in Chengde. The very best is the PUTUO ZHONG SHENG MIAO. This one, a smaller version of the Potala Palace in Lhasa, was constructed between 1757 and 1771. Inside are five stupas, a symbol of the five mountains on Wutai Shan. The XUMI FUSHOU MIAO is said to be dedicated to Mount Sumeru, the central mountain of the Buddhist universe, but may also relate to Xumi Shan located in southern Ningxia. The temple was built to honour the sixth Panchen Lama who visited Beijing and Chengde. PULESI is an interestingly constructed round temple, built for an envoy of Kazaks who visited Chengde in 1766. The PUNINGSI has a huge statue of the Buddha inside; the statue is about 26 metres high. Photography is not permitted. The Summer Palace, called BISHUSHAN-ZHUANG, is another Buddhist temple. To get to these places one can walk the short distance from the hotel to the Summer Palace, then catch bus 6 which takes riders to the northern temple. Or one can rent a bicycle from a news stand just south of the Chengde Hotel.

Temple, Chengde

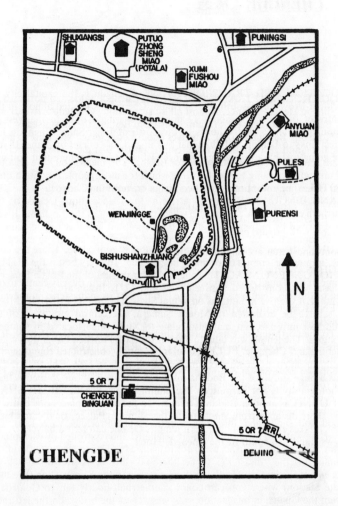

CHENGDU 成都

LOCATION AND TRANSPORTATION: Chengdu is the capital city of Sichuan Province of south central China. Chengdu is located almost in the centre of the province, about 12 hours by overnight train to the west of Chongqing, and about 4 hours to the north of Emei Shan. Chengdu has direct links to Beijing and Shanghai by rail and, of course, by plane. If you are going to Lhasa in Xizang Province (Tibet), it is from here that you will fly.

HOTEL: The only hotel for the foreign traveller in Chengdu is the JIN JIANG BINGUAN. When you arrive at the train station, located at the northern end of town, take bus 16 which runs in front of the Jin Jiang. If you have arrived by bus, simply walk to the west about half a km. One bed in a triple room costs Y9. As this is a huge hotel you can have more expensive rooms and better accommodation if you wish.

SIGHTS: Worth seeing in the city is DU FU COTTAGE, a replica of the home of the Tang Dynasty poet Du Fu. Take bus 5 from the city centre to the end of the line, then walk. There are two temples or monasteries in the city, WENSHUSI to the north (bus 16), and MARQUIS WU SI (walk from the hotel).

To the northwest of Chengdu lies the county town of GUANXIAN. It is here that is found the DUJIANGYAN IRRIGATION SYSTEM. This system is located on the Min Jiang and has a history of over 2200 years. Quoting a government pamphlet, "The Dujiangyan head-work is located at the foot of the Yulei Mountains to the west of Guanxian County town, and it is composed of three major projects: Yuzui Pier (The Fish Mouth), for dividing the water into two channels; Feishayan Spillway, for evacuating flood and sand; and Baopingkou Intake (The Precious Vase Tap), for diverting water to irrigate, which are regulated and controlled by each other. They are not only to divert water for irrigation but also to evacuate flood for minimizing the "disaster". To get there take bus 2, as shown on map, to the end of the line then walk the short distance to the Ximen Zhan (Western Gate Station) where you can board another half-hourly bus to Guanxian. From the Guanxian bus station walk west, cross the bridge on the left then walk west again to the big temple at the site of the irrigation system. This side trip will take the better part of a day.

South of Chengdu is EMEI SHAN. For more information refer to the hiking section of this book. To get there one can take a train, but it is far simpler to take a bus to Emei town. (Emei Binguan - Y3.50 per bed). Another place one should see while in this region is the huge statue of The Buddha located in the southern end of the valley at LESHAN. To get there take a bus from the Chengdu Bus Station for about a four hour ride. At the Leshan Station take a city bus to a point just south of town where is located the 71 metre high statue of DAFU (Big Buddha), one of the largest in the world. It was sculptured from the hard riverbank silt between 713 and 803 AD during the Tang Dynasty. Just north of Dafu are small ferry boats which will take you out into the river for a much better look at the statue, as well as carry you south several kms to where the MAHAO ROCK TOMBS are found. The only way to reach these tombs is by boat. There are three hotels in Leshan, the best being west of the main bus station by about 1 km; another just west of the bus station and a third near the Dafu. They are all inexpensive, just right for the budget traveller.

Elsewhere in the valley one can find several temples worth visiting. Just north of Chengdu, about 18 kms, is the town of XINDU with its 30 metre high pagoda built in the Tang Dynasty. Ask about the BAOGUANG SI when you arrive in Xindu. Take one of many buses going that way from the Chengdu bus station.

Located in the town of MEISHAN, 89 kms south of Chengdu, is the SANSU SI, a shrine dedicated to three saintly figures from the Northern Song Dynasty (420 - 589 AD). It was converted into a shrine in the Ming Dynasty. One could take a train to Meishan but the easiest way is to take a bus from the Chengdu bus station.

For those interested in pandas, you will be happy to know that the WOLONG PANDA PRESERVE is found about one day's drive to the northwest of Chengdu. To get there, you will need special permission and be escorted by a CITS guide in a CITS vehicle. The route goes through Guanxian, Yinziu and into the mountains at Wolong. CITS can advise you of the details. (The adventurous person could hitch hike that way; maybe?).

An alternate route to Chongqing and the river boat trip down the Chang Jiang is to take a bus from Chengdu in the direction of Chongqing. But stop at the two small towns called DAZU and ANYUE. It is worth the visit, especially if you are interested in Buddhist rock carvings. The CITS office in Chengdu can give you the latest word on transport and hotel facilities. It is likely that you will be on one bus most of one day getting there, then most of another day to continue to Chongqing. It could be a three day trip, at least for the casual traveller. Dazu is said to be better, having many caves with rock carvings and murals, all dating back to the Northern and Southern Dynasties (420 - 589 AD).

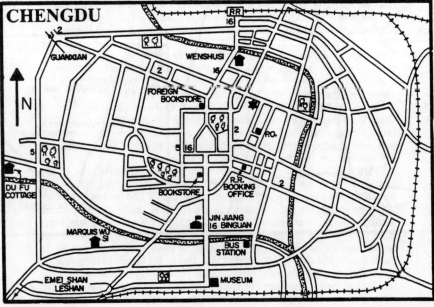

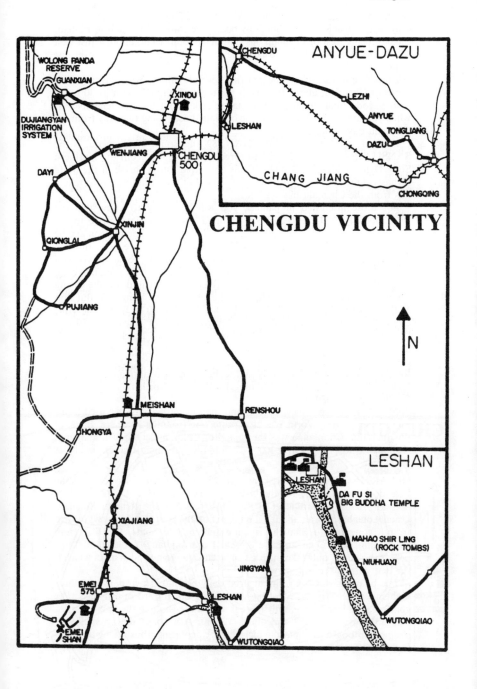

CHONGQING 重庆

LOCATION AND TRANSPORTATION: Chongqing (pronounced Chongching, formerly known as Chungking) is located in the southeastern part of Sichuan Province on the banks of the Chang Jiang (Yangtze River). Almost all independent travellers coming to Chongqing arrive by rail on the overnight train from Chengdu. For those with more time, leave Chengdu on a bus bound for Dazu, see the ruins there, then go on to Chongqing on another bus (see the Chengdu section for more information). Occasionally someone comes upriver on the boats but normally, for the foreign tourist, going downriver is far better because it is only three days down, but five days up.

HOTEL: From the train station ascend the steps to the top of the hill (or take the cable car), then either walk the 2 kms to the RENMIN BINGUAN or take bus 1 to the circle as shown on the map, then walk. The Renmin, actually an Opera House, is probably the best sight to see in this highly industrialised city. They have a large dorm room behind the stage for Y4 a night (men and women share). Alternatively, from the top of the hill you can take bus 1 in an easterly direction and stop at the CHONGQING BINGUAN. This hotel has smaller rooms, triples and quads, for Y6 to Y8 for each bed. This is better for married couples who want more privacy. To go directly from the train station to the docks from where boats leave for Wuhan, take bus 12.

SIGHTS: There are caves, natural and man-made, which were used as air raid shelters during World War II as protection from the Japanese. It was at this time that Chongqing was the capital of China under the Guomindang. Although Chongqing is over 3000 years old there are almost no ancient relics of its past.

DEPARTING: Foreign tourists may find it impossible to buy tickets at the boat dock ticket office for the boat trip down the CHANG JIANG. It is necessary to buy your ticket at the CITS office in the Renmin Binguan. Usually one has to wait about 2 days to get on the boat. To do the whole trip from Chongqing to Shanghai requires taking two boats, the first from Chongqing to Wuhan and the second from Wuhan to Shanghai. Most people, however, only take the boat between Chongqing and Wuhan which is the best part of the trip anyway.

The boat leaves Chongqing at 0700 daily and takes two days and three nights to reach Wuhan. Most budget tourists opt for 3rd or 4th class. The comfort level is the same, only there is a bit more room in the upper classes. The 3rd class is Y37.50 and 4th is Y25.80. Ask about the possibility of sleeping on board the boat the night before departing, thus saving a night's lodging.

Some travellers disembark at Yichang or Yueyang. (See p. 82 and 176).

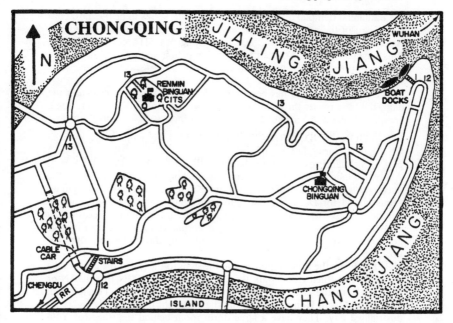

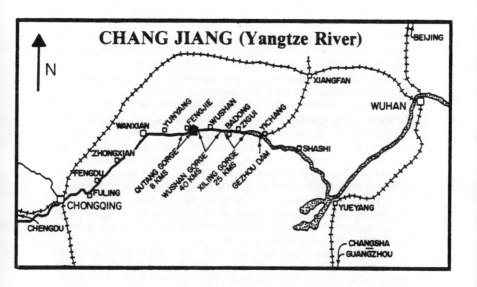

The best part of the river trip is the second day out of Chongqing. In the evening of the first day the boat stops at Wanxian for about 7 hours. Passengers disembark and walk around town and have dinner. In the early morning hours it leaves and enters the first of three gorges just after daybreak. The boat must pass through all gorges in daylight hours. Near Fengjie the boat enters the QUTANG GORGE. As you enter, you will see

81

the Baidimiao (temple) on the left hand side. This seems to be the most confining part of the boat trip, and perhaps the most picturesque of the gorges. A bit later the boat enters the 40 km long WUSHAN GORGE. The Yingfengguan (temple) marks the beginning of this section. The last of the gorges is the XILING which extends about 25 kms. This is the least spectacular of the three.

The GEZHOU DAM has been completed near Yichang. To get past the dam, the boat passes through the locks, lowering it about 25 metres. Some people disembark at Yichang or Yueyang, but most stick it out to Wuhan. If you want to continue on to Shanghai, buy your ticket immediately upon arrival. You will possibly have to wait two days in Wuhan to get on a boat for the last two days of the trip to Shanghai (total sailing time, Chongqing to Shanghai, is 5 days).

DALIAN 大辽

LOCATION AND TRANSPORTATION: Dalian, located in the northeastern province of Liaoning, is at the southern tip of the Liaodong Peninsula. It is possible to fly into Dalian from Harbin or Beijing, but most people take the train. The trains coming from Beijing first go through Shenyang, then south to Dalian. As an alternative, one can also take a daily ferry boat from Dalian to Yantai (located on Shangdong Bandao or Peninsula).

HOTEL: The expensive hotel is the Dalian Binguan, but for the budget traveller the best bet is the DUNGFENG BINGUAN which has various classes of accommodation in the same hotel. Get there by walking from the train station. The best rooms, with private bath and two beds, are priced at Y14 for each bed. Other rooms which are hard to come by have four beds for about Y5 each. These rooms on the 2nd floor have shared toilets.

SIGHTS: Dalian is a young city, first coming to prominence at the turn of this century as a concession to both European and Japanese trading concerns. The harbour was begun in 1899 and completed in the 1930's. It is now one of China's major harbours. Because of the many foreign businesses, one can see their influence in the style of the many public buildings in the downtown area. There are several churches. Around the one big traffic circle, where is located the Dalian Hotel, one sees many large buildings which were obviously designed by Europeans.

Other things to see include the locomotive plant located near the end of the trolley ("T") line. Stalin Square is interesting; take bus 2 from in front of the train station. Bus 2 also takes you to the beach resort of Xinghai while bus 5 takes you to the Fucha beach. If you'd like to buy some prawns, go to Tiger Park or Laohutan, where is located a street market for the sale of various seafoods. Dalian is also famous for its apples.

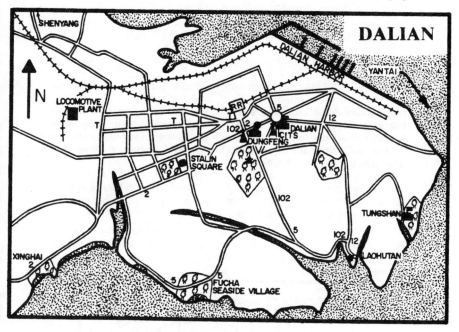

DAQING   大清

Daqing, located in the northeast of China in the province of Heilongjiang, is between the cities of Harbin and Qiqihar. The terrain of the area is flat at an elevation of only 150 metres. Daqing is a newly developed oil city which lies in the centre of the Sungliao Basin. Oil was first discovered in 1959. Today the city has close to one million people. There are many daily trains running from Harbin to Qiqihar, all of which stop at Daqing. Take bus 5 from the train station to the one and only hotel, DAQING DONG FENG BINGUAN, located at the far eastern end of the city. This city is new and, for the most part, planned and consists of several different centres. The reason for going to Daqing is to visit oil wells, oil pipelines or refinery. Since it is a spread out town you will probably want to hire a CITS or oil company guide and driver to take you to the various places.

DATONG　大同

LOCATION AND TRANSPORTATION: Datong is located in northern Shanxi Province, very near the border of Nei Mongol. The city lies at about 1200 metres elevation and has about one million people. Datong also sits on a "sea of coal". Because of the coal and the railway it has become a prominent and thriving city of north China.

One can reach Datong from Beijing on an overnight train. Most tourists take the 295 train which leaves Beijing at 2255 and arrives in Datong at 0710, thus saving a night in a hotel. There are also many daily trains coming from Baotou and Hohhot, and from Xian and Taiyuan in the south.

HOTEL: There is only one hotel in town, at least for foreign tourists, the Datong or YOU YI BINGUAN. From the train station take bus 15 which stops near the hotel. The cost for a bed in a dormitory is Y6 a night. Smaller, private rooms also are available.

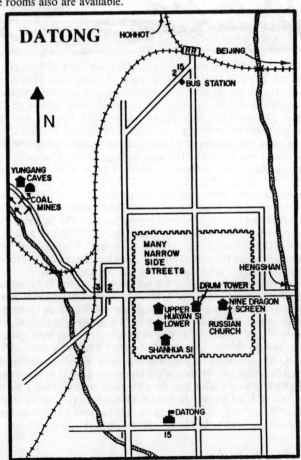

The Buddha sculptured in rock
at Yungang caves near Datong

SIGHTS: Inside Datong are several temples. There is the UPPER HUAYAN SI and the LOWER HUAYAN SI, both of which date back to the 5th century. The Upper Temple is one of the largest wooden temples still in existence in China today. There is also the NINE DRAGON SCREEN, over 500 years old. It is a wall with tiles of various colors depicting nine dragons.

The main attraction that draws tourists to Datong is the YUNGANG CAVES. This site consists of 53 caves carved out of a sandstone cliff-face that is about one km long. The largest statue towers 17 metres while the smallest is just a few centimetres high. You can explore the caves and examine the sculptured statues of The Buddha and the carvings of Hindu gods. You can enter these caves and take photos, something you cannot do in some other caves of China. The statues of The Buddha are reminiscent of the Graeco-Buddhist sculptures in northern Afghanistan and northern Pakistan. (Remnants of Alexander the Great's army that settled in that area in the 3rd century BC influenced the art of sculpture. Traders and Buddhist missionaries carried the art and religion along the caravan routes from India). The Yungang Caves were begun during the 5th century AD.

To get to the caves take bus 2 from the train station then, at the point indicated on the map, take bus 3. This bus runs on the highway near many coal mines. Ask to be put off at the Yungang Shir Ku (stone caves), a ride of 7 or 8 kms. From the hotel, take bus 15 to near the area from where bus 3 leaves, then walk to number 3. You will want to spend at least half a day on this trip as these caves are among the best in China.

For those interested in hiking, and especially those interested in China's nine sacred mountains, Datong is the jumping off point to Heng Shan Bei, located 65 kms to the south (see the hiking section in this book for details). At the base of Heng Shan is the XUAN KONG SI, a fascinating temple built on the cliff face. It is one of the best in China. You are supposed to hire a CITS guide and vehicle to get there but it is possible to hitch hike.

DUNHUANG 敦煌

LOCATION AND TRANSPORTATION: Dunhuang is located in the extreme western end of Gansu Sheng or Province. Dunhuang is also at the western end of the Hexi Corridor, which means "West of the Huang He (Yellow River)". It is also the end of the line for rivers that come out of the mountains and flow in a westerly direction. The Hexi Corridor forms a continuous line of oases from near Lanzhou to just west of Dunhuang. To get there take a train running on the Lanzhou-Urumqi line, stopping at Liuyuan. Then take one of several daily buses heading for Dunhuang. One can also stop at either Jiuquan or Jiayuguan, southeast of Liuguan, and take the 0700 daily bus to Dunhuang (bus starts at Jiuquan, then stops at Jiayuguan and Anxi). For those with less time and more money, a flight can be taken from Lanzhou.

HOTEL: For the budget traveller, perhaps the best place is the ZHOU DAI SUA (hotel), near where you will get off the bus. It has four- and five-bedded rooms, each bed costing Y4. The DUNHUANG BINGUAN at the eastern end of this small town has two sections, one for tour groups and the other for individual travellers. one bed in a quad room costs Y5. If you arrive in the middle of the rush season there are a few rooms available at the overflow hotel across the street west of the Dunhuang. It is usually quiet at the overflow, but you have to go to the Dunhuang to shower. It costs Y5 a bed. There is also a small hotel at the Mogao Grottoes.

SIGHTS: Dunhuang, known as Shazhou in the remote past, is a famous ancient city along the SI ZHOU ZI LU (Silk Road). As a prefecture it was first established in the thirtieth year of the reign of Emperor Wu of the Han Dynasty (111 BC). A gateway to the Western Regions, it served as a pivotal point of cultural interchange during the Han and Tang Dynasties. Along this Silk Road travelled caravans, their pack animals loaded with silk products from Chang'an (Xian). On reaching Dunhuang, the travellers would separate and proceed to take two different routes in their westward journey. The northern route, starting from the YUMEN GUAN (Jade Gate Pass) reached out to the Western Region via Turpan and Kucha (Kuqa) while the southern route, starting from the YANGGUAN (Yang Pass), stretched westward through Luobu Lake to Qarqan (Charchan) and Hotan. Dunhuang was thus the first stopover, too, for incoming traffic by way of the two passes, bringing in the Dawan horses, grapes and clover as well as Buddhist sutras from India.

The world-famous MOGAO GROTTOES or caves are 25 kms to the southeast of Dunhuang. Work here began in the year 366 AD. The additions and repairs made in the thousand years from the Northern Wei down to the Yuan Dynasties resulted in a honeycomb of caves and grottoes. A wealth of precious murals and painted statues represent various art styles of different

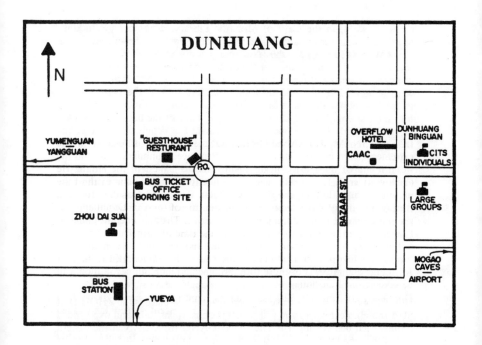

DUNHUANG

N

YUMENGUAN
YANGGUAN

"GUESTHOUSE"
RESTURANT

P.O.

OVERFLOW
HOTEL

DUNHUANG
BINGUAN

CAAC

CITS
INDIVIDUALS

BUS TICKET
OFFICE
BORDING SITE

ZHOU DAI SUA

BAZAAR ST.

LARGE
GROUPS

MOGAO
CAVES

AIRPORT

BUS
STATION

YUEYA

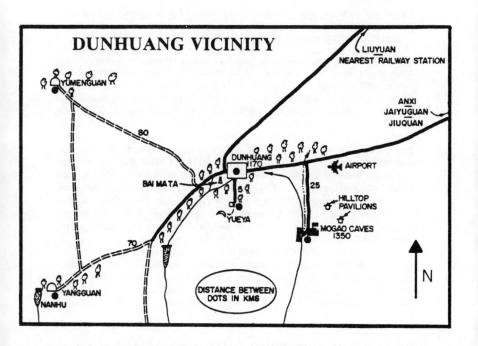

DUNHUANG VICINITY

LIUYUAN
NEAREST RAILWAY STATION

YUMENGUAN

ANXI
JAIYUGUAN
JIUQUAN

80

DUNHUANG
170

BAI MA TA

AIRPORT

5

25

HILLTOP
PAVILIONS

YUEYA

MOGAO CAVES
1350

70

NANHU

YANGGUAN

DISTANCE BETWEEN
DOTS IN KMS

N

times. In 1900, in the Cave of Monastic Library, a number of Buddhist scriptures, manuscripts and silk scroll paintings were rediscovered by the monk Wang Yuanlu. Since the caves were abandoned he settled in, diverted a small stream of water to run near the caves, planted trees, then set to work to bring the Mogao Grottoes to light once again. Early in this century the caves were plundered by art and museum collectors, but in the period of the People's Republic they have been preserved. Although erosion has taken its toll, there still remain 492 caves representing some of the best Buddhist cave art in the world. Sorry, no photos in the caves! For details on the caves buy the small booklet, The Mogao Grottoes, at the Dunhuang Binguan or at the caves.

To get to the caves, buy a ticket (best to buy the night before to ensure you get a seat) at the bus ticket office. Buses leave each morning in the busy season at 0700, and leave the grottoes at 1100. You might consider staying at the hotel at the grottoes, or even sleeping in one of the abandoned caves at the northern end of the 2 km long cliff of caves. The bus schedule changes, depending on the number of tourists and the time of year.

Interesting places to see outside Dunhuang are the Yumenguan and Yangguan. To get to these places one must hire a vehicle from CITS as there is no public transport. Because there are people living out there in or near both of these oases, hitch hiking on trucks might be possible. Just south of Dunhuang are some very large sand dunes, almost mountains. Making them even more interesting is a small spring and crescent-shaped lake called YUEYA (Crescent Moon). During the busy tourist season there are several buses each day going out that way. It is only 5 kms from town so you could walk or you could buy a bus ticket at the bus ticket office. All buses leave town at 1900. This gives people about 1½ hours to walk over the sand dunes to the lake near the edge of the oasis. The bus will return at 2100. In the off season, schedules will change.

Just to the southwest of town is a small pagoda called the BAI MA TA, or White Horse Pagoda. One can easily walk to this feature located in the middle of fields. It is 3 or 4 kms from the centre of town.

Refer to page 46 for BUDDHIST CAVES IN GANSU AND NINGXIA.

FOSHAN 佛山

Foshan is 16 kms southwest of Guangzhou in Guangdong Province. It is a small city of 300,000 people, usually visited by day trippers from Guangzhou. In Guangzhou there is a small bus station located on the east-west street just north of the Guangzhou Binguan. Buses leave about every hour for Foshan. There is one hotel, the FOSHAN BINGUAN, an old-fashioned relic. In times past, Foshan achieved considerable renown as a religious pilgrimage site. The name means Buddha Hill, in reference to the three statues of The Buddha which once stood on a small hill in town. In addition to the religious reputation it became famous as a pottery manufacturing site. It became well developed during the Song Dynasty (960 - 1279 AD). Later, it also manufactured ironware, and became a world famous port.

Today these same industries still continue as well as silk dyeing and printing. You might visit the Hongmian and Nanhai Textile Mills. As no city is complete without a temple or two, Foshan is no exception. You can see the Ancestral Temple (or Si) from the Song Dynasty, the REN SHOU SI, now an exhibition hall, and the ZU CI MIAO (temple). The latter is a Daoist temple from the Ming Dynasty (1368 - 1644 AD).

FUSHUN 撫順

Fushun is located in Liaoning Province about 60 kms east of Shenyang. The city is known for one industry, coal, which has been mined here for 2000 years. This city is not one of the normal tourist hangouts, but it is open and if you are interested in visiting a coal mine, that can surely be arranged. Best to stay in Shenyang and visit this city on a day trip. And the people will stare you to death!

FUZHOU 福州

An out-of-way city not normally visited by tourists, Fuzhou is the capital of the Fujian Province, located on the southeast coast of China. Fuzhou is linked to other cities by regular rail service and irregular boat service. There is not a lot to see here except people, but they do not represent any special group. There are a couple of pagodas in the city centre near Mao's statue. East of Fuzhou is GUSHAN (Drum Hill), at 1004 metres, with some temples on top. There is one hotel, the HUA ZHOU BINGUAN (Overseas Chinese Hotel). No dorm rooms here, but one bed in a double room costs Y8.

GONGXIAN 拱縣

LOCATION AND TRANSPORTATION: Gongxian, or GONGXIAN COUNTY as it is usually referred to in Chinese literature, is located about midway between Luoyang and Zhengzhou, in the extreme north of Henan Province. The area around Gongxian is one of the best attractions in China, although few tourists know of the place. To get there, take one of many trains each day running between Zhengzhou and Luoyang. Buses can also be used to reach Gongxian from the above two mentioned cities.

HOTEL: There is one hotel for tourists, the GONGXIAN BINGUAN, located about 2 kms due south of the train station. The bus station is also just south of the train station, but it is a lot less complicated just to walk the 2 kms to the hotel. The price is Y12 for one bed in a twin room with air conditioning. There are cheaper rooms but the staff prefers to put foreigners in the better rooms. If you can communicate you might get a less expensive room, one with a common toilet.

SIGHTS: Keep in mind that this part of China has the longest history of all. The Huang He or Yellow River Valley is where China first became a nation. Gongxian is part of the early history that can be traced back to 221 BC when China was first united by the first emperor of the Qin Dynasty, Qin Shi Huang Di. Magnificent tombs were built on the hilly land of loess (silt deposits) by the various Northern Song Emperors. All these famous historic sites have brought into vivid expression the features of the Huang He Valley culture.

Right across the road from the hotel is one of the royal tombs of the Song Dynasty (960 - 1280 AD), the YONGZHOU LING (Yongzhou Tomb). It, like all the rest, is in a corn field. It consists of a large mound, pyramid in shape. Just to the south of the mound are two rows of animal and human statues facing each other about 30 metres apart. The statues are about 3 metres tall; there are about a dozen on each side. If you walk directly south half a km, there is one more group of statues. If you can hitch hike or take a bus going in the direction of Luoyang, you will find perhaps the best preserved tomb of all, the YONGDING LING. It is 8 or 9 kms from the hotel, is similar to the tomb just mentioned but has more statues, making it seem a bit more impressive. Altogether there are 8 imperial tombs in Gongxian, spread out over an area within about 15 kms from the hotel.

About 9 kms from Gongxian town is the SHIR KU SI, or Stone Caves Temple. They were carved out of the side of Dali Shan, about 1 km from the Yiluo He. It is recorded that the temple was first built in 517 AD during the reign of Emperor Kiping of the Northern Wei Dynasty and subsequently enlarged into five caves in Eastern and Western Wei, Tang and Song Dynasties. It now has 256 shrines and 7743 Buddhist figures. This is one of the better examples of Buddhist art in China, although rather small. To get there one could proceed to the bus station and catch a bus going that way (about every two hours). It is less complicated to walk and hitch hike. There are many small tractors on the road that will stop not only for locals, but for foreigners as well. They are slow, but the scenery is interesting. Between about kms 4 through 6 one sees many CAVE HOMES dug out of the silt or loess along the river. Homes like these are all along the Huang He, from about Lanzhou to the China Sea. There are so many small tractors carrying bricks that you can get off, take a close look at the homes then catch another ride.

DU FU (712 - 770 AD) was one of the great realist poets of the Tang Dynasty in ancient China. Du Fu was born in a cave at the foot of Bijiashan near NANYAOWAN. There is a shrine or temple there today. At the Gongxian bus station you will find buses going that way.

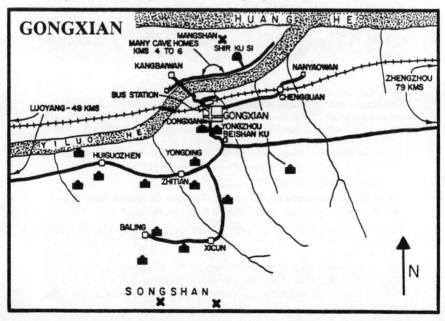

GUANGZHOU 广州

Guangzhou

LOCATION AND TRANSPORTATION: Guangzhou is more commonly known in the west as Canton. Guangzhou is the provincial capital of Guangdong Province, located on China's southeastern coast. If you enter China by land from Hong Kong, this will be your first stop.

Here is some brief information about some travel destinations and how to get there from Guangzhou. One can take a bus to Guilin, a total time of 40 hours which includes one overnight stop. A better way to reach Guilin is to take an overnight train via Hengyang, a journey of about 24 hours.

There are trains to Beijing, the fastest ones going through Wuhan. Train 16 departs Guangzhou at 2054 and arrives at 0601 in Beijing. Train 48 departs Guangzhou at 2240 and arrives in Beijing at 1032. It takes about 34 hours and costs Y67.80 for a hard seat.

One can take a boat to the city of WUZHOU on the ZHU JIANG (Pearl River), about 20 hours. The cost of Y4.80 includes a bunk with thin cotton pad mattress. As standard Chinese food is sold there is no need to take it with you. There is also a small store on board for snack foods. Hot water for your tea or coffee is always provided free of charge; this you will find is the case in every hotel, train and boat in China. The Chinese carry cups or glasses with lids, and sip green tea constantly.

There are express trains to Hong Kong costing Y18. Shenzhen is the Hong Kong-China border town.

Train 91   Departs 0830   Arrives in Shenzhen 1020
Train 93   Departs 1010   Arrives in Shenzhen 1200

There are slower trains too at a much lower price, Y8.60.

Train 101   Departs 1045   Arrives in Shenzhen 1337

Once you get to the border, you go through customs and immigration then take another train to Kowloon. The trains to Kowloon leave every half hour or so.

One can also take a Hovercraft from Whampoa, (a 30 minute bus ride from Guangzhou).

Depart 1245   Arrive Hong Kong 1545
Depart 1400   Arrive Hong Kong 1700
Depart 1445   Arrive Hong Kong 1745

Ferries also are available to Hong Kong. For the boat dock and ticket office, refer to the bottom left hand corner of the map.

There are also buses to Macao; you can get an entry visa at the border. From Macao you can take a ferry boat to Hong Kong. But do not rush to get away from Macao, it has many interesting things to see.

HOTEL: As you might expect, a city the size of Guangzhou has many hotels. Probably the best choice for the budget traveller is the LIU HUA BINGUAN right across the plaza from the Guangzhou Zhan or railway station. One bed in a large room is Y6; a bed in a triple room is Y8. The other hotels shown on the map are possibilities, but some are more expensive and lack big dormitory rooms; and others will not admit foreigners. You could check at the CITS office next to the station or the front desk at the Liu Hua for more information about the other hotels and what they offer. To get from the main railway station to the downtown area, around the Guangzhou Binguan, take bus 5 or 29.

SIGHTS: Not much is known of Guangzhou until the unification of China by the Qin leader, Qin Shi Huang Di in 221 BC. In the 8th century AD there were many Moslem traders in Guangzhou where they built a mosque. They were later driven out. In 1514 the first Europeans came (in this case the Portuguese). In 1699 the British East India Company established a trading post commonly known as a factory. Later concessions were granted. Shamian Island became a bastion for foreigners.

Some of the interesting things to see are as follows: SHAMIAN ISLAND, just mentioned, which has European style buildings. There is the CHINESE EXPORT TRADE EXHIBITION within walking distance of the main railway station. If you are in Guangzhou between April 15 and May 15, or between October 15 and November 15, you can see many displays of goods to be sold to foreign businessmen. But it is best to avoid this city during these times if you can, as accommodation is virtually impossible.

The LIURONGSI (Temple of the Six Banyan Trees) was founded in 479 AD, with the nearby pagoda being built in 537 AD. The pagoda stands 55 metres high and is octagonal in shape.

Also interesting is the HUAISHENG SI or mosque. This is reputed to be the oldest mosque in China, having first been built in 627 AD. The original building was destroyed; the one standing now was constructed in this century.

There is also a 49 metre high ROMAN CATHOLIC CATHEDRAL built between 1860 and 1863, designed in the traditional Gothic style as seen throughout Europe and the world.

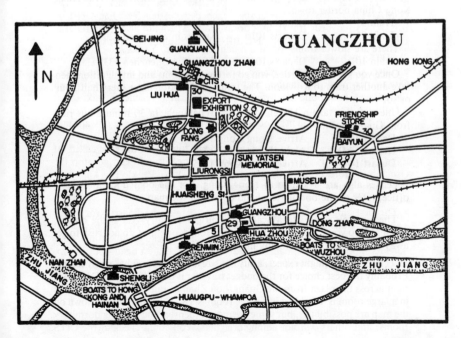

GUILIN 桂林

LOCATION AND TRANSPORTATION: Guilin is located in the northern part of Guangxi Province and is usually one of the first places tourists visit in China. Its fame comes from the limestone outcroppings in the region that resemble fangs or teeth. Normally tourists come here from Guangzhou. Most used is the train, but another way to Guilin is to travel from Guangzhou by boat (or by bus) to Wuzhou, spend the night then go by bus to Yangshuo, about 50 kms south of Guilin. Most people combine Yangshuo and Guilin as the scenery is similar. From Yangshuo, one way to Guilin is by the river boat on the Li Jiang (Li River). It takes about six or seven hours for this trip to Guilin. By using the Wuzhou route to Guilin you can avoid backtracking. The boat actually leaves Guilin in the mornings with tourists bound for Yangshuo; they are bused back to Guilin in the afternoon. In the past, the boat returned almost empty but now you can pay Y15 to Y20 for the up-river trip in the afternoons. This price is much less than the ride from Guilin to Yangshuo in the same boat.

HOTEL: There is a small but adequate hotel for tourists in Yangshuo, priced at Y9 for one bed in a room with private bath. You can walk there from the boat or the bus station. In Guilin, you can walk from the main railway station in a northerly direction to one of two or three hotels which offer low prices to budget travellers. Buses 1 and 11 also run on this main street. The OSMANTHUS has two big dorms, each bed costing Y5. The GUILIN BINGUAN has beds for Y6 in a dorm room. There are also the HIDDEN HILL, LI JIANG and RONG HU BINGUANS, all at higher prices.

SIGHTS: As has already been indicated, the primary reason tourists come to Guilin is to see the karst landscape. There are also several caves in the region. One that is rather outstanding and easy to get to is the LUDI YAN (Reed Flute Cave). It is found northwest of town and can be reached by taking bus 3 from the train station or anywhere along the main north-south street in Guilin. This cave is well lit; groups are escorted through a maze of stalactites and stalagmites.

There is another cave on the eastern side of town near the zoo, called QI XING (Seven Stars). To get a good look at the city you can go atop the Osmanthus Hotel or climb the DUXIU FENG (Duxiu Peak). This karst outcrop in the centre of town is in an enclosed park area. Take bus 1 or 11 to that area, or walk.

The best single side-trip from Guilin is to take the boat to (or from) Yangshuo, along 83 kms of the Li Jiang. Along the way you will pass small villages, rice paddies and of course the vertical pinnacles of limestone. Your hotel reception desk attendants can advise you of the latest details of this trip. Also, talk to fellow travellers about the latest conditions and information.

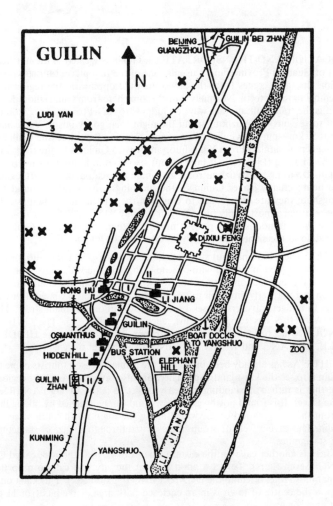

Many cities, such as Guilin, have bicycles for rent (J)

Families are restricted to one child (J)

Limestone peaks along the Li River

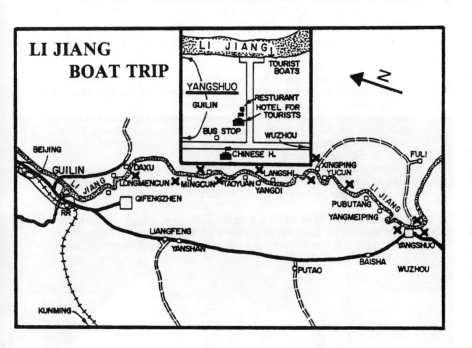

HAINAN DAO　海南島

● Hainan Dao

LOCATION AND TRANSPORTATION: The first thing to remember about going to Hainan Dao (Island) is that you must have permission given in your travel permit. It appears at this moment that permission is given to HAIKOU only, the island's largest city located on the north coast. A good way to reach the island is via the daily ferry from Guangzhou which takes about 24 hours. One problem is that it may be difficult to get permission in Guangzhou for this visit. Lots of rumors! Another way is to take a train from either Nanning or Liuzhou (only two trains, 161/162 and 312/313, make the run), to the city of ZHANJIANG, located on the Leizhou Bandao (Peninsula) just north of Hainan. From Zhanjiang a daily bus, or buses, run to Hainan at the very tip of the peninsula. From there a ferry sails to Haikou.

HOTEL: In Haikou stay at the HUA ZHOU BINGUAN with rooms and beds priced from about Y4 to Y8, depending on whether the room has a private bath.

SIGHTS: When permission to visit the island was granted in the early 1980's, the permission was only for the city of Haikou, but many individual travellers began travelling the entire island. As the police did not know how to react they allowed them to go. The latest word is that permission is given to Haikou only and that the people at the bus stations will not sell foreigners tickets out of the city. The alternative is to hire a CITS guide and driver to take you around the island. In Haikou you can visit night markets, food stalls, and temples which are much different from those found on the mainland. The isolation of the island environment has resulted in many different cultural features.

When the whole island opens you can visit such places as the highland town of BAOTING, the capital of the minority region of the Li and Miao peoples. As these people live more in the interior of the island you will not see many in Baoting.

The large port city of SANYA is on the south coast, a day's journey by bus from Haikou. A few kms to the west of Sanya is the beach resort of LUHUITOU. It may or may not be possible to hike to or climb the highest peak on the island, WUZHI SHAN, at 1867 metres.

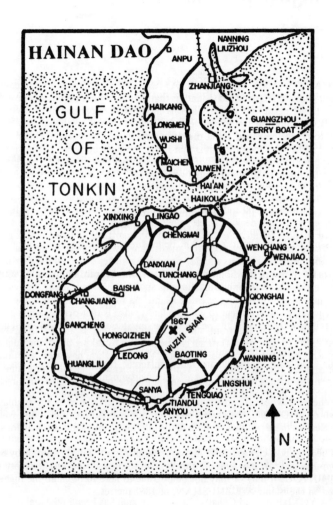

HANGZHOU 杭州

LOCATION AND TRANSPORTATION: Hangzhou is located in the eastern portion of Zhejiang Province not far west of Shanghai. It lies very near the mouth of the Qiantang Jiang (Qiantang River). There are many trains daily coming and going from Hangzhou. The Shanghai - Hangzhou train takes 3½ hours. If you are planning to go to Huang Shan or Jiu Hua Shan to the the west, this is the place from where many buses leave. Several buses leave Hangzhou each morning for Huang Shan; the cost is Y6.90 and takes 8 hours. At Huang Shan another bus will take you to Jiu Hua Shan. Hangzhou is at the southern end of the DA YUNHE (Grand Canal). You can board a nightly boat from Hangzhou to Suzhou, a journey of about 13½ hours. It leaves at 1800 and arrives at about 0730 in Suzhou. Cost is Y4.10 for bunk class. Below deck is where other passengers sit up all night in seats similar to those found on trains. Everyone on board has a seat or a bunk bed. On board you can buy prepared meals; kai‾ siway (boiled water) also is available. Buy your tickets the day prior at the ticket office on the canal, as shown on the map. Bus 53 goes to that area from the train station, or you can catch it from near the big bookstore, as shown.

HOTEL: There are two hotels for foreigners. The preferred hotel is the HANGZHOU BINGUAN on the northwest shore of Xi Hu (West Lake). Take bus 7 from the train station. Another hotel is the HUAGANG BINGUAN (dorms for Y4) which can be reached by taking bus 7, then bus 4, then walking northwest a short distance. The Hangzhou has large dormitory rooms at Y5 for each bed. This is the recommended place because almost every night there is singing and dancing at the theatre in the same building as the dorms. On about half the nights, hotel guests are allowed in free.

SIGHTS: There are several temples, one of which is right next door to the Hangzhou Binguan, and a number of parks. You could look into the possibility of visiting a SILK FACTORY. You can organize your own group then have the CITS office at the Hangzhou Hotel complete the arrangements. As of 1985, you could not go by yourself to a silk factory; you had to be part of a group. Perhaps you could join an existing tour group. Check into this at the CITS office.

DA YUNHE (Grand Canal): The Grand Canal has been in the making for about 2,400 years. It covers a full 10 degrees of latitude from north to south; it is approximately the same distance as is Florida from New York City. The Grand Canal is still used today from Hangzhou in the south to the Huang He (Yellow River), but in the north it dwindles. North of Tianjin it is completely dry. At one time it reached Beijing. The total distance covered is 1794 kms.

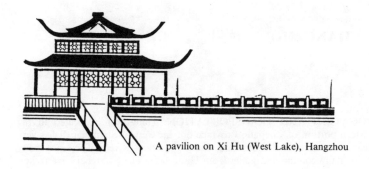

A pavilion on Xi Hu (West Lake), Hangzhou

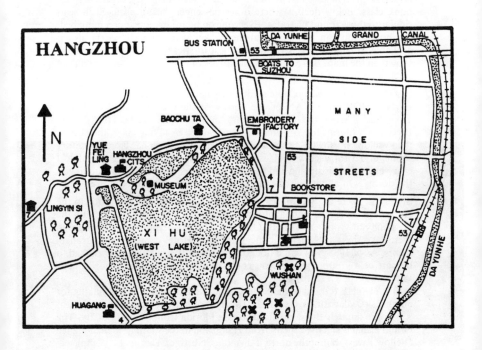

Hangzhou Tea picker (J)

Silk factory, Hangzhou (J)

HARBIN 哈尔滨

LOCATION AND TRANSPORTATION: Being the capital of Heilongjiang Province, Harbin is the political, economic and cultural centre of the province and the northeast. Its population is nearly 3 million, despite the fact the town was first incorporated in only 1898. Harbin is an important hub for railways. Although a river port, there is no passenger service on the Songhua Jiang (Songhua River). There are many trains each day from Beijing, a ride of about 19 hours on the fastest train.

HOTEL: For the budget traveller, the preferred hotel is the HUAZHOU BINGUAN. It is in a good location. The price is Y18 for one bed in a double room with a private bath. There are no cheap dorm rooms in town because there are so few independent travellers in Harbin. A short block away from the Huazhou is the GUOJI BINGUAN. You can walk from the train station to either of these, or take any trolley running up the hill in a southerly direction.

SIGHTS: There is not a lot to see in Harbin for the average tourist but it does have some interesting architecture. The Russians ruled this part of China's Dong Bei (northeast) when they pushed a railway through to Vladivostok across Manchuria. They were in Harbin long enough to erect many European style buildings. Many of these buildings are in the area of the hotels just mentioned, in the district north of the railway station. A place of interest is the RUSSIAN ORTHODOX CHURCH, as shown on the map. Take bus 3 from the hotels or the railway station. You will have to search hard for this church as it is in the middle of a block where newer Chinese apartment buildings have been constructed around it. Today, this onion domed church is a warehouse and totally neglected as an historic landmark by the Chinese.

If you ask a Chinese person what there is in Harbin to see, he will tell you to go to the CHILDREN'S PARK with its 2 km long miniature railway run by children, and to two parks along the Songhua Jiang. On the south side is STALIN PARK; on the north is SUN ISLAND PARK, reached by ferry.

HOHHOT 呼和浩特

LOCATION AND TRANSPORTATION: Hohhot is the capital of Nei Mongol (Inner Mongolia) and is located about half way between Baotou and Datong on the main rail line running west from Beijing. By rail it is about 5 hours from Datong, 14 from Beijing, and 4 hours from Baotou.

HOTEL: The HOHHOT BINGUAN, a ten minute walk from the station, is Y6. You can walk for 25 minutes to the XIN XI BINGUAN (New City Hotel) and sleep in a large dorm, a corridor near an indoor swimming pool, for Y3. There are no city buses which will really help you to either of these hotels.

SIGHTS: There are two interesting temples to see in the city. The DA SI (Big Temple), actually a large mosque, combines the architecture of Islam and traditional Buddhist China. Take bus 3 from near the Xin Xi Hotel. Also to visit is the WU TA SI (Five Pagoda Temple) which is small but unique.

Enquire about the MONGOLIAN RODEO or the camel and/or horse races. The racing grounds are on the north side of the city.

Most tourists going to Hohhot visit the Mongolian grasslands for an insight into the Mongolian way of life. You must do this as part of a CITS tour. You can join a larger group or organize one of your own, the cost depends on how many go and how long you stay. You can do one-day trips, but trips are usually of one or two nights (two or three days). Accommodation is in yurts (the Mongolian portable tents made of felt). The cost for a tour of three days and two nights is about Y70-Y80. You usually visit communes of herdsmen and see many camels, sheep, horses and donkeys on the endless plain.

The recommended time to go into the grasslands is during the summer. By September it can be very cold with a strong north wind blowing across the flat terrain. You can rent warm fur collared coats from the hotel in Hohhot for Y1 if you go during the cooler months. It is well worth the investment!

The DA SI
Hohhot

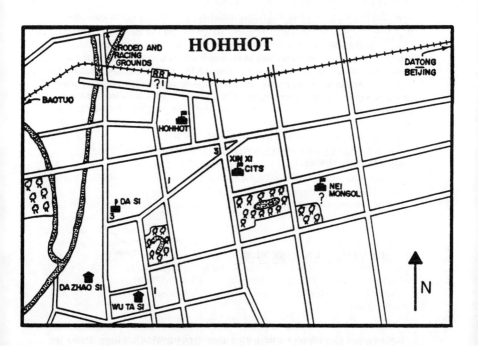

Mongolian yurts in the grasslands

HANDAN 邯 郸

Handan is located in southern Hebei Province on the main railway line between Beijing and Guangzhou. Handan is one of the oldest cities in China, dating back to 546 BC. During the Han Dynasty it was one of five important cities, the others being Xian, Luoyang, Zibo and Chengdu. In the city is the HANDAN BINGUAN with accommodation for Y8 a night. The most interesting site to visit is XIANGTANGSHAN DONG (Mt. Xiangtang Grottoes). These Buddhist caves were started in the Northern Qi Dynasty (550 -577 AD) and continued into the Ming Dynasty (1368 - 1644 AD). There are 16 caves with over 3,000 Buddhist statues.

JIAMUSI 佳木斯

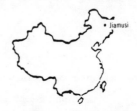

Jiamusi is located in the extreme northeastern corner of Heilongjiang Province in China's northeast. Jiamusi, which sits on the banks of Songhua Jiang (Songhua River), is about as far northeast in China as tourists can go. The people here are Manchu and Han, but it seems impossible to make the distinction. The one hotel in town is the JIAMUSI BINGUAN for Y18 a night (one bed in a double room). In this area you can see the southern fringe of the Siberian boreal forest which, in the Soviet Union, is called the taiga. Unfortunately, not much of the forest remains. The people in Jiamusi are so unaccustomed to seeing tourists that they fall over themselves trying to help you! If you enjoy people and far-out places, you might consider a trip here. There are several trains a day running to and from Jiamusi, from Mudanjiang and from Harbin.

JIAYUGUAN 嘉峪关

LOCATION AND TRANSPORTATION: JIAYUGUAN (Jiayu Pass) is located in the western end of Gansu Province, at the western tip of the Great Wall of China. It lies about half way between Lanzhou and Turpan on the only rail line connecting China Proper and the western territory of Xinjiang. Virtually everyone who arrives at Jiayuguan comes by train. There are about six trains daily making the run, each way. In the immediate area buses are used.

HOTEL: The JIAYUGUAN BINGUAN is located in the middle of town on the main circle. One bed in a dorm is Y5 a night. The CITS office is here. There are several restaurants in the area of the bazaar.

SIGHTS: It is not at the very end of the wall, but is it the last fort. The wall can be seen snaking across the desert in a southwesterly direction from the fort; you can see nothing running in an easterly direction.

The fort at Jiayuguan

To get from the centre of town to the fort, a distance of about 7 kms, there is one bus in the morning taking passengers directly to the fort. The schedule and number of buses each day varies with the season. There are also buses every hour or so making the run between Jiayuguan and Juiquan, about 30 kms to the southeast. Some people stay in Jiuquan and visit the fort on a day trip. There is one morning bus running to Dunhuang, beginning at 0700 in Juiquan; it also stops in Jiayuguan.

An information leaflet states: "Jiayuguan, wedged between the snow capped Qilian Shan and the Mazong Shan, assumes an imposing and menacing stance that has won it the title of 'the Impregnable Defile under the Sun'. It is China's best preserved ancient stronghold. Through this pass, caravans pushed ahead 2,000 years ago along the ancient SI ZHOU ZI LU (Silk Road), to central/west Asia and to Europe, transporting silk products from China and inaugurating trade and cultural exchange between east and west. Toward the latter half of the fifteenth century, however, the Silk Road traffic underwent a gradual decline as a result of the advent of sea transportation. In the Ming (1368-1644 AD) and Qing (1644-1911 AD) Dynasties, the Jiayuguan stronghold was used by the ruling class as a toll-house to extort money from people engaged in inland trade". The fortress or stronghold has a wall around it about 11 metres high and has two walls enclosing the inner sanctuary or living quarters. Inside is a temple and a place to buy souvenirs, postcards, food and drinks. It is an interesting place and should not be missed if you are in this part of China.

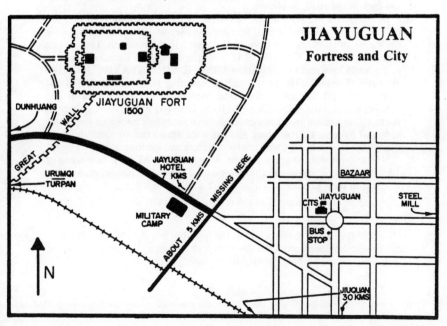

JILIN 吉林

LOCATION AND TRANSPORTATION: Jilin is located in the northeast of China in Jilin Province. It is the second largest city after Changchun. Getting there is virtually always by train. There are many trains daily from Changchun which run to the northeast and the city of Tumen on the North Korean border and to Mudanjiang in Heilongjiang Province.

HOTEL: Although there are two hotels in Jilin, only one can be used by foreign tourists. To reach the XIGUAN BINGUAN, take bus number 1 from the train station and alight at the traffic circle, as shown. You then walk about one km to the hotel. There are some beds available for as little as Y4 or Y5 a night in large rooms; or you may get a room to yourself for Y8. This is one of the few places in China's Dongbei (Northeast) that has cheap accommodation. The Dongguan Binguan does not accept foreign travellers.

SIGHTS: Jilin is one of the few places in the northeast which has something to see, at least from the tourist's point of view. Famous in this area are the "Three Treasures of Northeast China". They are sika deer antler from which blood tonics are made, sable or marten furs which rank among the finest in the world, and ginseng root which is used to make tonic for restoring vigor and health. All three products can be seen at the LONGTAN SHAN DEER FARM. Take bus 12 from the train station then walk or hitch hike south at the fork in the road, as shown.

In the JILIN MUSEUM, one can see a meteorite weighing 1770 kgs, one of 132 pieces recovered from a meteorite shower of 1976. Take bus 3 from the station or from near the Dongguan Binguan to this museum. There is also a large CATHOLIC CATHEDRAL near the Dongguan Binguan.

About 16 kms south of Jilin is the SONGHUAHU SKI AREA. It has two ski runs of about 3000 metres each, descending from an altitude of 934 metres. The lift is 1800 metres long. Nearby is FENGMAN town and HYDROELECTRIC POWER STATION. Take bus 9 from the traffic circle north of the Xiguan Hotel. Buses leave about every half hour and stop in the centre of Fengman. From there you can walk across the river to behind the dam to see timber being unloaded from barges and loaded onto railway cars.

It is also possible to see a Korean village, named ALADI, just north of Jilin. However, if you are heading eastwards, you will encounter many more Koreans in that direction.

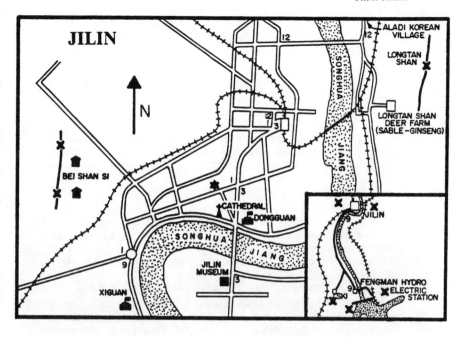

JINAN 济南

Jinan is not noted for its tourist attractions, but you may have to stop there if you are on your way to "greener pastures" on the Shandong Peninsula. Jinan is the capital of Shandong Province and the most prosperous city. It is also on the main rail line linking Beijing and Shanghai. There is a hotel, the JINAN BINGUAN, about 1 km from the train station, but it does not offer budget accommodation. The main thing to see in Jinan are the four BUBBLING SPRINGS for which the city is famous in China.

Turpan cemetery, one km. north of Turpan hotel (K)

JIUQUAN 酒泉

Jiuquan is just one of the many oases one passes when taking a train from Lanzhou to Urumqi in Xinjiang. Jiuquan is found in western Gansu Province and was part of what is called today the Si Zhou Zi Lu (the Silk Road). Marco Polo mentioned the town in his diary in the 13th century. A 4th century DRUM TOWER stands at the crossroads of the city. Also, you can visit the bazaar. The people here are Han Chinese, not the Uygurs you will meet in Xinjiang. There is a comfortable hotel where the cheapest beds are Y2.50 a night in large 25 bed dorms, or Y8 for a bed in a triple room. The Buddhist caves outside town are under military guard and not yet open to public viewing. From Jiuquan you can catch a once-hourly bus to nearby Jiayuguan, 30 kms away, and view the famous Jiayuguan fortress. When you arrive in Jiuquan, get off the train and take a bus the 14 kms to the centre of town. Presumably a bus will be around at the time of the arrival of your train.

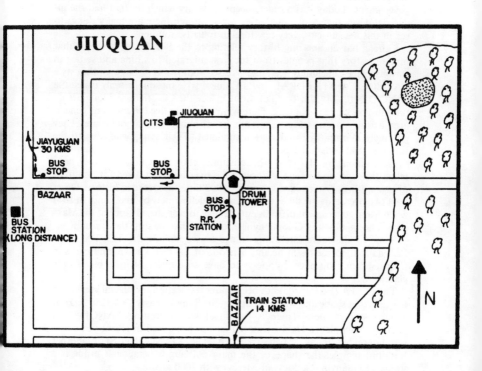

KAIFENG 开峰

LOCATION AND TRANSPORTATION: Kaifeng is located on the main rail line linking Xian , Luoyang, Zhengzhen and Shanghai. It is only about one hour to the east of Zhengzhou, in northern Henan Province. Virtually everybody visiting Kaifeng comes by train, of which there are many each day.

HOTEL: There are three hotels in Kaifeng, but the Sondu is off limits to foreigners at this time. The ones you can stay at are the KAIFENG which charges about Y20 per night, and the BIAN JING which charges Y4 for each bed in a quad room, and Y6 for each bed in a triple room. Take bus 3 from the train station to reach the Bian Jing, and bus 5 to reach the Kaifeng. The local CITS office is at the Kaifeng Binguan.

SIGHT: Situated in the lower reaches of the Huang He (Yellow River), Kaifeng has a population of over half a million. With a recorded history close to 3000 years, Kaifeng was the capital of seven dynasties and is one of China's six great ancient capital cities. The last time Kaifeng was capital was in 1127 when invaders from Manchuria leveled the city and drove out the government. Today it is a quiet, sleepy little city which has not had the industrial development of other cities. Even though there are many things to see in this ancient city, very few foreign tourists stop here.

Kaifeng has an amazing history relating to the Silk Road. It was at that time in history that peoples from the west migrated to China and settled in various places, including Kaifeng. We see today a very large Gothic style CATHOLIC CATHEDRAL and a Chinese style mosque, simply called the QING DIN SI (Muslim Temple). Long before the Christians and long before the Muslims came to Kaifeng, there were Jews who lived in the same general area as the mosque today; they numbered about 1000 at one time. They gradually intermarried and were assimilated. Their synagogue, lost to the flood in 1842, was not rebuilt.

Floods along the HUANG HE, sometimes known as China's Sorrow, have taken their toll on Kaifeng. Although the river has been diked for hundreds of years, it has broken its dikes at least 900 times in recorded history. On at least two occasions the dikes were breached deliberately by man: once in 1644 when Ming government officials cut the dike to stop the advance of the Manchus, and in 1938 the Guomindang broke the dike to stop the Japanese.

Some of the more interesting things to see include the TEI TA, (Iron Pagoda). At 55 metres in height, it is one of the best known landmarks in China. From a distance it appears to have an exterior of iron, but is only glazed tile.

The PO TA (Po Pagoda) has been under restoration for several years. It is hexagonal in shape and was built during the Song Dynasty (960-1280 AD). It is nine storeys high. There is the small but interesting YANQING SI (Yanqing Temple), a Daoist temple that has been used in recent years as a warehouse but today is being restored. The XIANGGUO SI is another Buddhist temple; the shape of the main building is octagonal; inside is a statue of Guanyin (Goddess of Mercy) with 1000 arms.

Old Kaifeng, the part shown on this map, has narrow streets that make it difficult for buses to pass. The wall surrounding the city is one of the better ones to be seen in China. Street vendors appear to be everywhere, mainly selling food. Because of this and because of the unusual temples, Kaifeng is well worth seeing.

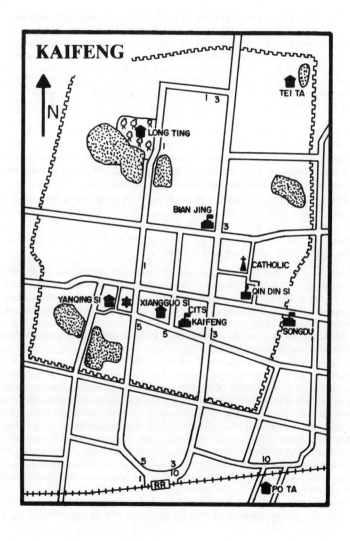

KASHGAR (KASHI)
喀什爾

Kashgar (Kashi)

LOCATION AND TRANSPORTATION: Kashgar is located in the extreme western end of Xinjiang, the most westerly province in China. Kashgar, the farthest west a visitor can go in China, lies very near the point in Central Asia where the USSR, Afghanistan, Pakistan and China meet. Getting there today is relatively easy; distance being the only hardship. There are flights from Urumqi which in turn is linked with the rest of China, the cost of a flight is approximately Y218. The 3 to 4 day bus ride costs Y38.30. One reason for the high cost of flying is that foreigners pay more than Chinese, similar to the price controls on train tickets. Many travellers take the bus one way for the experience, then fly back. Each morning there are about 3 buses leaving Urumqi bound for Kashgar, and each morning the same number leave Kashgar for Urumqi. They try to leave by 0900. In 1985 you could take a train to Korla then a bus the rest of the way to Kashgar, but it is more time consuming than taking the bus direct from Urumqi.

HOTEL: In Kashgar there is one hotel, the XIN BINGUAN (New Hotel). Getting there from the bus station requires about a half hour's walk, but most people hire a donkey cart of which there are many. Get three or four people together and the total cost is only about Y1.5 or Y2. The hotel also houses the CITS office and a restaurant.

SIGHTS: The history of Kashgar can be traced back more than 2000 years. In ancient times Kashgar was known as Shule where, according to the Persian Epic, the legendary Tushlan hero Abla Puziyafu built the capital of his kingdom. During the rule of Han Emperor Wu Di (about 200 BC) the Western Region came under the wing of the Western Han government. For 2000 years this Western Region has been more or less part of China but the influence has vacillated greatly.

By far the biggest attraction in Kashgar is the people. There are about 55 national minority groups in China. The UYGUR people who inhabit Kashgar, as well as most other bases in Xinjiang, are one of the largest groups; they number about six million. Although there are also Kazaks and Kirgiz, you may not recognize them unless someone points them out. The Uygurs (pronounced We-Ger) are a Turkish speaking people who in written history migrated from the Orhon River Valley of Mongolia. Although their language is somewhat similar to that spoken in Turkey, the language has been influenced over the centuries by its proximity to China. The Uygurs are the farmers who inhabit the oases; the KAZAKS raise sheep and cattle and, in summer, live high in the mountains with their flocks and herds. The KIRGIZ dwell mostly in the desert with their camels. The Kazaks number about one million while the Kirgiz are about 100,000 in population.

Although there are Han Chinese in Kashgar, their numbers are few and they keep a low profile. They are definitely a minority here. Some of the best places to meet the Uygurs are in the bazaars. Some tourists spend a week just walking around the bazaar looking at Uygurs! The best time to be in Kashgar is on Sunday for the SUNDAY BAZAAR, as shown on the map. The number of people there at midday is near 15,000. Counting the numbers coming and going and who might have attended at some time in the city, the number reaches maybe 20-25,000. Everything under the sun is sold or bartered! It is recognized as one of the most impressive markets in China.

Other things to see include the ID KAH MOSQUE, especially on Fridays at 1230 local time (1430 China Standard Time). This is when the Muslims gather for their weekly prayers; the place is full. Women are usually not allowed inside. People who have been to Afghanistan or northern Pakistan will see striking similarities with this mosque, the people and the bazaar. Further to the east, within walking distance of the hotel, is the ABAKH HOJA TOMB and mosque. A cemetery just to the east is well worth the walk, or jump on one of many donkey carts going that way. August and September would be ideal times to visit Kashgar because they have some of the best melons in the world at that time. Watermelons are called XI GUA, while honey-dew melons are called *hami gua* after the name of the town in eastern Xinjiang.

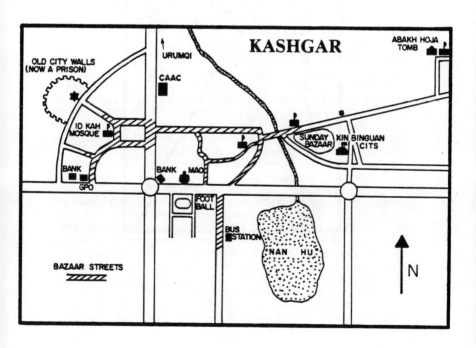

115

Outside Kashgar are several sites that might be interesting if you have the time. One is the SAN XIAN SHIR KU (Three Immortals Stone Cave). There are three caves; you will have to take a ladder with your CITS vehicle to reach them. To the east of town about 30 kms are the ruins of the ancient city of HANOI. Hanoi reached its apex during the Tang (618-907 AD) and Song (960-1280 AD) Dynasties. The best part of the ruins would be the MOR TEMPLE. If you can get several people together to form a group you could go to the big mountains southwest of Kashgar, namely the famous MUZTAGATA. You will have to make arrangements with CITS.

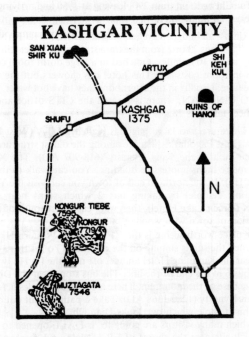

Refer to page 47 for BUDDHIST CAVES IN XINJIANG.

KUNMING 昆明

LOCATION AND TRANSPORTATION: Kunming is located in southwest China in the province of Sichuan. It sits on a plateau at about 1800 metres, making it one of the most desirable cities, climate wise, in China. It has a spring-like climate the year round. Getting to this city of 2 million is almost always by rail, but people in a hurry sometimes fly in or out from places like Chengdu, Beijing, Xian and Shanghai. Most people arrive in Kunming on train 79 from Shanghai and Guilin, arriving at 0640. That same train (#80) leaves Kunming at 1640 bound for Guilin and Shanghai. Many people leave Kunming for Chengdu on train 290, leaving at 1950 and arriving in Chengdu at 1918, about 24 hours later.

HOTEL: Almost all budget travellers stay at the KUN HU FAN DIAN (Kun Hu Hotel). Take bus 23 or 2 from the train station, or better still walk the one km north in about 10 minutes. One bed in a large dorm room costs Y3.50; a bed in a twin room costs Y6. This hotel has showers but the water is cold most of the time. Usually in the afternoons they have hot water. To reach the KUNMING BINGUAN, where is located the CITS office and the nearby CAAC office, take bus 23.

SIGHTS: There are two large pagodas, called XI TA (West Pagoda) and DONG TA (East Pagoda), which are among the oldest structures in the city, having been built in the Tang Dynasty (618-907 AD). The Xi Ta is a 13 storey, 36 metre high, impressive building. You can walk to these from the hotel (Kun Hu). In the northern end of town you can visit the YUANTONG SI (Yuantong Temple) by taking bus 2 which stops near the LU HU BINGUAN (Green Lake Hotel), then walk east. Just south of this temple is an old section of town with wooden buildings.

Another place worth seeing is the XI SHAN or Western Hills. Go in the morning when the sun is shining on the cliff face. To get there take bus 5 or 26 from near the Kunming Hotel and get off near the Lu Hu, where one can then take bus 6 to the end of the line. The bus stops near the Dian Chi (Dian Lake) at the base of the mountain. There are several temples here dating back to the Yuan Dynasty (1280-1368 AD). Take a pathway cut out of a cliff-face to a Buddhist temple which overlooks Dian Chi.

A city which many visitors are going to, is DALI, opened to foreigners in early 1984. It sits near the shores of ER HAI (Two Lakes), a lake ranking sixth in size among fresh water lakes in China. As the city is at a high altitude the nights are cool. Just northwest of the city is a peak reaching 4122 metres which is snow capped at times. Another nearby mountain is considered sacred by Buddhists. It is called Chicken Foot. At one time there were 200 Buddhist temples on it, most of which were ruined during the Cultural Revolution (1965-1976). Getting to Dali requires two day bus ride from Kunming, one night being spent in a hotel on the road. Inquire at the CITS office about tickets and departure location. Dali is an excellent location to observe some of the minority peoples of China, the Bai and Li.

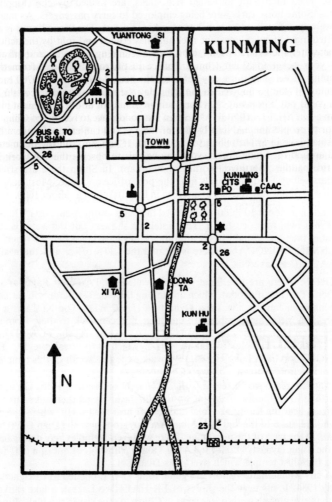

There are many interesting places to visit outside the city. The best known is SHILIN (Stone Forest), located about 126 kms southeast of Kunming. The road to Shilin traverses a mountainous region where much of the soil is reddish in colour. This colour contrasts with the valleys which are clothed in rice fields, some green, some brown. The latter await the peasant's scythe. Carts, piled high with harvested rice stalks, are hauled by clip-clopping horses. Some horse carts were being employed to carry passengers. As many as twelve people would be hunched together in a cart. The Stone Forest is an uplifted mass of solid limestone rock that has eroded and split by the action of rainwater and wind. The tall, eroded rocks stand upright, grey and naked. Buy your ticket to Shilin from an office just across the street from the Kunming Hotel. Buy it the day before as the buses leave at about 0700 each morning. If you go and return the same day the round-trip ticket costs Y7. You could buy a one-way ticket and stay in Shilin for about Y4 a night in a dorm at the SHILIN BINGUAN. Shilin is a good place to see one of China's minority people, the SANI, a branch of the Yi. You can encounter them by the small lake in Shilin selling souvenirs and, if you walk on the perimeter road around the Stone Forest, you may be able to observe them at work in the rice paddies (northwest corner of the map). In Shilin there are street vendors selling food and meals near the post office and lake. Most people coming to Shilin stay the day and return in the afternoon at about 1600. The bus ride to Kunming takes about three hours.

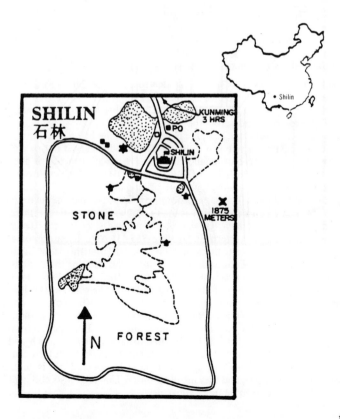

LANZHOU 兰州

Lanzhou

LOCATION AND TRANSPORTATION: Lanzhou is the capital of Gansu Province and is located in the eastern end of that province. You might say Lanzhou is situated at the western boundary of what we normally call China Proper. To the east is the densely populated region China is noted for; to the west is the desert - the relatively unpopulated area. Beyond Lanzhou is the frontier region. There are about eight trains per day running to Lanzhou, about six of which run beyond, to Xinjiang. If you are leaving Lanzhou going to Xining, only one train runs daily, train 301. It leaves the main Lanzhou Station at 1516 hours and arrives at Xining at 2029. It is usually better to buy your ticket the day before and catch the train at LANZHOU XI ZHAN (Lanzhou West Station) at 1534 hours. With your ticket you will be given a seat. The Xi Zhan is only five minutes walk from the You Yi Binguan. There are about four other trains leaving Lanzhou for Xining, but they run about every other day.

HOTEL: The You Yi Binguan (Friendship Hotel). It is pronounced Yo E. One bed in a large dorm costs Y6 a night. If your train goes to the Lanzhou Xi Station, you could walk to the hotel. If you get off the train at the main station, take bus 1 for a 30 minute ride. Lanzhou, a very long city, stretches for 20 kms along the Huang He (Yellow River).

SIGHTS: BAI TA SHAN (White Pagoda Mountain) or Bai Ta Si. You can climb to the topmost temple of this temple complex for a fine view of the city. Take bus 1 to near the temple (as well as other buses), then walk the short distance north and across the river.

BINGLINGSI (Bingling Temple). This is one of the better Buddhist cave complexes in China. There is a statue of The Buddha carved out of a cliff face with an assortment of smaller figures. The main attraction is the 27 metre high statue of a seated MAITREYA BUDDHA. Rough-cut from the cliff, it was finished by adding a mixture of mud and straw to fill it out and form the finished look. This same procedure is used elsewhere in the western region of China because the climate is so dry. Being under a cliff, and thereby protected, it remains today. Repairs have continued since the cave temples were first begun in the Western Jin Dynasty (385-431 AD). These are some of the oldest Buddhist cave temples in China. Apart from this large Buddha there are smaller statues and some caves with murals. Getting there can be a problem. Summer is an acceptable time to go to Binglingsi, as you have to take a boat on the lake behind the Yong Jing Dam. The water level is low at other times of the year. Buy your ticket at the CITS office in the You Yi Hotel the day before. You will ride a bus about 70 kms from Lanzhou to Yong Jing then board a boat for a 3 hour cruise to the Binglingsi. You will have about two hours there. It is advisable to take your own lunch and a water bottle; drinks are not always available but in season fresh fruit can be purchased. This trip costs Y20, and takes about 11 hours. There is another slower boat for Chinese, and they use older buses. That tour costs about Y18. The CITS tour seems to be more convenient.

If you are there and the boats are not running, you might look into an alternate route. You can take a bus, or maybe hitch hike, to a place called Yang Ta, another 69 kms from Yong Jing. From there a trail runs down the canyon to the Binglingsi. But to do this route will likely require an overnight stay somewhere. Ask at CITS.

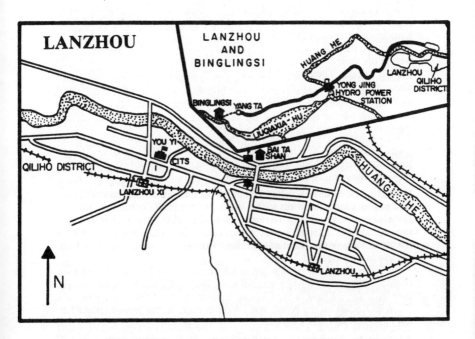

Refer to page 46 for BUDDHIST CAVES IN GANSU AND NINGXIA.

LHASA 拉萨

• Lhasa

LOCATION AND TRANSPORTATION: Lhasa, capital of XIZANG (Tibet) AUTONOMOUS REGION lies on the banks of a tributary of the YARLUNG ZAMBO (Brahmaputra River) at 3,800 metres.

On September 1, 1984, Lhasa was opened to foreign independent travellers. To reach Lhasa you leave from Chengdu. You have three alternatives: a) Travel by bus, a 10 day trip. b) Train to Golmud, then a 30 hour bus trip to Lhasa. Take water and food. c) Fly for about US$130.00 from Chengdu.

Lhasa airport, 80 km from town, is served by a bus that meets the plane. Don't miss the bus! As you may suffer breathlessness and a headache at the high altitude, take motion sickness tablets. Include in your baggage warm clothing, a hat, sunglasses and lip salve. The temperature on the plateau fluctuates. The days can be hot; the nights, cold.

To leave Lhasa you can return to Chengdu or travel overland to Kathmandu, Nepal. To go to Nepal you must obtain a visa at the Nepalese consulate in Lhasa. It costs Y30. Next, obtain an exit permit from the Lhasa office of the Public Security Bureau. The cost is Y6. To buy your bus ticket to your first destination, XIGAZE, go to the bus station next to the CAAC office. One road goes direct to XIGAZE: the fare is Y17. Another goes via GYANZE where you stay overnight. Near GYANZE, two fortresses sit on isolated hills. The road passes a turquoise lake and climbs the 5000m KAMBA pass. Magnificent panoramas of the Himalayas can be seen from the towns of Pagri and Tingri.

In Xigaze look for a truck going to Khasa. As the 15-20 hour trip to Khasa could be dusty, wear a white surgical mask (buy in Lhasa) or a handkerchief over your face. Khasa is the Chinese frontier town. From Khasa you walk 10km to Kodari on the Nepal side of the border. A bus from KODARI to KATHMANDU takes 6 hours.

ENTERING TIBET FROM NEPAL: As of September 1985 it is only possible to enter Tibet from Nepal on a packaged tour.

HOTELS: DIYI BINGUAN (No. 1 Guesthouse), located near the Potala. Y5. DISAN BINGUAN (No. 3 Guesthouse) located 7km out of town. This hotel's rate can be as much as 20 times the rate at DIYI.

SIGHTS: By far the most famous sight in Lhasa is the POTALA PALACE, the former winter residence of the Dalai Lama. The Potala was first built in the eighth century by Songtsan Gampo and was named the Red Palace. That structure is long gone and the one we see today was built by the fifth Dalai Lama (1617-1682). It took 50 years to build and is said to contain 1,000 rooms, 200,000 statues and 10,000 chapels. There are tombs within the palace, the best ones being the tombs of the fifth and thirteenth Dalai Lamas. The Potala is built on a hill overlooking the city and can be seen from all parts of the valley.

About 3 kms west of the Potala is the NORBU LINGGA, or Jewel Park. It is the former summer palace of the Dalai Lama. It is now open to the public; on weekends people throng here for picnics.

Lhasa has two cities, the old and the new. The new part is where the expensive hotel is located; the old part has the cheaper hotel and all the places you will want to visit. Just inside the old city is the oldest and holiest of all the temples in Lhasa, the JOKHANG SI. This temple, first founded in 652 AD during the reign of Songtsan Gampo, has been expanded at times since. It combines architecture of Nepal, China and Tibet. Inside is a 2 metre high statue of the Sakyamuni Buddha. The street encircling this temple is where you will find one of the biggest bazaars in Lhasa, the Bargor Bazaar. Expect to haggle here.

Seven kms north of the Potala Palace is the SERA GOIN (Sera Monastery). The bus leaves from outside the Jokhang. The Sera Monastery sits on a hill overlooking the valley. Many of the Tibetan rebels were headquartered here during the bloody riots of 1959. It has four temples behind which several huge statues of the Buddha are carved into the cliff face.

Near the Sera Monastery it is possible to view the traditional Tibetan funeral custom. This custom requires that a corpse be dismembered and the bones, including the skull, be crushed, and the remains fed to vultures and wild dogs. Reasons for this strange burial are that the ground is generally too hard during much of the year for graves to be dug and the scarcity of wood in this treeless land rules out cremation. Arrive at dawn just east of the Sera Monastery on weekday mornings to see bodies butchered on a large flat rock. Follow the canal.

About 10 kms northwest of town you will find the DREPUNG GOIN. The bus leaves from outside the Jokhang. The Drepung Goin is where the Yellow Hat sect of Tibetan Buddhism was founded in 1416. This monastery at one time was the biggest in the world, said to have housed 10,000 monks, but today has only 300. This place may or may not be open for the foreign visitor.

GYANZE is located to the southwest of Lhasa and, like many cities and towns in Tibet, has a fortress or citadel sitting atop a small hill. It has an interesting Golden Temple with a white stupa, similar to those found in Nepal.

If you can make it to XIGAZE, do so. This is the second largest city in Xizang Province, and is the seat of the Panchen Lama. The rein of the Panchen Lama began in 1641-42 when Mongol armies invaded Tibet to insure the rule of the Yellow Hat sect when they were struggling for power and influence against their adversaries, the Red Hat sect. The Mongols put into power, or rather kept in power, the fifth Dalai Lama, known as the Great Fifth. As a kindly gesture the fifth Dalai Lama created a new institution by bestowing the name of Panchen Lama upon his aged and revered teacher, the Abbot of the Tashilumpo Monastery near Xigaze. Panchen Lamas are chosen in the same manner as Dalai Lamas. When either of these leaders dies a search begins throughout the land for his reincarnation. The chosen male child has to possess the same mystical qualities as the lama who has just recently died; these set him apart from ordinary mortals. Some signs are that the new lama has large ears, upward-slanting eyes and eyebrows, and that one of his hands should bear a mark like a conch-shell. Their choice is usually a child of two or three from a lower class family. The reason for choosing the lama from a lower class rather than a noble family is to ensure that one family cannot take the title and treat it as a hereditary crown. The last of the Panchen Lamas went to Beijing in 1965 and has lived there ever since. The Tashilumpo Monastery still stands today near Xigaze and is one of the more important in the province.

LUOYANG 洛阳

• Luoyang

LOCATION AND TRANSPORTATION: Luoyang is located in north central Henan Province on the main rail line linking Xian and Zhengzhou. Many trains pass Luoyang daily; getting transport is easy. Across the square from the main railway station is the long distance bus station where you can buy tickets for a town such as Dengfeng.

HOTEL: The one hotel in town for foreign visitors is the YOU YI BINGUAN (Friendship Guesthouse). Walk about 200 metres from the front door of the train station and board bus 2 which runs along the street north of the YOU YI. One bed in a large dorm room costs Y4.

SIGHTS: LONGMEN SHIR KU (Dragon Gate Stone Caves). These caves stretch along the banks of a river for about one km. The many different sized caves total 1,352. There is one very large opening in the cliff, presumably a cave at one time, which now has a collapsed roof. It contains some large carved images of The Buddha, two statues of Bodhisattvas and four fearsome figures of other gods. The tallest is 17 metres. This particular cave or temple, called FENGXIANSI, was completed in 675 AD in the Tang Dynasty. This entire complex was started in 494 AD by Emperor Xiao Wen of the Northern Wei Dynasty when he moved to Luoyang from Datong. The complex took over 400 years to complete. To get there take bus 10 from near the hotel for the 30 minute ride.

BAI MA SI (White Horse Temple, a Buddhist temple). Take one of several buses across town to reach a place called Xiguan, where you will catch bus 6. (See map for the buses which will get you to Xiguan). Take bus 6 to the end of the line, which is right in front of the temple.

Luoyang is one of the oldest cities in China. It has a written history dating back to about 2100 BC when it was the capital of the Xia Dynasty. It was also the capital of the Zhou (1122-770 BC), the Han (206 BC - 220 AD) and the Tang Dynasty (618-907 AD). It was in 937 AD when the capital was moved to Kaifeng that Luoyang lost its prominence and was never the same after that. Today Luoyang is a very clean and proud industrial city.

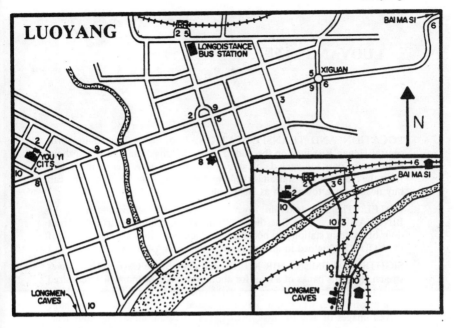

龙门   Longmen caves, Luoyang

Beijing (Peking) duck (J)

Wuzhou. Homes are constructed in brick; wood is not plentiful (J)

126

MUDANJIANG 牡丹江

LOCATION AND TRANSPORTATION: Mudanjiang is located in China's Dong Bei, or northeast in the extreme southeastern corner of Heilongjiang Province. This is a city of nearly a million people. Trains run directly westward to Harbin; others run north-south in the direction of Jiamusi to the north, and to Tumen (on the Korean border) to the south.

HOTEL: There are three hotels in town; the one with a CITS office is the MUDANJIANG BINGUAN. Get there by walking out of the train station and turning left. It is not far. There is a bus, also. The cost of one bed in a double room is Y21; there are no economic dorm rooms.

SIGHTS: About the only thing to see in Mudanjiang is about 1,000 other people gathering around you! There simply are not many foreigners in this area thus the curiosity. JINGPO HU (Lake) is of interest. This large lake on the Mudan Jiang (Mudan River) was formed by a lava flow creating a blockage across the river. It is the largest barrier lake in China, being 45 kms long, and is in a relatively pristine setting with forests surrounding the lake. At the northern end of the lake are villas and a hotel. At the lava dam are the Hovering Mansion Waterfalls where the water spills over the lava, creating quite a spectacle. Inquire at the hotel and CITS office about buses going there, and lodging at the lake.

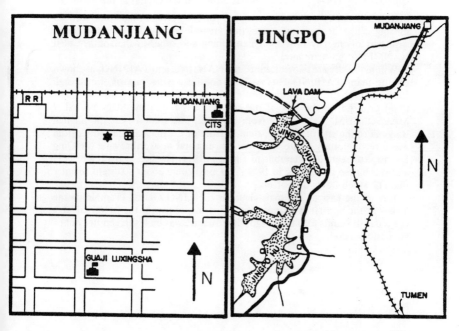

NANJING 南京

LOCATION AND TRANSPORTATION: Nanjing is located in the southwest corner of Jiangsu Province on the bank of the Chang Jiang (Yangtze River). It is the capital of the province. It also lies to the northwest of Shanghai on the main rail line linking Shanghai and Beijing. Literally dozens of trains pass this city each day.

HOTEL: The cheapest hotel in town is the SHENGLI or VICTORY HOTEL. Dorm rooms are about Y5 or Y6 a night. Take bus 1 or 33 from the train station. The next cheapest place is the DING SHAN BINGUAN, located on a small hill in the northwest part of town. It has dorm beds for Y8 a night. Take bus 1 or 33 from the station, transfer to bus 16, and walk nearly a km; or, bus 10 from the station, and walk nearly two kms. If these are all full try the NANJING BINGUAN, but this one has no dorms or cheap accommodation. Take bus 33, then 16.

HISTORY: Nanjing (Southern Capital) has a history dating back to the Xia Dynasty (2205-1706 BC) and before. Off and on, Nanjing has been the capital of China since the Three Kingdoms period (220-265 AD). It was also the capital until the end of the Sui Dynasty (589-618 AD), then again in the Southern Tang (618-907). It was chosen the capital city in the Ming Dynasty (1368-1644 AD) and was declared a southern capital for a time during the Qing Dynasty (1644-1911 AD). It has also been the capital in this century.

SIGHTS: The city wall has been extant for 600 years but has some sections missing. There are two main gates that are well preserved: one in the northwest part of the city near the Chang Jiang and other in the south, called NANMEN (Southern gate).

Within the city are two museums, the NANJING and TAIPING, as shown on the map. TAIPING PALACE is not far to the east of the Shengli Binguan. Perhaps the most interesting places to see and visit are some tombs (ling) on a hill to the east of the city. Here is found the SUN YATSEN MAUSOLEUM. Take bus 9 from the main intersection near the Shengli Binguan to the end of the line, right in front of the mausoleum. Sun Yatsen was a revolutionary figure who was instrumental in overthrowing the Qing Dynasty to create the Republic of China in 1911. He died in Beijing in 1925 and was buried in Nanjing in 1929. You must climb about 400 steps to enter tha hall which holds his coffin.

Just to the east of the mausoleum is the LING GU SI (Temple of the Valley of the Spirits). The most obvious structure here is the LING GU TA (Pagoda). It stands 61 metres high; the structure was built this century out of steel and concrete.

West of the mausoleum are two places of interest. First is the MING-XIAOLING (Little Ming Tomb). Being in a rather dilapidated condition not many people visit it. Just to the south of this tomb is the street with the GUARD OF HONOUR, also known as the SPIRIT WAY. Two rows of statues of animals guard the entrance of the tomb. The larger than life animals consist of camels, horses, elephants, lions and mythical animals. Some are standing, others crouching. This same type of Guard of Honour can be seen at the Ming tombs north of Beijing, and in Gongxian County, east of Luoyang in Henan Province.

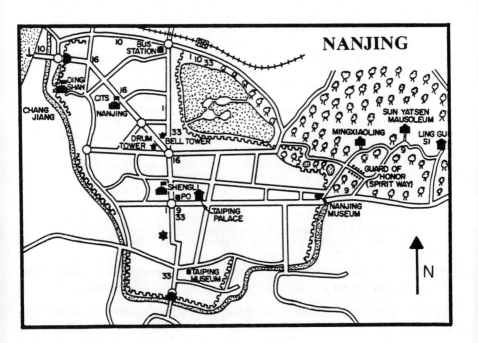

NANNING: 南寧

LOCATION AND TRANSPORTATION: Nanning is the capital city of the Guangxi-Zhuang Autonomous Region, one of China's most southerly provinces. It is also on the rail line running to Hanoi in Vietnam. About three trains a day run as far as Nanning, and a couple of others run south toward Vietnam.

HOTEL: Several hotels are in Nanning; the CITS office is in the MINGYUAN BINGUAN. Most travellers stay in the YONGJIANG BINGUAN, reached by taking bus 5 from the train station. The cheapest bed costs Y7 per night in a triple or quad room.

SIGHTS: If you are in China in winter, it would be an excellent place to spend some time as the region is tropical. As the city is relatively new, dating mainly from 1949, it has little to see in the way of old buildings or temples. However, older buildings stand near the train station and west of the Nanning Hotel. Not in Nanning itself, but in the surrounding countryside you may encounter national minority people. Guangxi is an autonomous region for the ZHUANG people. The Zhuang are one of the Tai tribes whose numbers total nearly 13 million, one of the largest minority groups in China. Ask about the GUANGXI INSTITUTE FOR NATIONALITIES located northwest of town.

YILING DONG (Yiling Caves) are 32 kms north of the city. Inquire at CITS about buses heading that way. In the vicinity of Nanning are several places open to foreigners, including the old fishing port of BEIHAI, an eight hour bus ride away.

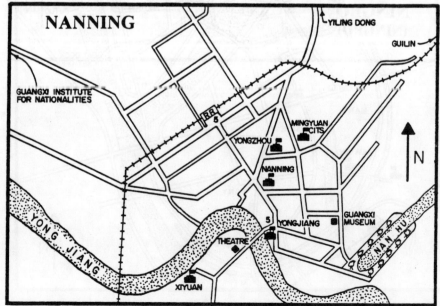

NINGPO 宁波

Ningbo

LOCATION AND TRANSPORTATION: Ningpo is located in eastern Zhejiang Province at the confluence of two branches of the Yong Jiang. Even though Ningpo is inland it is a major port of China. Several trains each day are scheduled for Ningpo, most of which pass through Hangzhou. You can leave Ningpo by a ferry which sails for Putuo Shan, one of China's nine sacred mountains. This mountain is located on an island east of the city. See the hiking section of this book for more details.

HOTELS: Stay at the HUA QIAO, one km from the train station. As there are no dorm rooms in this hotel you will be placed in a double room, at Y15 for each bed; but that includes a color TV.

SIGHTS: Ningpo has an interesting old part of town - the part shown in the centre of this map and along the river. Chinese junks ply the river. There are a number of canals but most are out of town. Just north of Ningpo is the oldest wooden structure in China south of the Chang Jiang - the BAO GUO SI (temple). The original structure, built in the Tang Dynasty (618-907 AD), was destroyed; the temple you now see dates from 1013. To get there take bus 11 from just over the bridge and to the left, as shown on the map. The last bus each day leaves at about 1500 hours.

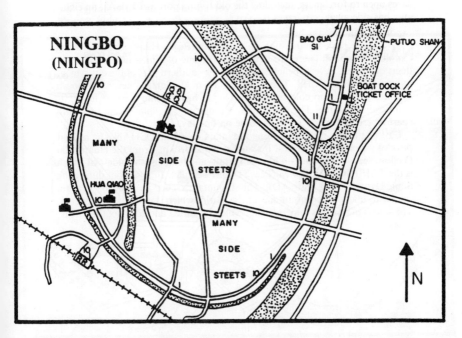

QINGDAO 青岛

LOCATION AND TRANSPORTATION: Qingdao is a city of a million people located on the southern side of the Shandong Peninsula, in Shandong Province. At least half a dozen fast trains, plus several local trains, come and go each day from Qingdao. All trains must pass through Jinan before arriving here. You can also arrive or depart Qingdao by ship. Several times a week boats go to Shanghai; a third class ticket costs Y10.

HOTEL: The HUIQUAN, the hotel most used by foreign tourists, is expensive and has no dorm rooms. The CITS office is in this hotel. Take bus 6 from the train station. The ZHANQIAO (or maybe it's called the Huazhou Binguan) just east of the train station has cheaper rooms. For one bed in a double, the cost is about Y12. Sorry, no dorm rooms! But with the influx of more tourists, cheaper accommodation may be forthcoming.

SIGHTS: One of the main sights to see is the old part of the town. Before 1898, Qingdao was only a small fishing village. In that year China ceded the peninsula to Germany as a trading port. It was then built into a city and port by the Germans. Today the central part of the city, shown on the map, has many European style buildings and churches, and the port area is one of the best in north China. The Germans held the city until the end of World War I, then for a while it was used by Japan. Finally after 1949 ownership reverted to China. The Germans not only left behind interesting old buildings, but also a brewery. The QINGDAO PIJIU is famous throughout China. Some is exported. Pijiu means beer.

Within the park surrounding Taiping Shan (Peace Hill) is one interesting temple or pagoda. There are two museums, one of which has marine products displayed. Several beaches lie along the southern part of the city which, in summer, are crowded. This city enjoys a mild climate - never too hot in summer and not too cold in winter. Thus it has become a resort town, its main claim to fame. There are many European style villas along the south coast where high party officials come on holiday.

East of the city is an interesting mountain called LAOSHAN, the highest peak of which is 1133 metres. It stands a few short kms from the Huang Hai (Yellow Sea). The mountain has many trails and temples, the oldest of which is the TAIPING DAOIST SI (Peace Daoist Temple), first laid out during the Song Dynasty (960-1280 AD). This mountain's core is made of granite, similar to many other mountains of the world, which is mined and exported. The Laoshan also has mineral water which is bottled and sent to other areas.

QIQIHAR 齐齐哈尔

Qiqihar is a city in the northeast of China, in Heilongjiang province. For foreign tourists, it is as far in the northwest of Heilongjiang that one can officially travel. One noteworthy item to mention is the large wildlife refuge where you can see some unusual birds.

HOTEL: The one hotel contains the CITS office. There are no inexpensive beds.

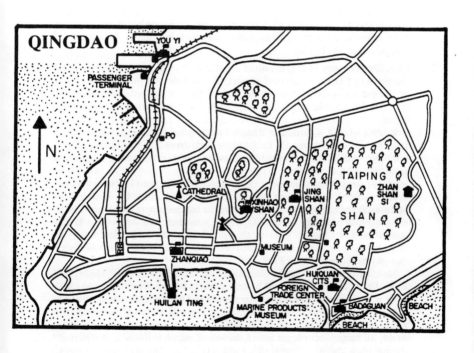

QUFU 曲阜

LOCATION AND TRANSPORTATION: Qufu is located in central Shandong Province about half way between Shanghai and Beijing. It is near, but not on, the main rail line connecting these two major cities. To reach Qufu (pronounced Chufu), one must get off the train at YANZHOU then take the one (half-hourly or once-hourly) bus leaving the train station running to Qufu. The bus stops at the station in Qufu and, in most cases, makes another stop at the drum tower and Kong Family Residence. Dozens of trains a day pass Yanzhou.

HOTEL: There is one binguan, located inside the KONG FAMILY RESIDENCE. One bed in a double room costs Y15 a night. There is another hotel near the Yanzhou railway station for much less, about Y6 a night for one bed in a quad room.

SIGHTS: The city of Qufu, one of the oldest in China, is famous for being the home of KONG FU ZI (CONFUCIUS), the famous thinker and educator of ancient China who lived at the end of the Spring and Autumn period (770-476 BC). Today, Qufu is only a town but with some rather famous sights.

KONG MIAO (Confucian Temple) was erected for the first time in 478 BC, the year after Kong Fu Zi died.(He lived from 551 to 479 BC). It was built and rebuilt throughout the successive dynasties, reaching the present scale in the Ming and Qing Dynasties. Occupying more than 20 hectares of land, the temple has nine courtyards extending for one and a half kms from north to south. This is one of three Grand Palaces in China; the other two are at Taian at the base of Tai Shan, and the Forbidden City in Beijing. To list all the halls and pavilions is impossible here, but there are dozens of imperial steles (upright columns with writing on them), one long line of thirteen Tablets Pavilions, and many more. This whole grand temple exists so people can pay homage to Kong Fu Zi.

Next to this temple is the RESIDENCE OF THE DESCENDANTS of Kong Fu Zi. Kong Fu Zi lived in near poverty but all his direct descendants were honoured with pensions from the Han (206 BC - 220 AD) to the Qing Dynasty (1644 - 1911 AD). The buildings you will see are actually from the Ming Dynasty. Because of the protection given by imperial governments nearly all family records are intact, as well as many artifacts of everyday life dating back many centuries. In most cases you can only peep through windows at room furnishings.

About 4 kms north of the Kong Miao and family residences is the KONG LIN (Confucian Forest) and the KONG LING (Tomb of Confucius). The road connecting these two areas is lined with cypress trees said to date back to the Yuan Dynasty (1280-1368 AD). The Kong Lin, reputed to be the largest man-made forest in China, consists of cypress trees. The tomb of Kong Fu Zi is a mound of dirt about 5 metres high with a line of animal statues leading to the tomb; as well there is a small temple. At the western end of the Kong Lin are found the tombs of most of the descendants of Kong Fu Zi.

In the eastern part of Qufu is the FUSHENG SI, as well as the mausoleum of King Shao Hao which is known as the Chinese Pyramid. King Shao Hao presumably dates back to the Xia Dynasty (2205-1766 BC). This is four kms east of Qufu and is said to be the only pyramid tomb in China. In the area is NISHAN, the birthplace of Kong Fu Zi.

Inside and around the Qufu sights are food and drink vendors. Waiting at the entrances are young men with cycle rickshaws looking for passengers; getting around the area on the map is therefore, easy and fast. As the area between Qufu and Kong Lin is open farmland, and interesting, you may consider walking the four kms, at least one way.

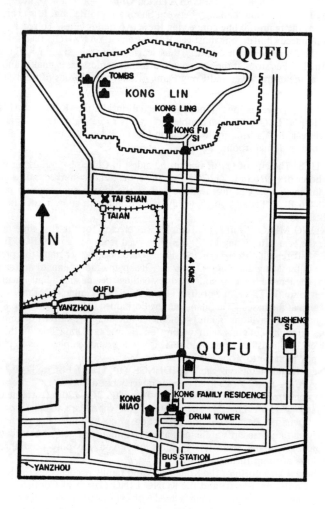

For details about TAI SHAN, see page 190

SANMENXIA 三門峽

Sanmenxia (Three Gates Gorge) is located about 125 kms west of Luoyang on the main Luoyang - Xian railway line. This name is taken from the Huang He (Yellow River) where it separates into three channels and rushes through the mountains. What makes this place interesting is that several temples have been built over the centuries. More important to historians are the walk-ways on the cliffs overlooking the river which, in earlier days, were used by trackers to pull boats upstream through the gorges. These walk-ways are similar to those seen in the Chang Jiang gorges. Now many of these relics of the past have been lost by the building of a dam and hydro-electric station at the site.

Since all trains stop here you could get off one train, see the gorges, get on another train and continue on to Luoyang or Xian, thus seeing the sights in a day. Since this place is open officially you will also find a hotel for foreigners.

SHANGHAI 上海

LOCATION AND TRANSPORTATION: Shanghai is located on the east coast of China. It is part of the Shanghai Shi, or Municipality, which is directly under the control of the Beijing central government. It is considered one of 29 provinces in China.

All railroads in eastern China lead to Shanghai. It is one of the biggest and most crowded cities in the world. The railway station is one of the busiest in the country, if not the busiest. You will have to buy your train ticket at CITS, similar to the procedure in Beijing, and you will have to pay the full tourist price in FEC's. As you may have learned already, in small stations you can sometimes use RMB, or people's money. Sometimes they will give the people's price for a ticket instead of the tourist price, especially if you can speak a few words of the language. When you want to get on a train to leave, go to the north side of the station; the south side is for arrivals.

Many people arrive from Hong Kong by boat, or leave to go to HONG KONG by boat. For boat tickets from Shanghai to Hong Kong contact the CITS office at the Peace Hotel (Heping). The ship leaves every 11 days. It has movies and good food. The fare is Y90 in the dormitory, a price which includes all meals; it takes 3 days to reach Hong Kong. On board also is a small store which sells snacks such as cookies, candy, nuts and soda pop.

The large dorm holds 20 to 40 passengers and can get noisy at night with players of mahjong, and from cassette recorders. The next class up has cabins with 3 double bunks which offer security and a quieter voyage.

There are also occasional boats sailing to Dalian in the northeast and to Qingdao on the Shandong Peninsula. You can leave Shanghai for Kobe (Japan) by ship. The voyage takes 2 days.

HOTEL: The cheapest hotel seems to be the PU JIANG BINGUAN which has beds for Y6. Take bus 65 from just north of the train station. If you are going to the CITS office in the PEACE HOTEL take this same bus, but get off further down the line. Some travellers have said that the Peace Hotel has beds for Y6 as well. Also, the JIN JIANG offers beds for Y6. Take bus 41 from near the train station.

SIGHTS: Perhaps the most interesting thing to see in Shanghai is the waterfront area called the BUND. This main road along the river front is dotted with European style buildings dating back to the time when this city was a foreign trading concession.

The home of Sun Yatsen is here, and a place where the Communist Party of China held its first National Congress.

See Tai Chi in the early morning in Huangpu Park near the Bund. Buy theatre/acrobats tickets from CITS at Heping (Peace) Hotel. In the area encircled by Renmin Road and Zhonghua Road is "Chinatown" of old, with its temples, tea houses and street vendors. For inexpensive food, visit the restaurants selling pastries and bowls of noodles just off Nanjing Road (south side) near Fujian Road.

A recommended restaurant in "old Shanghai" is Green Waves Restaurant. It is near the Yu garden, off Fuyu Road. Go to the second floor.

Across the road from the Jin Jiang Hotel is the old French Club in which is a video game room. In the dance hall the off-key orchestra plays waltzes.

You can do a boat tour of the city and/or take a 50 km trip to the river mouth. Contact CITS.

To get to the Railway Station from the Bund take bus No. 65 (The bus stop is almost opposite the Friendship Store along the Bund).

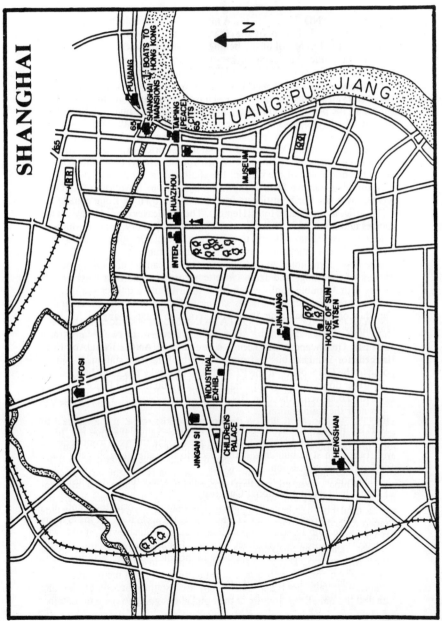

SHANHAIGUAN 山海关

The small city of Shanhaiguan (First Pass Under Heaven) lies at the eastern end of the Great Wall of China. Just east of this city is where the Great Wall was built jutting into the sea. For a detailed account of the city and wall in the region, see the hiking section in this book.

SHAOXING 紹興

LOCATION AND TRANSPORTATION: Shaoxing is located between Hangzhou and Ningbo on the main rail line between the two. Many trains pass daily; many people stop for a short day trip on the way to or from Hangzhou or Ningbo.

HOTEL: The Shaoxing Binguan is within walking distance of the train station. There are no buses going there from the station. Just get someone to point out the direction of the hotel (binguan). One bed in a triple room is Y5.

SIGHTS: As the city is not on the normal tourist route, it may appeal to some travellers who prefer fewer tourists. This small city is rather old, has a long history and is criss-crossed by canals. Shaoxing is linked by canal to Hangzhou and the Grand Canal region. It has some similarities to other eastern cities such as Suzhou and Wuxi. Shaoxing is also the birth place of one of China's greatest modern writers, Lu Xun. There is a museum dedicated to his life and works. Shaoxing claims to be the place where the mythical ruler of the Xia Dynasty (2205 BC - 1766 BC), Yu the Great, or Jade Emperor, died. His tomb and temple can be visited in the nearby GUIJI SHAN (Guiji Mountains) to the southeast of the city.

In the vicinity of Shaoxing are the YAN DANG SHAN (Wild Goose Marsh Mountains). This is a rather small mountain range; it has not been seen on any maps. There is a lake at an altitude of 1,040 metres and many streams, waterfalls, pools and trails. There are also the monasteries, the Ling Yan and the Ling Feng. Inquire at the hotel about going to these mountains.

SHENYANG 沈阳

Shenyang

LOCATION AND TRANSPORTATION: Shenyang is the capital of Liaoning Province, the most southerly of the provinces of the northeast or, as we commonly call it, Manchuria. It is a large industrial city of 3 million and is the first major rail centre in the northeast. It is about 12 hours from Beijing by train.

HOTEL: Liaoning Binguan is the hotel in Shenyang for foreigners at this time. As this hotel is in the northern suburbs, take trolley 6 from near the train station. One bed in a double room will cost about Y15 a night. Sorry, no dorm rooms in Shenyang.

SIGHTS: In the old part of Shenyang you can see the IMPERIAL PALACE built between 1625 and 1637. Although only about 1/20th the size of the Forbidden City in Beijing, it is worth visiting. It was built by Nurhachi, the self proclaimed first emperor of the Qing Dynasty. That was in 1616. It took several of these Manchu leaders to finally conquer all of China and officially begin the Qing Dynasty (1644-1911 AD). The Qing Dynasty was a foreign, or alien-ruled, period in China as was the Mongol Yuan Dynasty 1280-1368 AD. Shenyang was the capital of the Manchus in 1625; in 1644 it was relegated to being a regional capital while the capital of China was Beijing. Around the Imperial Palace is the old part of town, but not the city wall which has long since disappeared.

Nurhachi is buried in the eastern part of the city at the DONG TA or East Pagoda. He died in 1626 after a short rule. He was succeeded by his son, the second Qing Emperor, Abakai. Abakai died in 1643, the year before the Manchus finally subdued all of China. Still considered the second emperor, he is buried in the BEI LING or Northern Tomb, just north of the Liaoning Binguan. The Manchus of this Manchu Dynasty were gradually assimilated into the Chinese culture. Today we, as foreigners, find it impossible to distinguish a Manchu from a Han Chinese. (94% of Chinese are considered Han, after the Han Dynasty).

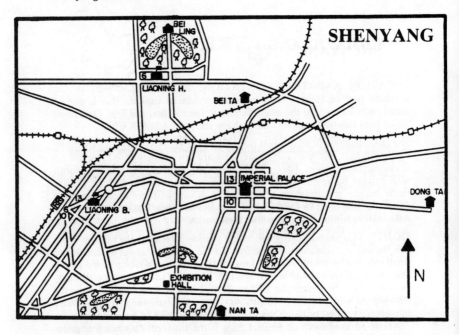

SHIHEZI 石河子

LOCATION AND TRANSPORTATION: Shihezi, a desert oasis about 150 kms west of Urumqi in Xinjiang Province, is a city of nearly one million people. Those who have travelled by bus from Urumqi to Kashgar know that the route passes one oasis after another, along the southern side of the Tian Shan (Heavenly Mountains). Shihezi is a similar oasis, but it lies on the northern side of the Tian Shan on the edge of the Junggar Pendi or Basin.

The history of Shihezi is short. It was originally a Guomindang garrison under Chiang Kaishek, but surrendered in 1946. Since they were forced to remain in place, they at once began to construct a series of dams and irrigation projects. The city now is one of the major industrial and agricultural centres in Xinjiang. Its cotton mill processes cotton grown in the area. Being a city open to foreigners it has a hotel.

SHIJIAZHUANG 石家庄

• Shijiazhuang

LOCATION AND TRANSPORTATION: Shijiazhuang, found in the southern part of Hebei Province, is the provincial capital. This is one of many cities located on the main Beijing to Guangzhou rail line. Dozens of trains pass this way each day on perhaps the busiest line in China.

HOTEL: The one hotel in town is the SHIJIAZHUANG BINGUAN in the southwest part of the city. Because there are few tourists here there are no dorm rooms available. They will automatically put you into a double room with private bath, but as there are other rooms available without private baths inquire and insist on getting a bed in one of these cheaper rooms. Standard rates are Y18 for each bed in a double room. Take bus 6 from the train station to the end of the line, then walk.

SIGHTS: This town has grown in recent years as a result of the railway. Outside the city are features worth seeing. To the southeast about 40 kms is the small city of Zhaozhou. About 3 kms south of this town is one of the oldest bridges in China and the world, the DA KU QIAO (Great Stone Bridge), usually called the Zhaozhou Bridge. It was built during the Sui Dynasty (589-618 AD) in about 600 to 610 AD. This 51 metre long, 9 metre wide single-span vaulted bridge is made of 28 separate rows of huge stones.

About 50 kms north of Shijiazhuang is the town of Zhengding and the LONG XING SI. This is perhaps the oldest monastery in China in its original condition. Inside this temple is a 24 metre high bronze Buddha with 42 arms. It was cast in 971 AD during the Song Dynasty (960-1280 AD). To reach Zhaozhou or Zhengding inquire at the CITS office in the hotel. However, in the case of Zhengding you can take a passenger train, one with high numbers (400 and 500's), to Zhengding Station and perhaps walk from there.

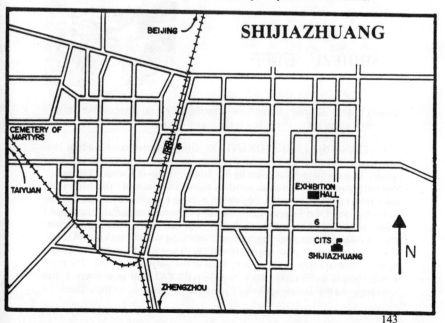

SUZHOU 苏州

LOCATION AND TRANSPORTATION: Suzhou is located on the main Beijing-Shanghai railway, about one hour from Shanghai. If you are heading towards Nanjing, it is only about 3 to 4 hours. Suzhou is on the DA YUNHE (Grand Canal) on which is a regular boat service from Suzhou to Hangzhou. See under Hangzhou for details about the canal. Several boats leave Suzhou each day at about 1730 and arrive in Hangzhou at about 0700. The lower decks of the boats have seats for those who want to sit up all night. Otherwise, it costs Y4.10 for the overnight trip in a quad room. There is little room in which to move around on these boats. Meals are served and there is a small shop selling snack foods and cigarettes. Buy your ticket the day before; either walk from the hotel or take bus 1 to the boat dock/bus station.

HOTEL: There are three hotels in Suzhou that accommodate foreigners. The biggest, and the one with the CITS office, is the SUZHOU BINGUAN. Take bus 2 from the station then walk or finish the trip on bus 4. This hotel has 8 bed dorm rooms for Y5 a bed. Plan to arrive in the morning otherwise they may be full; then you will have to pay a higher tariff, maybe Y20. Along the street to the west of the Suzhou is the NANLIN BINGUAN. Reportedly you can get one bed in a triple room for Y8. A hotel in the centre of town is the LEXIANG. Bus 1 from the station may be the best way to get to this one. It has beds for as low as Y8 a night. To repeat, try and arrive in the city in the morning hours to be sure of getting a cheaper room.

Canal in Suzhou, the "Venice of China"

SIGHTS: Lots of things to see here in Suzhou. Several things make Suzhou an interesting place to visit; they are the gardens and canals and, to a lesser extent, some temples.

The gardens in Suzhou comprise ponds, arched bridges, artificial hills constructed of rocks, trees and shrubs, and winding pathways. You never know what miniature landscape you will see around the next corner. Gardens of this nature originally were restricted to the wealthy nobles. Today they are open to the public. If you are limited in time and want to see just the best, go to the LIUYUAN (Lingering Garden), the best garden in Suzhou. Take bus 2 from the station or from near the hotels, and ride it in a circle to where you can get on bus 5. Take bus 5 to Liuyuan. By riding bus 5 to the end of the line you will reach HUSHAN, or the HUQIU SI (Tiger Hill Temple). This is said to be the burial place of a king who lived in the sixth century BC. The main attraction is a seven storey brick pagoda (HU TA) built in 961 AD. It has similarities to the leaning tower of Pisa in Italy because of its lean. There are

虎丘

Huqiu Si (Tiger Hill temple), Suzhou

many other gardens to see as well as several other interesting temples. There are two temples in the southwest corner of the city called the RUIGUANGSI and KAIYUANSI. Near the city centre is the twin pagoda, called SHUANGTA. You can only see this one from the street.

As you are walking around the city you will see many canals not shown on this map. Be sure and get a better map at the train station or the hotel you are staying in. Because of the canals, the city can be likened to Venice. Whitewashed brick homes line the narrow canals. Long, narrow barges carry produce and building materials. Men stand at the stern, propelling the barges forward with oars, using a criss-cross motion.

You can join a tour group going to a silk factory and/or a weaving or embroidery factory. Or you can organize your own little group and go by car or small bus, depending on the size of the group. The cost is only Y6 each for a half-day tour to a spinning and an embroidery factory. Each group must have an English-speaking (sometimes French or Spanish) guide and a driver and car. Since silk originated in China, it is a pity to visit China without seeing the silk industry. Any tour of this important industry is well worthwhile.

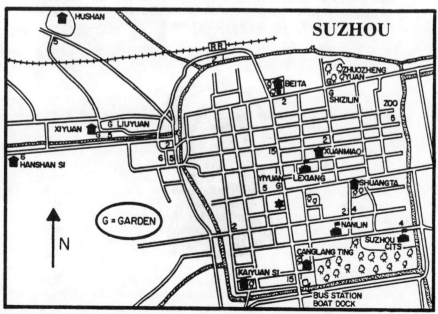

TIANJIN 天津

LOCATION AND TRANSPORTATION: Tianjin, about 150 kms southeast of Beijing, is the capital city of the City State of the same name. Tianjin Shi is one of three city states in China, directly under the control of the central government of Beijing. The other two are Beijing and Shanghai. Tianjin, on a main rail line connecting Beijing and Shanghai, is two hours from Beijing by fast train.

HOTEL: There are several hotels in Tianjin; the main one where tourists stay is the TIANJIN BINGUAN. To get there take trolley 96 or bus 13 from near the train station. Check out other hotel possibilities along the same street as the Tianjin Hotel. Another one for foreigners is the Di Yi or Hai He Binguan.

If you are tired of waiting around in Beijing to get a travel permit, the Gong Anghee (Public Security Bureau) in Tianjin is very good, and fast. Take bus 35 from near the station, then walk.

SIGHTS: This city of 4 million people is highly industrialized. Since it was founded as a military post in 1404 it has no ancient relics. It is an important city because it has become the port for the capital, Beijing. At one time the Grand Canal (Da Yunhe) passed through here, but now it has dried up. The year 1858 marked the arrival of Europeans; the city became a treaty port. It was after that period that many of the European style buildings were built, something for which the city is noted. The city is known for its carpets; there are eight carpet factories in the city. The city also has a fine arts museum and an "old Chinatown"; you might enquire about it.

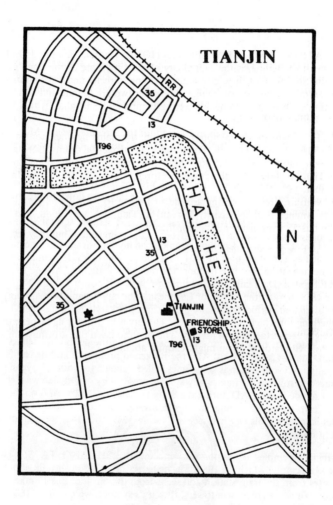

TAIYUAN 太原

LOCATION AND TRANSPORTATION: Taiyuan sits in the middle of the province of Shanxi and is that province's capital city. It is about halfway between Beijing and Xian, being about 13 hours away from Beijing by overnight train. Because it is on a main rail line one can find a train at about any hour of the day or night.

HOTEL: There are two hotels in Taiyuan for the foreign traveller. Most used seems to be the YINGZE BINGUAN, about 10 minute walk directly west of the train station on the main street in the city. There are also buses. As comparitively few tourists visit Taiyuan, cheap dorm rooms are not available. You may have to pay between Y15 and Y18 for one bed in a double room. With a little bargaining you may be able to get the price down to the student rate of about Y10 a night. The other hotel is the BINGZHOU BINGUAN, about a five minute walk from the train station. There are several other high rise hotels along this main street in front of the train station but they seem to refer all foreigners to the Yingze.

Taiyuan sits in the middle of the Taiyuan Basin at an altitude of 800 metres. It is much drier than areas to the east, thus it has occasional droughts. The Taiyuan Basin is abundant in coal and iron reserves; as a result, this city has become rather industrialized. It now has about two million people.

Taiyuan, called Jinyang in ancient times, is an old city. Built in 497 BC, it has a history of over two thousand years. During the period of the Eastern Han Dynasty (206 BC - 220 AD) the Bingzhou prefecture had its capital in Jinyang, and so Taiyuan is sometimes called "Bing" for short. Jinyang was reduced to ruins in the flames of war. The present city of Taiyuan was rebuilt and extended in 982 AD during the Song Dynasty (960-1280 AD) on the site of a town called Tangming, north of Jinyang. (Jinyang was located where Jinci is today). This city had city walls until 1949, then they were gradually taken down.

SIGHTS: Temples of importance include the SHUANG TA SI (Twin Pagoda Temple) which, in 1985, was being restored. You can walk about 15 minutes from the train station and see it from the outside. Bus 19 takes you about half way. These twin towers, the city's symbol, were built in 1608 AD and stand 50 metres high.

Also inside the city is the Chongshan Si, but this temple is rather ordinary. It has a couple of bronze lions, cast in 1391 AD, guarding the entrance. Just north of town are two temples, the Duofu Si and the Doudaifu Si.

South of the city are found some impressive temples. It is 92 kms by train from Taiyuan to the small city of Pingyao, and another 6 kms to the west, to the SHUANGLIN SI (Twin Forest Temple). This temple has stood there for about 1,500 years, from the time of the Northern Wei Dynasty (420-589 AD). The most remarkable artistic achievements in this monastery are moulded figures which number more than 2,000.

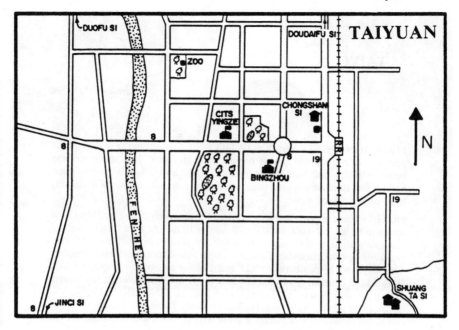

Perhaps the best places to visit are the hardest to get to. To the west of Jinci Si, in the mountains, are two sites, the LONGSHAN SHIR KU (Dragon Mountain Stone Caves) and TIANLONGSHAN SHIR KU (Heavenly Dragon Mountain Stone Caves). Most people would hire a CITS guide with driver and vehicle to reach both of these Buddhist caves sites, but it is possible to see both in one day on foot (maybe?). To reach Jinci Si where is located a hotel (ask CITS people if foreigners can stay there), take bus 8 from the main traffic circle in Taiyuan. Catch it at the little plaza or square, as you will not get a seat further down the line. It is a 45 minute ride. From the entrance of the Jinci Si, walk south a little, then west, then up a winding road into the mountains. It is 11 kms to Longshan caves and the other must be in the near vicinity. But ask the exact location before you leave the CITS office in the Yingze Hotel. The Longshan grottoes are Daoist caves while the Tianlogshan caves are Buddhist. This latter contains a huge open air statue of a sitting Buddha which appears to be about 30 metres high. If you are interested in Buddhist cave art and statues, this should be on your list of sites to see.

At Suzhou   (J)

Taiyuan: Tianlong Shan (J)

About 60 kms southwest of Taiyuan stands another rather important temple which was left intact during the cultural revolution of the 1960s and '70s. This is the XUANZHONGSI. Founded in 472 AD, it was historically important in spreading the Pure Land sect of Buddhism in China. It, like so many other temples in China, has many halls with many statues of the Buddha. To get to this isolated temple you can take a bus from Taiyuan to the small city of Jiaocheng then, unless you are with a tour group, you will have to walk the 4 kms to the temple. This last 4 kms is barely reachable with a good vehicle. Near the temple is a monk's cemetery with a "forest of stupas".

About 25 kms south of Taiyuan is the JINCI SI, one of the better temples in all of China. Construction on a large scale began about 1,500 years ago. Among its numerous relics are sculptures, stone inscriptions, statues and figures of the Song Dynasty (960-1280 AD). The courtyards boast old cypress trees, one of which is said to have been planted during the Zhou Dynasty (1122-770 BC). It developed a heavy lean but now has supports. Within the temple complex is a spring emitting enormous amounts of water.

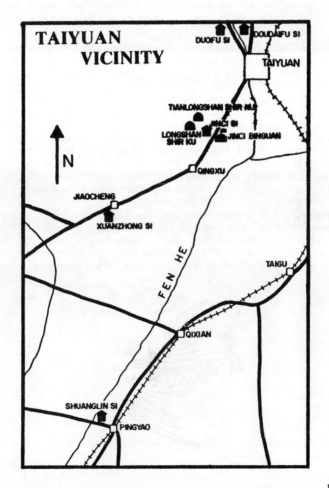

TIANSHUI-MAIJISHAN

Tianshui-Maijishan

LOCATION AND TRANSPORTATION: Tianshui is located on the main rail line about half way between the cities of Xian and Lanzhou. The only way of getting to this place is by train, of which about a dozen a day pass through.

HOTEL: In 1985, Tianshui and the ultimate destination of Maijishan were closed to foreigners of European ancestry. Hong Kong residents and other Overseas Chinese only were allowed in. In 1985, although the restoration on Maijishan was complete and ready to accept tourists, it seems the thing they were waiting for was the building of a hotel acceptable to the foreign traveller. When a hotel is complete, foreigners will be allowed to visit this town officially. That should be soon.

SIGHTS: The Buddhist rock caves complex called MAIJISHAN SHIR KU (Corn Rick Mountain Stone Caves) is regarded as one of the four best in China. This outcropping is composed of a soft and easily excavated con-glomerate rock. It has sheer cliff faces on two sides where the workers must have been held secure by ropes attached to the cliff top. The cave decoration was started in the 5th century as were most other Buddhist cave temples in China. These caves contain clay figures and wall paintings. Two large statues of the Buddha nestle under the cliffs on each of the two sides. The setting is in the mountains in a fairly wet area. Everything has been protected by overhanging cliffs. Today, since restoration, there are cat-walks to all the caves and the statues. All the cave entrances have locked doors such as we see at Dunhuang. You can take photos from the outside but not inside the in-dividual caves.

Try to arrive on an early morning train such as train 143 from Xian which arrives at 0611 in Tianshui or train 148/145 from Lanzhou which arrives at 0529. From the station, where you can store your baggage, walk south to the bus station and catch the 0830 bus to Maijishan. There is one also at 1100. It takes less than an hour to go the 32 kms; then the bus returns about noon.

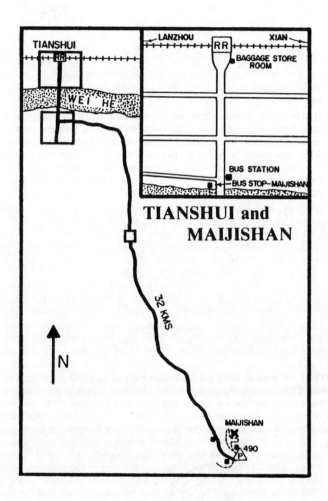

TURPAN 吐鲁番

LOCATION AND TRANSPORTATION: Tur-pan is the Uygur name, Tur-a-fan is used by the Han Chinese. Turpan, located in Xinjiang Province, is just south of the eastern half of the Tian Shan. The rather famous Bogda Shan is the highest peak north of Turpan. Just to the south is the Turpan Pendi (or Basin), the lowest place in China at − 154 metres. Turpan is not far from the end of two railway lines: the main one running to Urumqi, the other ending at Korla. You can reach Turpan on one of about six daily trains. The train station is not in Turpan but in a town called DAHEYON - about 30 kms to the northwest. To get from the train station to Turpan you will have to catch the bus at 0800 or at 1700. If your train arrives at 0830 you could join other tourists and hire a bus or truck, or walk about 2 kms south of the station to where the road to Turpan turns east, and hitch hike. Hitching is fairly easy, at least for foreigners.

If you are heading west to Urumqi after your stay in Turpan it is probably better to take the bus rather than bother going back to the train station to take a train. There are several buses each day to Urumqi, most of which leave in the mornings. The 5 hour ride costs Y4.90. If you want to go to Kashgar, you will have to go to Urumqi and catch the bus from there. A train service serves Korla, just west of Bosten Hu (lake). It may be possible to take a train to that point then hopefully continue by bus to Kashgar. However, we recommend you go to Urumqi where you will be assured of a seat without having to wait.

To get around the Turpan Oasis you can either hire a small donkey cart for short distances or you can arrange with CITS for longer rides, such as to Gaochang.

HOTEL: There is one hotel in Turpan which accommodates all classes of tourists. The new rear section is modern with air conditioning; the older part is actually a former caravanserai. You will probably stay in the older part which has beds in dorm rooms with two to six beds. Each bed costs Y4. The ground level rooms have fans, at least in summer, when temperatures are 40 °C and more. It is better to request a room in the basement as these rooms are small, cooler, and have two beds. Speaking of heat, many travellers recommend you stay away from Turpan in the heat of the summer, but it is bearable. As it is a very dry heat you would be advised to do your visiting and travelling in the mornings or evenings. One advantage of visiting Turpan in the late summer is to take advantage of the 'hami gua', a sweet honeydew-type melon that ripens at that time of year.

The CITS office is located in the reception office of this hotel, along with a small store and a canteen. The canteen serves soft drinks and beer to tourists while you sit under a canopy of grapevines. In the evenings, at least in summer, you will be treated to music and dancing in one of the courtyards, again under the grape arbor. A small admission fee is collected. The performers are local Uygur people. This definitely is a highlight of the trip to Turpan. You can also buy cassette tapes of the music in the small store for Y5 each. The sound of this music has shades of both Chinese and other Asian influences.

SIGHTS: Perhaps the main reason for going to Turpan is to see the people. The Uygurs are a Turkish speaking group who are in the majority in Xinjiang Province. The name of this province is actually "Xinjiang Uygur Autonomous Region". These people number nearly six million in the province and are the vast majority of the people living in Turpan. In the middle of the 9th century large numbers of Uygurs moved to Turpan from the Orhon River Valley in Mongolia. The majority of Uygurs look very Caucasian; in fact, with their looks and language, it would be very difficult to distinguish them from their relatives in Turkey (except that the men do not wear the customary mustache as in Turkey). The women are colourfully dressed. Their clothes have no similarities to those worn by Chinese women in the same community. Usually they wear scarves on their heads, pantaloons, (sometimes long, sometimes short), and a dress over the pantaloons. No veiled women were seen in Turpan as one sometimes sees in Kashgar and some Asian and North African countries. The best place to see the people is in the main bazaar. Men generally love having their photos taken, but be a bit more polite when it comes to photographing the women. The children are the friendliest of all. The bazaar is busiest in the morning hours and again in the evenings.

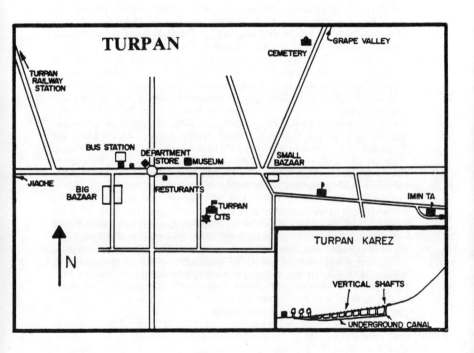

Another fine place to encounter the Uygurs is to walk out of the hotel to the small bazaar (see map), then walk down the narrow street in the direction of the IMIN TA or SUGONGTA (Imin Mosque). This walk is through a residential neighborhood reminiscent of those found in other Asian countries. The large mosque has two parts: the prayer hall and a minaret. This minaret, or 'ta' (pagoda) as the Chinese call it, is round and is 44 metres high, tapering towards the top. Inside in the centre is a spiral pillar that bears the weight of the pagoda. The pillar also provides a staircase for visitors to ascend to the top. This mosque was built by Sulieman in 1779 during the Qing Dynasty (1644 - 1911 AD).

Jiaohe was the capital of the Kingdom of Che Shi Qian during the second century BC to the mid-5th century AD. When Gaochang came under the rule of the Qu family, Jiaohe became a prefecture. The Anxi supervisory office of the Tang regime was established in Jiaohe. Later it moved to Qiuci (Kuqa, today) and was abandoned in the Yuan Dynasty (1280 - 1368 AD).

You can ride a donkey cart to Jiaohe or you can organize a group of other tourists and go there with CITS help. You can visit Jiaohe, the karez and the grape valley in one evening. CITS likes to take you to a commune in the GRAPE VALLEY. The place they will take you to is a covered grape arbor. Walk around and see the grape-drying buildings and the lovely clear-water river running through the valley.

Just to the north of the main town centre of Turpan and just to the north of the irrigated areas one can see an interesting feature called the KAREZ. This is an irrigation system that originated in Persia. It is called *"qanats"* or *"kanats"* in Iran today. The karez consists of a series of wells and tunnels. Water is tapped from the water-saturated alluvial fans that lie between the mountain base and the nearly flat valley bottoms. Workers dig a series of holes in the ground to where water is abundant then connect these wells by tunnels. The finished product is an underground tunnel from the mountain base to the beginning of the oasis where the water emerges to fill ditches and canals. The water is clear, cool and pure; it is used for agriculture and drinking. The karez is the lifeblood of Turpan. There are many of these karez, but if you ask to be taken to one they (CITS) will usually take you 7 or 8 kms from the centre of town to the northwest to see a good one. On the road to this particular karez one can see tree-lined country lanes filled with donkey carts and children playing in the canals.

For those interested in old city ruins, Turpan is an excellent place in western China to see them. About 10 kms west of Turpan town centre are the ruins of JIAOHE. Jiaohe stands on an island surrounded by two small river valleys. On either side of the main street which runs from north to south are traces of crowded structures. No doors face the street front. Communication to the street was through alleys. At the northern end of the ruins is a monastery; figures of The Buddha are still faintly visible.

Refer to page 47 for BUDDHIST CAVES IN XINJIANG.

The next morning you can visit the ruins of Gaochang, Baijikalika Buddhist caves and the Hastana tombs. The Y22 cost is well worth it.

The site of GAOCHANG is in a rough square with a circumference of six kms. The city wall is well preserved. Its base, made of rammed earth, is now little more than 11 metres high. The wall has buttresses at regular intervals; outside is a moat. Gaochang was divided into the inner city, the outer city, and the palace city. The layout is similar to Chang'an (Xian's former name). Outlines of buildings remain. A large monastery in the southwestern part of the city is in good condition. Visitors can walk along the corridors and enter the halls. The doors, windows and niches are well preserved. All the buildings were constructed with rammed earth or sun-dried bricks. The upper part of doors and windows are arched, a feature found in the Turpan Basin of today.

The Tang Dynasty (618 - 907 AD) set up the Gaochang prefecture in 640 AD and renamed it Xizhou. In the mid-9th century the Uygurs moved from Mongolia to Gaochang and made it their capital. It was abandoned in the 14th century. In Gaochang evidence has been found of Buddhist and Nestorian Christian influence dating to the 5th century AD.

Near Gaochang are two Buddhist cave complexes, one of which is closed. The closed one is Shengjinkou. The one you can visit is Baijikalika or Thousand Buddha Caves. There are seven caves here, all with murals. The wall murals are in a bad condition, ruined by Muslim fanatics. It is still worth a visit; the frescoes date from the Tang Dynasty (618 - 907 AD).

Also in this area about 30 kms east of Turpan town are several tombs, apparently those of the ruling class of Gaochang. There is not much to see here in the HASTANA TOMBS except the holes in the ground and burial chambers. You are not allowed to take photos inside.

Because of the abundance of fresh fruits and vegetables around August and September, some travellers prefer this time to visit Turpan. As Turpan should be a highlight of a trip to China, plan to stay as long as possible.

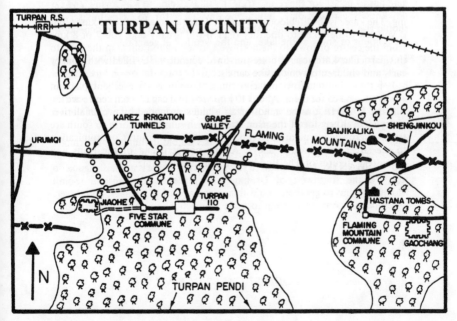

URUMQI 乌鲁木齐

• Urumqi

LOCATION AND TRANSPORTATION: U-rumqi in Uygur, Wu-lu-mu-qi in Chinese. The city of Urumqi is the largest settlement in the Xinjiang Uygur Autonomous Region. It is located in the north central part of the province between the eastern and western portions of the Tian Shan (Heavenly Mountains). Urumqi is at the end of the railway line that connects the rest of China. From Beijing it takes about three days to reach Urumqi. There are trains also from Shanghai, Xian, Zhengzhou, and Lanzhou. Six fast trains in all reach Urumqi, plus a local train or two. You can also fly to Urumqi from Beijing. The fast trains going to Urumqi are nearly all hard sleeper cars; the distance is long and can be tiring. You must book a sleeper in advance as they sell out quickly. This can be done three days in advance.

If you are going from Urumqi to Kashgar, buy your ticket the day before departure at the bus station shown on the map. Bus 8 passes closer than any other to this station, but bus 7 passes nearby as well. The Kashgar buses, travelling in convoy, should leave Urumqi at 0900 but they may not leave until 1000. The fare is Y38.30 for the 3½ day trip.

If you are going to TIAN CHI (Heavenly Lake) in the mountains to the northeast of Urumqi, you should buy your ticket the day before at the small ticket booth about half a block east of the post office. This taxi stand sits right next to a park; bus 7 passes right by. Round-trip tickets cost Y7.50; a date has to be set for the return trip. If you are going to stay awhile and do not know the return date, buy a one-way ticket for Y5. This bus service should run from about June 1 through September, but it would depend on the amount of snow at the lake, and the weather in general.

HOTEL: There are several hotels in town. The BEI HUA ZHUN is a very high building, green in color. Get there from the train station on bus 8. It has beds for Y4.50 a night in a quad room. The HUA ZHOU BINGUAN has triples and quads for Y4 a night. Take bus 10 from the station, then walk or take bus 7. There is another hotel half a block in front of the train station where Hong Kong travellers often stay.

SIGHTS: Urumqi is a rather new city; it has no old monuments or temples and offers nothing architecturally outstanding. You could climb to the top of HONG SHAN (Red Mountain) to survey the city, There is a small pagoda on top. To the southwest of Urumqi is a place called Nanshan (South Mountain), but to get there you will have to have a CITS vehicle and driver. Often people come to Urumqi to make connections to go somewhere else.

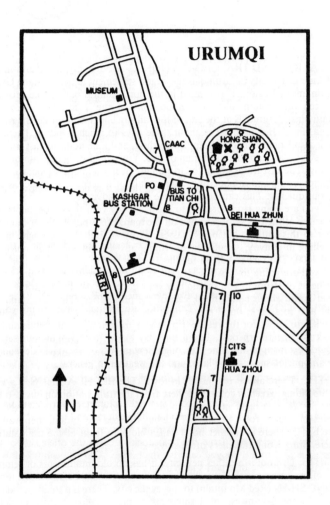

WUHAN 武汉

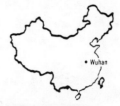

LOCATION AND TRANSPORTATION: Wuhan is located about half way between Beijing and Guangzhou. It is one of the busiest rail centres in the country, connecting two of China's most important cities. It is also the capital of the province of Hubei, and lies on the banks of the Chang Jiang (Yangtze River).

Most people coming to Wuhan either pass through on the train without stopping, or arrive on the river boat from Chongqing. The boats from Chongqing arrive each afternoon. Boats leave daily from Wuhan to go upstream to Chongqing; this trip takes 5 days. Most prefer the 3 day trip downstream from Chongqing. You can also go downstream to Nanjing and Shanghai. The trip to Shanghai takes two days. It is not much slower than the lengthy roundabout trip by train, but is much cheaper.

HOTEL: There are several hotels to choose from in Wuhan. One is the JIANGHAN, a five minute walk from the main Hankou Train Station. It has quad rooms for Y6. Another hotel near the station is the AIGUO BINGUAN with singles from about Y7. This is one of the few hotels in China that has rooms for singles. It is in an old building and is a friendly place. The SHENGLI has quad rooms for Y6 also. From the boat docks take bus 30 then walk to either of the two mentioned hotels. The CITS office is in the XUANGONG BINGUAN. The staff there invariably want to put you in a more expensive room although there are cheaper rooms available.

SIGHTS: Wuhan has a population of 3 million. It is comprised of three cities: Hankou, Hanyang and Wuchang. Of the three, Hankou is the more important. The whole area was only a village until the Treaty of Nanjing made it a treaty port; then came an influx of various Europeans and the place blossomed. The coming of the railway also made the city grow. In 1957 the WUHAN BRIDGE was completed; it spans the kilometre-wide Chang Jiang. The bridge is about 1.5 kms long and handles both rail and road traffic. This is probably the best sight to see in Wuhan. You can reach the base of this bridge by taking a ferry from the boat docks area to the other side of the Chang Jiang. From there you can visit the bridge. Also you can take bus 14 and visit one of the best parks in Wuhan.

For more about the YANGTSE RIVER trip, see pages 81, 82 and 176.

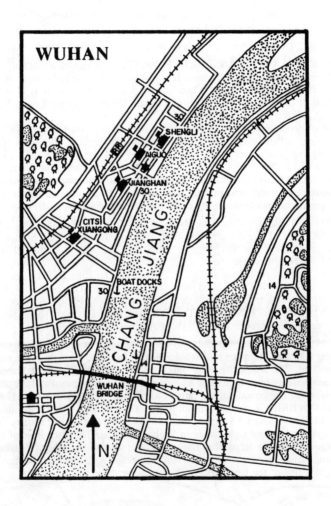

WUXI 无锡

LOCATION AND TRANSPORTATION: Wuxi sits on the main Beijing-Shanghai rail line about half way between Nanjing and Shanghai. Dozens of trains pass daily; the fast trains take only about 2 hours to reach Shanghai. The DA YUNHE (Grand Canal) runs through the city.

HOTEL: There are several hotels in Wuxi, but a couple of them are out of town near Tai Hu (Tai Lake). There are two, maybe three, hotels in the centre of town - one of which is where the CITS OFFICE is located. It has an older section with dorms and public toilets, but they usually try to put you in a twin room with private bath. If you do get a dorm, it is about Y6 a night. There is another hotel just south of the CITS hotel, and two on the lake. The TAIHU BINGUAN is the most used by foreigners, some of whom have paid only Y6 for a bed. Take bus 2 from the station then walk. Another hotel is the LIYUAN by the garden of the same name. Take bus 2 from the station then bus 1 from the round-about near the centre of the city.

SIGHTS: The two most famous sights in Wuxi are the canals running throughout the city and beyond, and the third largest lake in China, TAI HU. Wuxi is one of the oldest cities in China having a history dating back to the Zhou Dynasty (1122 - 770 BC). It had tin mines in its early history until the tin ran out 2000 years ago. It is located in the "land of fish and rice" and is barely above sea level; the place is well watered, thus the use of canals. The Grand Canal still supports boat traffic. One can take a boat tour on Tai Hu. There are gardens near the lake, the most famous of which is the LIYUAN or Li Garden. By taking bus 2 from the station you can visit the XIHUI PARK which has a large temple complex with a tall pagoda. Wuxi has also become famous since the Ming Dynasty (1368 - 1644 AD) for its clay figures. You can visit a factory there today. Wuxi is also a silk producing area, and tours can be arranged.

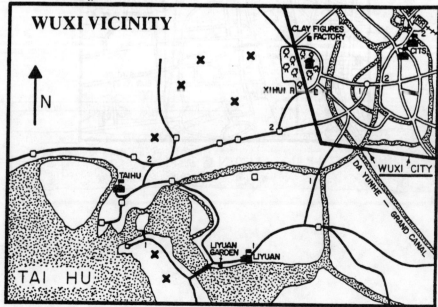

WUXI VICINITY

WUZHOU 梧州

Wuzhou is a small city located about half way between Guangzhou and Guilin; it is in the province of Guangxi. The standard route is to take a boat from Guangzhou, stay overnight at the WUZHOU BINGUAN then, on the following day, continue to Guilin and Yangshuo by bus. The hotel, a 30 minutes walk from the boat dock, costs Y2.50 a night in a dorm. If you are heading for Guangzhou, the downstream boat arrives in Guangzhou at about 0400. This means you have one night's accommodation on the boat and you have all the day to travel around Guangzhou or continue to Hong Kong at a good hour.

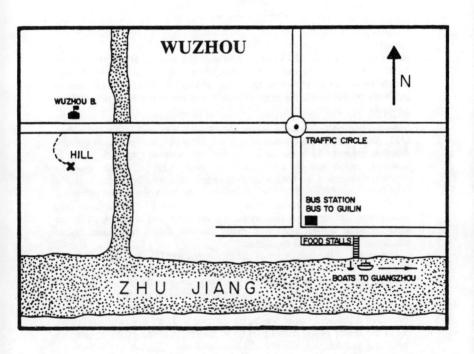

XIAMEN —厦门

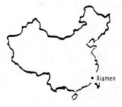

LOCATION AND TRANSPORTATION: The city (and the island) of Xiamen, sometimes known as Amoy, is situated directly west of, and across the Formosa Straits from the island province of Taiwan. Xiamen is in the province of Fujian. Because of its southerly position it is rather warm the year round. Most people arrive at Xiamen via the railway. There are direct connections with Shanghai. One can also take a boat to or from Hong Kong but this is an expensive trip considering the cost of everything else in China.

HOTEL: The HUA ZHOU BINGUAN is the one hotel for the foreign traveller. For about Y5 you can have a bed in a triple room. Take bus 1 from the train station (not shown on this map). If you are at the main bus station just walk to this hotel; the same applies if you are at the ferry terminal.

SIGHTS: For the most part the attraction in Xiamen is the city itself. Its history is relatively short; the first accounts say it was built into a garrison in 1387. After that time it developed into a trading port and gradually became more prominent. As many of its citizens went overseas to such places as Sumatra, Japan and the Philippines, for many years there has been an overseas connection. In 1842 Xiamen became one of the five treaty ports. In 1980 the city was opened to tourism and since has become a special economic zone for foreign investment. Because of its history of foreign trade, the architecture and streets of the city have taken on a special flavour. It has a Mediterranean appearance with many narrow side streets that makes wandering around rather enjoyable.

Just south of the main part of the city is NANPUTUO SI (South Putuo Temple) which has a history of over 1000 years. Nearby is the Xiamen University and a museum. Near the hotel is a mosque. Perhaps the best side trip from the city itself is a ferry ride to the island of GULANGYU. This is a small island covered mostly with trees; it has many narrow roads. As cars are forbidden a quieter, slower atmosphere prevails. There are two beaches. A hill in the centre of the island rises to 90 metres, offering excellent views of the island and Xiamen. On the island are two old churches worth visiting.

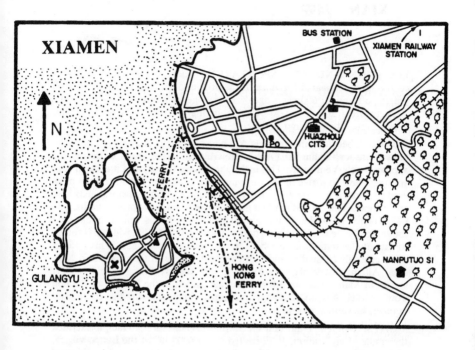

XIAN 西安

LOCATION AND TRANSPORTATION: Xian, located in the south-central part of Shaanxi Province, is the provincial capital. From about 2500 years ago to about 600 years ago Xian was the terminus of the Silk Road.

There are trains going to Xian from major cities such as Shanghai, Guangzhou, Chengdu and Beijing.

HOTEL: There are three hotels to choose from in Xian. Very near the railway station is the JIEFANG BINGUAN. It has beds in dorms for approximately Y8 a night. This is the cheapest in the city but it is often full; you may have to arrive in the early morning to get in. The next hotel most used by foreign tourists is the RENMIN (People's). The cheapest beds here are in triple rooms; a bed is Y14 a night. These rooms have private baths. The CITS office is in this hotel, along with many shops selling books and souvenirs. There is a hotel right next to the BELL TOWER which has rooms for about the same price as the Renmin, about Y14 a night. This hotel is more centrally located to most of the sights to see in the downtown Xian area. All the hotels are easy to reach with the excellent public transport system in Xian. Take bus 3 from the train station to the Renmin or the Bell Tower Hotel. And of course get a Xian city map showing bus routes and numbers as soon as possible.

SIGHTS: Xian is an important site in Chinese civilization; in fact, it is termed the cradle of civilization. It all started about 6000 BC at the Banpo village. The next important step in Xian's history was in 221 BC when the first emperor of the Qin Dynasty made Xian the capital of all of China. The man was Qin Shi Huangdi. Xian was the capital of China from the Qin through to and including the Tang Dynasty which ruled from 618 - 907 AD. Barring some interruptions it was the leading trading city in China, being the ter-minus of the SI ZHOU ZI LU (Silk Road). Later, when sea transport im-proved, Xian's importance gradually declined.

Within the city are several sites worth visiting. The BELL TOWER is located at the junction of the city's main streets. It has been restored; visitors can ascend the stairs and look around. This particular one dates to the 16th century. Just to the west is the DRUM TOWER. You can enter this old structure and walk to the top level. It is now a type of museum and souvenir shop for tourists.

Xian at one time had hundreds of temples, mosques and even a few Nestorian churches, but today there is only one mosque, the QIN DIN SI (Muslim temple). This mosque was first built during the Tang Dynasty (618 - 907 AD), but was restored in the 14th century.

Only a couple of blocks south of the Bell Tower is the SHAANXI MUSEUM, on the grounds of a former Confucian temple. It is one of the best museums in the country. Most of the artifacts are from the tombs in the immediate area. One of the most unusual sections of this museum is the Beilin, or Forest of Steles (stone tablets with engravings). This collection con-tains over 2300 steles from all the dynasties beginning with the Han (206 BC - 220 AD). If you are staying in the Jiefang or Renmin Hotel, take bus 3 to the museum.

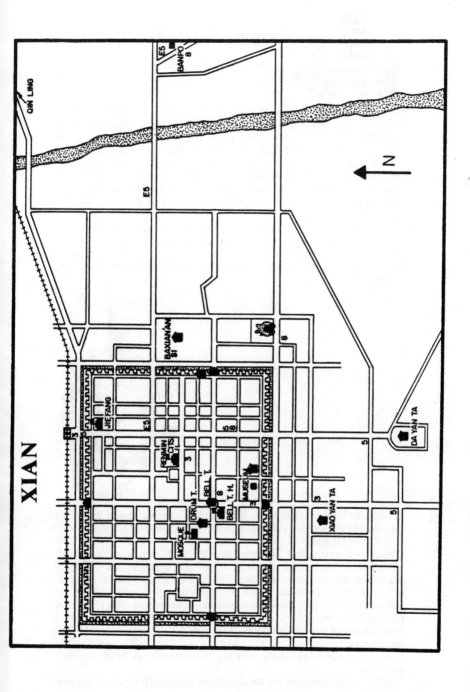

大雁塔

Big Wild Goose pagoda, Xian

Just south of the walled portion of the city is the XIAO YAN TA (Little Wild Goose Pagoda). Take bus 3 from the train station, the Renmin Hotel or the Bell Tower. Not far from there is the DA YAN TA (Big Wild Goose Pagoda). Get to this one by taking bus 5 from the train station. This seven storeyed pagoda was built in the seventh century AD to house Buddhist sutras (prayer texts) brought from India. Climb inside the staircase for a view of the city. Looking to the northeast you may discern a mound, the tumulus of Qin Shi Huangdi. This may be visited during the tour to the terra-cotta soldiers.

There are four main city gates in the well preserved city wall. Any of the gates are worth visiting although they are all similar in appearance. The city wall is about 10 to 12 metres high. In the city are several temples such as the BAXIAN'AN SI and the ruins of the XINGPING PALACE of the Tang Dynasty.

Terra cotta (clay) solider, Xian

The most famous site to see in Xian, a place everyone should see while in the city, is the museum which houses the TERRA COTTA SOLDIERS of EMPEROR QIN SHI HUANGDI (died 210 BC). He was the founder of the Qin Dynasty that ruled China from 221 to 206 BC. He was the man who unified China, standardized money, weights and measures and writing. He linked and extended the Great Wall. To visit the archaeological site of the terra-cotta soldiers consider a tour. The tours depart between 0700 and 0730 and return about 1700. The one you join may visit the Hua Qing Hot Springs Park (3 to 4 hours; you can bathe), tumulus of Qin Shi Huangdi (20 minutes), site of terra cotta soldiers (50 minutes) and Ban Po neolithic village (45 minutes).

Buy your ticket in advance at Jie Fang Hotel or your own hotel. The cost is about Y6.

CITS runs a tour from the Renmin Hotel that spends longer at the terra-cotta soldiers.

Stone barge in the pool at
Hua Qing Hot Springs, near Xian.

Your stops on the tour may include:
● Hua Qing Hot Springs Park. Swim in the mineral water baths. Visit the large pool which has the barge made of stone. At the forward end are mythical beasts in stone (see sketch). Walk up the pathway to the hilltop for an overview of the township and fields; it takes about one hour to get to the top. Visit the museum at the springs concerning Chiang Kaishek. Chiang Kaishek, leader of the Nationalist forces, was at the resort in 1936 when he was betrayed by one of his generals. He tried to escape but was arrested. He was later released after he agreed to have his forces join the Communists against Japan, the foe that was attacking China. The event is known in Chinese history as the "Xian Incident".
● Tumulus of Emperor Qin Shi Huangdi, founder of the Qin dynasty that ruled China from 221 to 206 BC. The walk to the top of this artificial burial mound takes a few minutes. Later, at the terra-cotta soldiers exhibit, you will see a diorama of the layout showing the position of the tumulus in relation to the site of the terra-cotta soldiers. The tumulus, which has not yet been excavated, is sure to contain treasures.

It is thought from the name Qin (pronounced Chin), the West began calling the country China.

About two kilometres from the tumulus is the subterranean vault estimated to contain 6,000 terra cotta (clay) warriors, plus horses and remains of chariots. The site has been roofed over. You are forbidden to take pictures of this clay army. You will notice the facial features of each soldier is different; about 500 in battle formation have been exposed. This complex is part of the tomb of Qin Shi Huangdi.

Just outside this main display are two small buildings housing some of the warriors and chariots in one, and a bronze chariot with horses and driver inside the other. You have to pay extra to see this latter building, but it is worth it.

● Ban Po Neolithic Village is located ten kilometres east of Xian. You will see traces of village houses dating back to 6000 BC. The post holes are visible, as are earthen floors. A reconstructed hut has been erected. The area is roofed over. Boardwalks serve as viewing platforms as you wander through the village. An on-site museum displays artifacts. Apart from being visited on a tour it can be reached by taking electric trolley bus No. 5. Or take bus 8 from the Bell Tower.

On the smaller map showing the vicinity of Xian one can see a number of other sites of historical interest. Most of these are tombs of former leaders of China or ruins of palaces of leaders over the past 2200 years. There is also a number of temple sites. Inquire at the CITS office for information about getting to these places. To see any number of these in a reasonable length of time, it will be necessary to be a part of a tour.

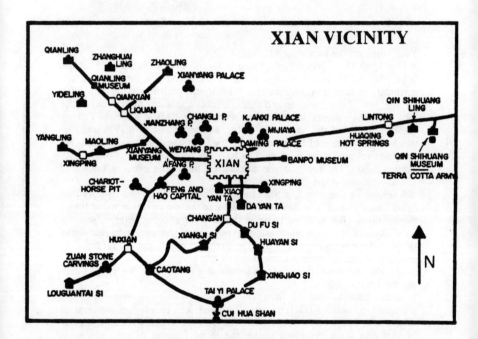

XILINHOT 錫林浩特

The Mongolian city of Xilinhot is located about 500 air kms north of Beijing in the province of Nei Mongol. This city, open to foreign tourists, can be reached only by air. By going to this city one can see a region where few other tourists have been. It would be an excellent place to see the grasslands where the formerly nomadic Mongolians lived. Today most Mongolians in China have been settled in communes and cities.

In the 17th century when the Yellow Hat sect of Tibetan Buddhism spread into Mongolia, they built a number of monasteries or lamaseries. Although most of these have gone they were the foundation of many of today's towns in that area. The lamaseries grew large and powerful and owned most of the land and cattle. The monks of these lamaseries were fully one fifth of the population and employed another fifth. Today the lamaseries are gone and in their place are the headquarters of the Banners (similar to a county, but which represent various tribes). Xilinhot owes its existence to one of these former lamaseries; Xilinhot's population is now about 100,000 people. The monastery, BEIZIMIAO, is still extant and is perhaps the biggest tourist attraction. It now has a carpet factory employing monks and outsiders.

XINING 西宁

LOCATION AND TRANSPORTATION: Xining is located in the extreme eastern side of the province of Qinghai. It is also just to the west of Lanzhou in Gansu Province. The only way to Xining is by rail. There are four fast trains and one slow train to Xining from Lanzhou, but three of the four fast trains travel every other day only. You will have to check at the CITS office to be sure about which trains leave on what days. The fast train takes about five hours to Lanzhou; nine hours in the local train. Three of the four fast trains go on to Beijing, Qingdao, or Nanjing.

HOTEL: The XINING BINGUAN Is the one hotel in XINING. When you get off the train someone will probably approach you and direct you to the bus run by the hotel. The hotel helps tourists get from the station to the hotel. The fare for this bus is only slightly more than for the number 9 bus which also runs in front of the hotel. Take the hotel bus; it is less crowded. When leaving town you could take bus 9 from the hotel to the station.

SIGHTS: One good reason to visit Xining, especially in summer, is for its cool weather! The city, at 2260 metres, offers a cool respite from the summer heat of the rest of China. Since the city is on the edge of Tibet you will find a few non-Han Chinese, but not many. A minority group you will encounter are the Hui. They are Han Chinese Muslims who speak Putonghua (common language). Many of the men wear small, white skull caps and long beards. On occasion you will see Tibetans, but they usually live higher in the mountains around the Taer Si.

While in Xining you can visit a large mosque, the DONGGUAN SI (East Pass Temple). Friday at noon would be an excellent time to view this mosque as that is the weekly prayer time.

Another place of interest would be the temple on Bei Shan, called the BEI SHAN SI (North Mountain Temple). It is a small temple perched on the face of a cliff. Some of the rooms are caves dug out of the cliff-face. Just walk west from the hotel then north, across the tracks, and follow a small road to the base of the hill, then walk up.

There is a market place or bazaar on the hill about due south of the hotel. This older part of the city around the bazaar is interesting.

Walk west, then south of the hotel for about one km to where you can board a bus bound for the Tibetan temple or monastery of TAER SI. This temple, open to foreign visitors, is located in the town of HUANGZHONG. You will stop in the centre of the town near an outdoor basketball court. (It is here you board the bus later to return to Xining). The cheapest hotel in town, the HUANGZHONG BINGUAN, is just across the street. One bed in a quad room costs Y4 a night. If you walk south and up the main street, you will come to Taer Si (Taer Temple). Within this monastery is another hotel. Most foreign tourists stay in this one for Y7 a night. Most rooms are twin bedded rooms which offer more privacy. It is more expensive, but as monks used to stay here there is that added special appeal. This hotel is very quiet with rooms surrounding a courtyard. They have experienced water problems

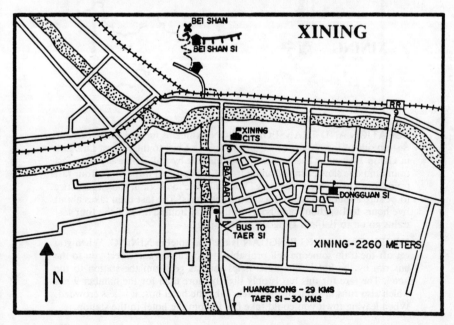

but the problems will surely be rectified. You may not feel the need for showers anyway as the elevation of Taer Si is nearly 2700 metres. Taer Si or Lamasery, founded in 1560, is the birthplace of Tsongkhapa, the founder of the Yellow Hat sect of Tibetan Buddhism. Taer Si is one of the six major lama temples in the Tibet region.

The glaze-roofed temples, halls, pagodas and monks' residences constitute an integrated architectural complex in a combined Han-Tibetan style. The temples are decorated with butter sculptures, superimposed appliques and frescoes known as "three wonders" for their exquisite craftsmanship and unique style.

Along the road between the bus stop and the monastery are many restaurants. In the early mornings and evenings they are generally closed because most tourists (Chinese) or pilgrims come to the Taer Si during the daytime only. So, eat there before late afternoon or eat at a hotel restaurant. Along this same street closer to the monastery are dozens of small souvenir shops selling Tibetan handicrafts and trinkets.

For those wanting to venture further from Xining you can travel with a CITS guide and driver. You can go to Qinghai Hu (lake) or possibly other temples or monasteries in the region. With a little luck you could even hitch hike to some of the surrounding areas. Pick up a regional map at the hotel.

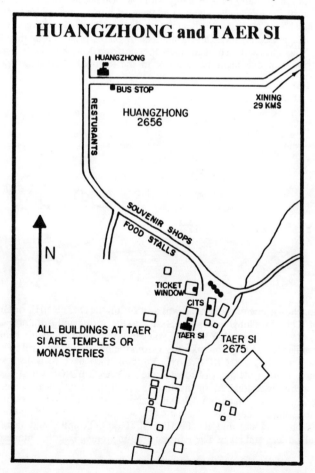

HUANGZHONG and TAER SI

HUANGZHONG

BUS STOP

XINING 29 KMS

RESTURANTS

HUANGZHONG 2656

SOUVENIR SHOPS
FOOD STALLS

N

TICKET WINDOW

CITS

TAER SI

TAER SI 2675

ALL BUILDINGS AT TAER SI ARE TEMPLES OR MONASTERIES

YAN'AN 延安

Yan'an is a small city located in north central Shaanxi Province. It is where Mao Zedong, Zhu De and Zhou Enlai made their headquarters during the years 1937 - 1947. The story started in 1934 in Ruijin in Jiangxi Province when the Communist party and its leaders were forced out and had to begin the LONG MARCH. There were about 100,000 men and women to begin with. They marched for one year, crossing eighteen mountain ranges and fourteen rivers. In October, 1935, they arrived in the town of Wuqi, just northeast of Yan'an. Two years later the Communist Party set up their headquarters in Yan'an. During the Long March they amassed 50,000 troops, making it necessary for them to farm in order to live. During the ten years at this location the party leaders, along with the local population, lived in caves dug out of the loess hills. These same types of homes can be seen today all over northern China, especially along the Huang He (Yellow River). Today there is a museum, hotel, and a number of places preserved as they were when Mao was there. You can reach Yan'an from Xian by bus. It is a two day trip, with one night being spent in the town of Huangling (Yellow Tomb).

YANGZHOU 扬州

Yangzhou is one of the canal towns as it sits on the DA YUNHE or Grand Canal. This city's long history traces back to the Spring and Autumn Period (770 - 476 BC). To reach Yangzhou you can take a bus from either Nanjing or Zhenjiang. In Yangzhou take bus 3 from the bus station and ask to be let off near the XIYUAN BINGUAN. You will then have to walk a short distance. Also in the heart of town is the LUYANG BINGUAN.

Yangzhou is considered the most northerly of the canal towns, the others being Zhenjiang, Changzhou, Wuxi, Suzhou, and Hangzhou. The canal is an interesting place to visit. There are also several temples including the SHI TA (Stone Pagoda) and the FAJINGSI (Fajing Temple); and there are several gardens and lakes. The Fajingsi is a functioning Buddhist monastery.

YANTAI 烟台

LOCATION AND TRANSPORTATION: Yantai is located near the eastern end of the Shandong Bandao or Peninsula, in Shandong Province. It is located on the coast and has one of the better harbours in the north of China. You can reach Yantai (meaning smoke tower) by rail from Qingdao and the rest of China, and by ferry service from the cities of Dalian, Qingdao, Tianjin and Shanghai. The boat to Dalian leaves daily, but boats to other destinations leave on a less frequent basis.

HOTEL: There are two hotels in town, but it appears that most tourists are diverted to the ZHIFU BINGUAN in the eastern suburbs off this map. There is another hotel very near the boat docks terminal called the YANTAISHAN BINGUAN.

SIGHTS: Yantai is a city with a history of about 2200 years. The first emperor of China, Qin Shi Huangdi of the Qin Dynasty (221 - 206 BC) visited during this time. The year 1398 AD saw a garrison established. Not much of note happened in Yantai until the last century when it was opened to foreign trade. Today Yantai is a summer resort town but has some factories including several clock factories. It is in an apple growing region, it has a beach and is a cool hideaway from the scorching plains of China during summer. There is not much to see in the way of antiquities but if you like seafood, you will find plenty.

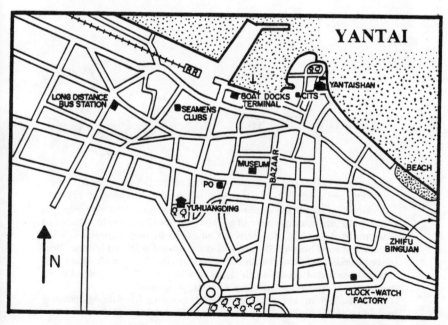

YICHANG 宜昌

If you are taking the Chang Jiang (Yangtze River) boat trip from Chongqing to Wuhan, the boat will stop at the city of Yichang. Yichang is about two-thirds of the way downstream from Chongqing and is just a couple of kms beyond the Gezhou Dam. There is very little to see in Yichang; it is simply a transit point for most. Some people get off the boat and take a train to Luoyang via Xiangfan. If you decide to disembark, something of interest is the Gezhou Dam. This dam and water control project is the first giant dam on the Chang Jiang. It is built across the river just beyond the last of the river gorges at the point where the river meets the plain. The dam includes a hydro electric plant with 21 sets of turbo-generators, navigation locks, spillways and scouring sluices. One spillway was put into use in 1981.

To see the dam you can take a bus from the centre of Yichang to the dam site. You can view most sections of the installation without problems. If you do not stop in Yichang you can see from the boat the navigation locks in action as the Chang Jiang boats pass through the locks.

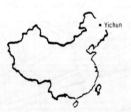

YICHUN 宜 春

Yichun is located in the extreme north of the province of Heilongjiang, in China's Northeast, or as they call it, the Dong Bei (East North). This small city is the furthest north of any city in China open to foreign tourists. It is not far south of the China-USSR border and the Amur River, and is rather close to the Siberian taiga. It is at a similar latitude as Ulan Bator in Mongolia. The climate is such that on the north slopes of hills you will see forests. On the open plains there are no trees, mainly because of man.

To get to Yichun take a train from Harbin or even from the Mudanjiang or Jiamusi side.

YINCHUAN 银川

• Yinchuan

LOCATION AND TRANSPORTATION: Yinchuan is the capital of the Ningxia Hui Autonomous Region. Ningxia is located in north central China on the fringe of the Gobi Desert. Yinchuan is located in the northern part of Ningxia, very near the banks of the Huang He (Yellow River), and on the main rail line linking Lanzhou with Baotou and Hohhot. Because this region does not have the high population as other parts of the People's Republic, there are only two long distance trains daily leaving the station in Yinchuan. There are also flights to Beijing.

HOTEL: The one hotel in Yinchuan for the foreign traveller is the YI SOUA BINGUAN. It has recently been renovated and is gearing up for more tourists. The people in this hotel were very friendly. They have at least one room costing Y6 a night; this is a twin room sharing a common bathroom with shower. To get there from the train station take bus 1 to a point near the hotel, then walk around the corner to the Yi Soua.

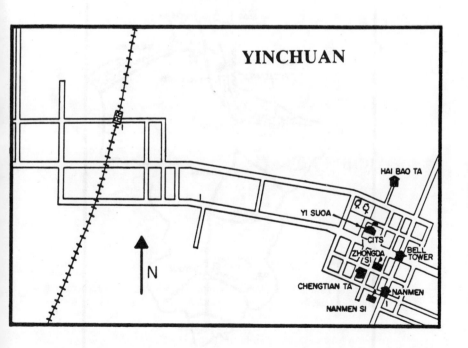

SIGHTS: There are two very tall and unique pagodas in Yinchuan. To the north of the hotel is the HAI BAO TA and to the south, the CHENGTIAN TA. Both of these structures are near 60 metres in height and have staircases to the top where visitors can climb and view the city.

There are two major mosques in the city. The NANMEN SI (South Gate temple or Mosque) is very near the city's south gate. You can reach it by taking bus 1 from near the hotel or the train station. This one has the look of a south Asian mosque with five domes on top. Not far to the north of this one is the ZHONGDA SI (Big Central Temple or Mosque). It may appear to the casual foreign visitor to be a Buddhist temple. This temple or mosque is similar to other mosques located to the east and south of Ningxia. Yinchuan also has two interesting structures which are often called gates or bell towers in other cities. They are shown on this map as temples.

There is a number of other interesting sights outside Yinchuan, and in the province of Ningxia. Those sites near the capital are open to foreigners as long as you can go out and come back in one day. In some cases they may be open only if you are in the company of a CITS guide. You can get this information at the hotel. There are even better sites in the south of Ningxia, but they may still be closed to foreigners, except tourists of Chinese ancestry.

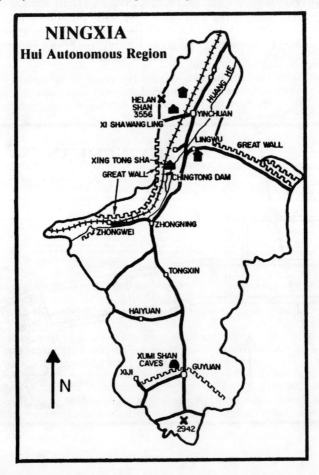

About 37 kms to the west of Yinchuan are the SI SHA WANG LING (tombs). With perseverence they can be found. Try taking bus 10 from Yinchuan to Ge Pu Zhan and walking or hitching from there. This is open to foreigners. Somewhere northwest of Yinchuan and near the mountains is another pagoda-type building. To the south of Yinchuan within a day's trip by public bus is the CHINGTONG GORGE HYDROELECTRIC POWER STATION. You can take a bus to see the dam and a place called the XING TONG SHA in a one-day trip. At Xing Tong Sha are the YI BAI LING BA TA (pagodas) numbering 108 in all; these are 78 kms south of Yinchuan.

Further to the south are the cities of Guyuan and Longde and some interesting Buddhist caves. As stated, this is the part of Ningxia which has a majority of the Hui peoples. This you should find interesting when it is opened up. The caves, called the XUMI SHAN SHIR KU (Xumi Mountain Rock Caves), are 303 kms from Yinchuan and very near Guyuan. One of the caves has a statue of The Buddha which is 19 metres high.

Around the small city of Zhongwei are some other sites, but they are covered under Zhongwei.

Ningxia is one of five national minority autonomous regions in China. The other four are Nei Mongol, Xinjiang (Tibet) and Guangxi. Ningxia has a total population of about 4 million of whom about 32% are the HUI minority. The Hui peoples are Han Chinese who practise Islam. Their religion sets them apart from other Han Chinese, not the language or some other factor. Most of the Hui people live in the south of Ningxia where the population is over 90% Hui.

The Huang He flows through Ningxia. This is one of the regions of the country where irrigation was first practised. Irrigation works date back more than 2000 years. Ningxia has abundant deposits of coal, petroleum, limestone, mica and asbestos.

ZHANGZHOU

• Zhangzhou

Zhangzhou is located in Fujian Province about 50 km inland, westward, from the island of Xiamen. This small city sits at tidewater height on the Jiulong Jiang (river). The old part of town near the waterfront has interesting old buildings.

Not far from the main market in town you will find, at the base of Nan Shan, the NAN SHAN SI (South Mountain Temple). First built in the early years of the Tang Dynasty (618 - 907 AD), it has a 5.3 metre high stone statue of The Buddha as well as Indian Buddhist scriptures from the Song Dynasty (960 - 1280 AD).

Zhangzhou is connected by rail to Xiamen and the rest of China, including points north and Shanghai. There are many trains a day. If you are going to Xiamen you could try the bus to Longhai then a ferry across the bay to Xiamen. There is one hotel in Zhangzhou just west of the bus station. From the train station walk south less than a km or take a cycle rickshaw. One bed in a triple is Y6 a night.

ZHENGZHOU 郑州

LOCATION AND TRANSPORTATION: Zhengzhou, the capital of Henan Province, is a large city located on the main rail linking Beijing with Guangzhou. Zhengzhou is also on the rail line connecting Xian and Shanghai, thus the amount of traffic in and out of this station is among the heaviest in the country. The Huang He (Yellow River) flows by the city's northern limits.

HOTEL: Of the three hotels in town, independent travellers usually stay in the ER YUE CHE BINGUAN (February 7th Hotel). The cheapest beds, in a quad room, are Y5 a night sharing a common bath. Although you can easily walk to this hotel from the train station you can also take bus 2. The hotel is next to the twin towers called the ER YUE CHE MONUMENT (February 7th Monument). You may not be able to get into the ZHONGYUAN BINGUAN, but it is close to the station as well. Bus 2 ends its run near the ZHONGZHOU HOTEL, another possibility.

SIGHTS: Zhengzhou was founded in the Shang Dynasty (1766 - 1122 BC). In 1955 some remains of this ancient city were discovered. It was the capital city of China during the Shang Period along with Anyang and Qufu. After that period it sank into oblivion until the railway came through the city near the beginning of this century. Some of the old city walls can be seen as shown on the map, but there is little left. The Er Yue Che Monument, the city's symbol, was built to commemorate a February 1923 uprising of railway workers. The uprising was crushed by a local warlord. Overall, you can see all there is to see in half a day or less. Most people put their luggage in the railway baggage room, spend a short time in the city then take another train out.

ZHONGWEI

LOCATION AND TRANSPORTATION: Zhongwei is the largest town in the western region of Ningxia Province. It is located just north of the Huang He (Yellow River) and is on the main rail line linking Lanzhou, Yinchuan and the cities of Nei Mongol. As for transportation there are only three trains daily passing Zhongwei going in either direction. Train 44 is the only express; there are two local or slower trains as well.

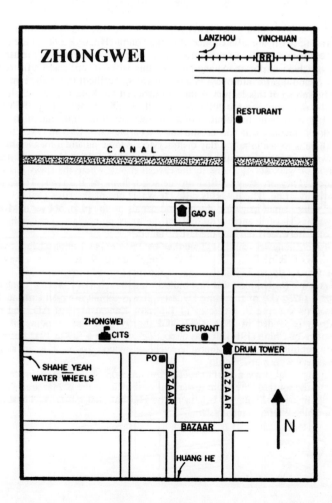

HOTEL: Since Zhongwei is a small city there is one hotel for both Chinese and foreigners. It is the ZHONGWEI BINGUAN with quad rooms for about Y6 or Y7 per bed, with a common bath. It has double rooms with private baths as well for about Y12 or Y14 a night per bed. As there are no city buses you will have to walk the one km or so from the train station or take a donkey cart.

SIGHTS: Zhongwei lies in the green lush valley of the Huang He, but also in an area of dry land at the edge of the Gobi Desert. The landscape and natural features of the area affect the type of things you can see and do. If you contact the CITS office they can help you get out of town and see sand dunes to the northwest of Zhongwei. You could also see the DESERT SANDS RECLAMATION PROJECT along the railway line and Huang He, just north of Shahe Yeah. However, you can see these sand control methods along the railway line as you ride out of Zhongwei by train to the west. The main control features include the placing of straw on and around sand dunes to slow the movement of the sand during windy conditions. You can also arrange to see some camels in a camel commune located in the desert just north of Zhongwei.

Other things outside Zhongwei which you can visit yourself without any guides are firstly the inflated sheepskin rafts on the Huang He. They are used to cross the river where there is no ferry. This place is about 5 kms south of Zhongwei. The rafts are made of inflated sheepskins placed under a frame of poles, in exactly the same way as is seen today in northern Pakistan. You can either walk or rent a bicycle at the front gate of the hotel.

Secondly, probably the best place to visit outside Zhongwei is the SIWAY CHA or water wheels, about 15 or 20 kms west of town. You can hitch hike on small tractors or trucks or you can rent a bicycle. This trip takes about half a day; you can see and ride the ferry across the river and have a look at a crock-pot factory. From the ferry terminal at SHAHE YEAH, you will want to ride or walk about 2 kms to the east, then ask where the siway cha are located. They are easy to find on the south bank of the river. There are several in a line. These wheels raise the water out of the river channel and pour it into small irrigation ditches and canals on the plain above the river. Nowadays gasoline engines do most of the water pumping and only a handful of waterwheels remain, the last of an era.

Inside Zhongwei you should see the GAO SI or Gao Temple. Even if you are tired of seeing Buddhist temples this one is a must to see. In some ways it is similar to all others but it is one of the most unique structures in China. This temple (or temples) was first built during the reign of Emperor Yong Le (1403 - 1425 AD) of the Ming Dynasty. It was rebuilt after an earthquake caused its collapse in the reign of Emperor Kangxi in 1710 AD, and repeatedly expanded in 1823, 1882, and shortly after the founding of the Republic of China (1911). It was almost destroyed in a fire in 1942 but was again rebuilt. It is built almost entirely of wood. Today it is an active monastery with many monks.

Zhongwei also has a drum tower at the junction of the two main streets. Just to the south of the drum tower and post office is the bazaar area. Most people living in Zhongwei belong to the Hui national minority. These are Han Chinese who practise Islam.

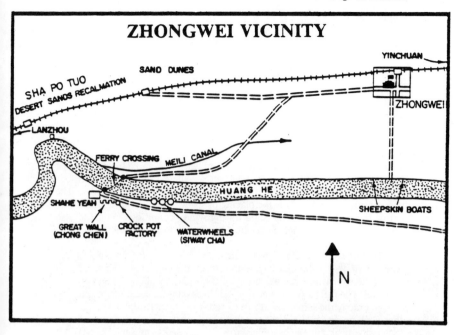

ZHONGWEI VICINITY

ZUNHUA 遵化

Zunhua in Hebei Province is located about 125 kms east of Beijing. Actually, this is not a city, but is a large group of imperial tombs of the Qing Dynasty (1644 - 1911 AD). It is not on any rail line; the only way there is by bus from Beijing. Five of the tombs are for emperors, fourteen for empresses, and others are for concubines and other women in the royal families. These tombs are sometimes known as the DONG QING LING or Eastern Qing Tombs. The scene is similar to that seen at the Ming Tombs just north of Beijing. The region has extensive stone carvings and stone structures. The central path to the tombs is lined with stone figures and animals like those of the Ming tombs. They represent ministers, generals, horses, unicorns, elephants, camels and lions. This is called the "Guard of Honour" or "Spirit Way". These tombs, like the Ming tombs, are underground but are more elaborate with stone carvings and inscriptions. The underground tomb of Yu Ling has been repaired and is open to the public. Of all the tombs of the Qing Dynasty, the one for Dowager Empress Ci Xi has the best surface structure. She was the lady responsible for the marble boat at the Summer Palace in Beijing. To get to these tombs inquire at the CITS office in Beijing about transportation and the possibility of a hotel on the site.

Bogda Shan: Main summit, 5445 metres, as seen from the north west (K)

See page 218 for details.

THE HIKING GUIDE

CONTENTS

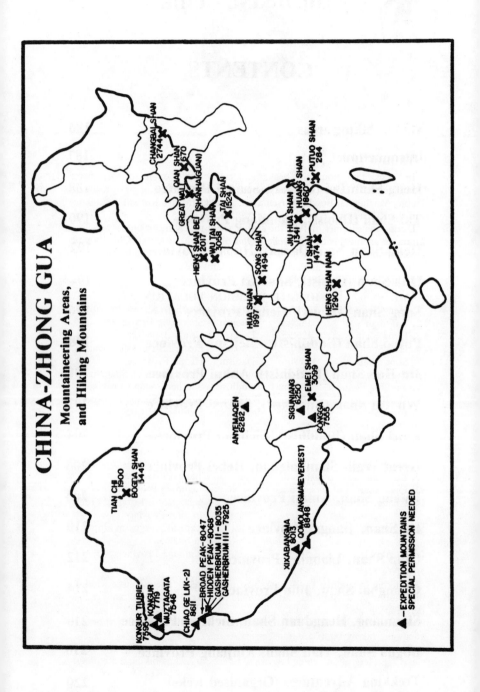

CHINA-ZHONG GUA

Mountaineering Areas, and Hiking Mountains

CHANGBAI SHAN 2744

670

GREAT WALL (SHAN-HAI GUAN)

HENG SHAN BEI 2017

TAI SHAN 1524

WU TAI SHAN 3058

PUTUO SHAN 284

HUANG SHAN 1860

JIU HUA SHAN 1341

SONG SHAN 1494

LU SHAN 1474

HUA SHAN 1997

HENG SHAN NAN 1290

ANYEMAGEN 6282

SIGUNIANG 6250

EMEI SHAN 3099

GONGGA 7555

TIAN CHB 1900

BOGDA SHAN 5445

KONGUR TIUBIE 7595

KONGUR 7719

MUZTAGATA 7546

CHIAO GE LI(K-2) 8611

BROAD PEAK - 8047

HIDDEN PEAK - 8068

GASHERBRUM II - 8035

GASHERBRUM III - 7925

XIXABANGMA 8013

QOOLANGMA(EVEREST) 8848

▲ = EXPEDITION MOUNTAINS
SPECIAL PERMISSION NEEDED

186

INTRODUCTION

In 1984, ten mountain peaks and areas were open to foreigners: Qomolangma (Everest), Xixabangma (Gosainthan), Kongur, Kongur-Tiubie, Muztagata, Bogda, Anyemagen, Gongga (Minya Konka), Siguniang and the K-2 region.

During the summer of 1984 the author spent nearly five months travelling China as an independent traveller. One object was to climb China's nine sacred mountains. Although he visited all, he was able to climb only eight.

In addition to these nine, six other mountains are described plus the Great Wall hike. Details are as follows:

NAME	HEIGHT	RELIGION	LOCATION
1. Heng Shan Bei	2017m	Daoism	Northern Shanxi Province
2. Tai Shan	1524m	Daoism	Shandong Province
3. Heng Shan Nan	1290m	Daoism	Hunan Province
4. Hua Shan	1997m	Daoism	Eastern Shaanxi Province
5. Song Shan	1494m	Daoism	Henan Province
6. Putuo Shan	284m	Buddhism	Island south of Shanghai
7. Jiu Hua Shan	1341m	Buddhism	Southern Anhui Province
8. Wu Tai Shan	3058m	Buddhism	North of Shanxi Province
9. Emei Shan	3099m	Buddhism	Sichuan Province
Other hikes include:			
10. Great Wall			Shanhaiguan (eastern end of the wall at the sea)
11. Huang Shan	1860m		Southern Anhui Province
12. Lu Shan	1474m		Jiangxi Province
13. Qian Shan	670m		Liaoning Province
14. Changbai Shan	2744m		Near North Korean border. In Jilin Province.
15. Siguniang	6250m		Expedition-type mountain in Sichuan.
16. Bogda Shan	5447m		Xinjiang Province

HIKING TIPS

If hiking in summer (mid-year), buy an umbrella. There is little wind on the mountain in summer; an umbrella will keep you cool and reduce perspiration.

As many of the hiking paths are stepping-stone trails, running shoes are adequate; hiking boots are unnecessary.

On the nine sacred mountains small hotels provide bedding and food. Carrying a tent and sleeping bag are not necessary when hiking these mountains.

Heng Shan Bei (Daoist), Shanxi Province

悬空寺导游图 Hanging monastery

Heng Shan Bei, or Northern Heng Shan, is the most northerly of China's nine sacred mountains. Located not far south of Datong, it stands 2017 metres high. It can be reached by train from Beijing and Taiyuan.

Most people going to Heng Shan first go to Datong where, incidentally, are located some of the best Buddhist caves in China. To reach Heng Shan, take a morning bus from Datong. The bus goes via Hunyuan and should drop you off at the parking plaza, at 1600 metres, at the base of the cliffs. A few minutes walk will take you to the amphitheatre of temples and monasteries. At present, as there is no lodging on or near the mountain, most people make it a one day excursion from Datong. However, being a rather dry area, sleeping out of doors is possible; no one should object.

If the mountain is closed when you arrive, but you're still hell-bent on climbing it, you might try what the author did. He hitched from Datong to Hunyuan and finally to Xuan Kong Si (temple). There's a fair amount of traffic on the road, thus hitch hiking is good. After seeing this spectacular cliff temple (Xuan Kong), a policeman said he couldn't go beyond the tunnel, so the author returned to Tao Jazhou and asked children about another trail. Yes! So he walked on one of several terraced field paths into a canyon where several trails came together. So the author climbed Heng Shan by this northern route which is used by only half a dozen people a day. He then hitched back to Hunyuan and took a bus to Datong (same day). There's a small spring at about 1500 meters, but start out with a water bottle if it's a warm day. Later on, when restoration is completed, there will be food and drinks available on the mountain, at least on the normal route. At present few people go to the summit, but instead visit the temples as shown. These are among the most interesting mountain temples in China because several are under overhanging cliffs. Xuan Kong Si is surely the best and most unique temple in China, it being on a cliff face. All tourists can visit this latter temple, if you're with a C.I.T.S. guide out of Datong.

Map: When the mountain is open to all, you will be able to buy simple maps in Datong, Hunyuan and on the mountain.

Heng Shan Bei (Daoist), Shanxi Province

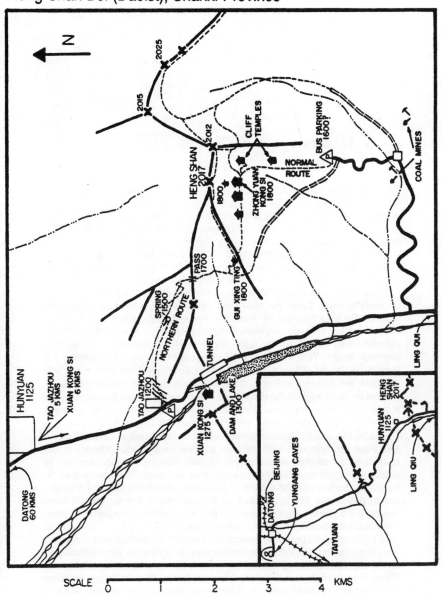

Tai Shan (Daoist), Shandong Province

Tai Shan •

For sketch of TAI SHAN, see page 136

The mountain featured here is Tai Shan, at 1524 meters. Tai Shan is one of the five Daoist mountains in China, and is the most easterly of the group. It is located on the main rail line which runs between Beijing to the north, and Shanghai to the south. At the base of the mountain is a small city called Taian which owes its existence to this small and compact range. Tai Shan is the most climbed of all the nine sacred mountains in China and is also likely to be the most climbed mountain in the world. Its location on the previously mentioned rail line puts it in easy reach of many Chinese, and nowadays many foreign tourists as well.

Because of it's popularity all trains, even the expresses, stop at Taian. There are many hotels in Taian, but as of 1984, only one accepts foreign tourists. To reach the Tai Shan Binguan, or Hotel, walk out of the train station (huo che zhan) and turn left to where one sees the bus stop sign for bus number 3. This will take you to the hotel located near the beginning of the main trail to the mountain. This same bus actually runs between the two main trailheads used for climbing Tai Shan. So at the end of your hike, if you have taken the western route down, you can catch bus 3, which will stop at the hotel near the other end of the line.

From the hotel walk on the street north a short distance to the gate which is the beginning of the normal route. Along this wide and stone paved trail are many vendors selling food and drinks, souvenirs, film and photographs.

The hike is about 12 kms. The elevation at the bottom is about 225 metres; you climb an estimated 7000 steps on a paved path to 1524 metres. A fast climber not interested in sightseeing or photography can accomplish the round trip in five to six hours. Plan on an all day trip as there is much of interest - the people and the scenery. It is possible to spend a night on the summit in one of the temples. Check on lodging before leaving the Tai Shan Binguan. To shorten your trip you can ride a bus to about the halfway point, then reach the summit ridge in the lift or teleferico.

It's recommended to use the western route on the return which begins at Zhong Tian Men. One can walk down the trail or road, passing a fine waterfall and pool on the way. Remember, it's warm at the base of the mountain and cool at the top. Climb from April through October. Also visit the Tai Miao or Temple in Taian, one of three palace-style buildings in China (the other two are the Imperial Palace in Beijing and Kong Miao in Qufu).

Map: The author found three different maps which he bought at the train station and hotel.

Tai Shan (Daoist), Shandong Province

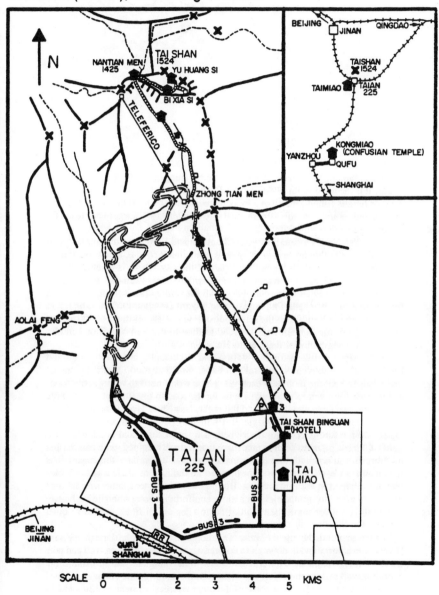

Heng Shan Nan (Daoist), Hunan Province

This mountain in Hunan Province is called Heng Shan Nan or Heng Shan South. It is the most southerly of the five Daoist mountains in China. The highest peak or *feng* is called Zhou Rong Feng at an altitude of 1290 metres. Of all the nine sacred mountains, this is perhaps the least interesting, largely because of a motor road to the summit.

Heng Shan Nan is located between Changsha and Hengyang in central Hunan province. The author arrived in Hengyang from Guangzhou (Canton) on a train, then took city bus #1 to the northern part of the city where is located the bus station for travellers going north. There are many buses each day going in the direction of Heng Shan. (One can also get off the train in Heng Shan, then take a ferry across the river and find buses going toward Hengyang). You'll be left at the bus station of Nan Yui on the south side of town. Walk north about 400 meters to a large gate through which is the road leading to the Nan Yui Si or Temple, which is the beginning of the way to Heng Shan.

On the street between the bus station and the temple are many shops and hawkers selling souvenirs, umbrellas, maps, pins and food. You'll be one of thousands to visit the mountain each year. You won't need to worry about food as there are food vendors everywhere along the road to the summit. Also, there are several places in which to spend the night, Ban Shan Ting being the largest. Rooms are large and dormitory style. But there may be smaller rooms for couples, especially for foreigners. Dormitory beds are very cheap and bedding is provided. Chinese pilgrims seldom take more than a small handbag, with camera and toothbrush, and not much else (but everyone takes an umbrella as this mountain is in that part of China that receives the heaviest amounts of rain). The author took a tent and camped in the rain and fog. But no one saw the tent; otherwise he may have been asked to instead sleep in a more comfortable hotel or boarding house. Camping is not recommended as flat camp sites are difficult to find in quiet places.

From Nan Yui to the top is 12 kms. The round trip can thus be done in one day. If you're in a hurry and don't want to spend a night on the mountain you can take a bus or truck from the Nan Yui Si to Ban Shan Ting, at Km 7. From there everyone walks along the good road to the top. If spending time on the mountain, one might visit Nan Tai Si or some of the other temples. Film sizes 126 and 135 can be bought on the mountain (B + W). The bottom of the mountain is warm and humid while the top is cool--dress accordingly. Shorts are accepted in China.

Map: Only in Nan Yui can one buy small Chinese maps similar to this one.

Heng Shan Nan (Daoist), Hunan Province

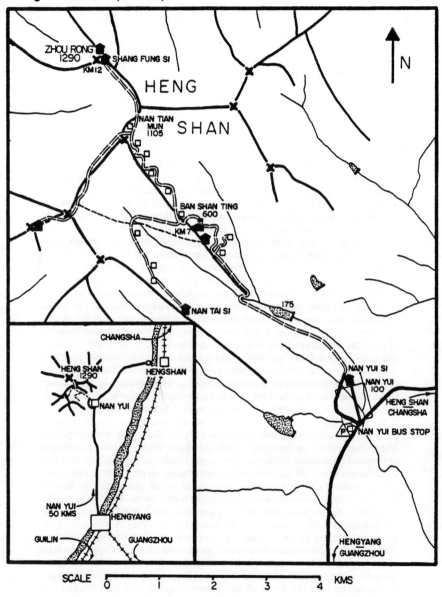

Hua Shan (Daoist), Shaanxi Province

Hua Shan is one of five sacred Daoist mountains of China. This one is located on the main rail line running between Xian and Luoyang, and very near where the Huang He (Yellow River) makes its eastern turn after running south. There are several elevations given by various sources; some say the peaks are as high as 2500 meters, but the author is using the altitude given by the National Geographic map, *Peoples of China,* that says the elevation is 1997 meters. One source also stated that the Zhong Feng (Central Peak) is the highest, but another book indicated Nan Feng (South Peak) may be the higher.

But no matter what the altitude, Hua Shan is a remarkable mountain. As with about all of the sacred mountains of China, it too is a mass of solid granite, at least the central portion. It's probably the most beautiful of the nine, and in many ways is similar to Huang Shan located in Anhui Province. As with all the sacred mountains, this range too has many temples (si) and pavilions (ting). But there's one small problem. It's officially closed to foreigners of European ancestry. Hong Kong and other tourists of Chinese ancestry are allowed on the mountain, and European and North American workers living in China are allowed; but blond haired, blue eyed people like the author are excluded (1984). The reason being presumably, is that there have been accidents on the mountain. In some places rock steps have been cut into the vertical granite, and chain hand holds installed, but in cold weather it can be icy and dangerous, thus the discrimination.

So the author was at the mountain base, but was told to go to Xian for permission, but that permission never materialized. At the end of his journey he hadn't the time to go back and climb, so this is what you can do if you're determined on climbing anyway. Arrive at the Hua Shan Railway Station, either from Luoyang or Xian (take one of the slower passenger trains that stops here), and walk along the tracks to Hua Shan Da Men and look at the situation in daylight. Then store unneeded baggage at the train station. After dark, it'll be possible to skirt the gate, perhaps walking in the stream bed. Since the trail to the top is about 20 Gong Li (kms), it can be done in one day, but you'll have to stay on the mountain one night. It's a good trail and can be followed in the dark, but don't plan to stay in one of the boarding houses, as they will ask for I.D. Just rough it for one night, then make the climb next day, and return. But if you can manage, stay more than one day as it's one of the most photogenic hikes around. There are people selling food and drinks all along the way. Climb Hua Shan from May to October.

Map: There are maps for sale at the train station and at stalls at the Hua Shan Da Men, (gate).

194

Hua Shan (Daoist), Shaanxi Province

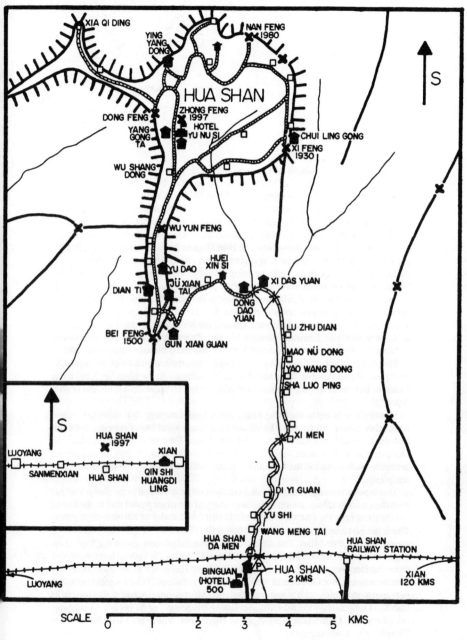

Song Shan (Daoist), Henan Province

Song Shan is the name of an entire mountain range in central China. The range is divided into two parts: Tai Shi Shan to the north of Dengfeng, whose highest peak is Junji Feng, at 1494 meters; and Shao Shi Shan to the west of Dengfeng (one map indicates the highest peak there rises to 1520 meters, but Junji Feng is regarded as the highest in the Song Shan). Song Shan is located between Luoyang (with the Longmen Caves) and Zhengzhou. Song Shan is the central range of the five Daoist mountains, lying between Hua Shan to the west, Heng Shan (Bei) to the north, Tai Shan to the east, and Heng Shan (Nan) to the south. Most people coming to the Song Shan visit the temples only; very few get out to climb the peaks. The author met about a dozen other people on his climb of Junji. Instead, the number one tourist or pilgrim attraction is the Shaolin Si (or Temple). This is perhaps the most famous temple in China. It was founded originally in 495 AD, and is the birth place of Zen Buddhism and the founding location of the martial arts, or Kung Fu. Besides Shaolin Si, the Zhong Yue Miao (or temple) is deluged with visitors, and the Song Yue Si is the most picturesque in the range.

The author climbed Junji Feng on day one, then the rains came eliminating the next hike. He was told of some very bad trails leading into the Shao Shi Shan from Shaolin, but never got the chance to explore (May a reader do a hike and send a report?).

Most people going to the Song Shan, arrive from Luoyang, but many also leave from Zhengzhou, all by bus. There are also many local buses running between Shaolin Si and Zhong Yue Miao, with Dengfeng as the central gathering place. In Dengfeng is a new hotel called the Song Shan Binguan. It has all classes of accommodation and is the best place to stay while exploring the mountains and temples.

This is what the author did: he got an early start, and walked to the Song Yue Si, then the Lao Mu Dong which is the beginning of the stone paved trail to the top of Junju Feng (peak). There are several old ruins and water at about 1050 metres. There are no temples on top, but another trail follows the ridge line south to the area of Zhong Yue Miao. The author walked this ridge route to Zhong Yue then got a bus back to the hotel (hiking time 8 hours). The trail is easy to follow except from the farm houses (1000) to Huang Gua Feng (there are many trails here and small canyons), but the general direction is easy to follow. Take a water bottle full between water holes as it's warm and humid. Most people should walk straight to Lao Mu Dong and do the hike without seeing the Song Yue Si as it's a very long hike for some. Climb here from April to November. There are many buses from Dengfeng to Luoyang daily.

Map: Buy simple maps at the hotel, Shaoling Si, or Zhong Yue Miao. Also history books.

Song Shan (Daoist), Henan Province

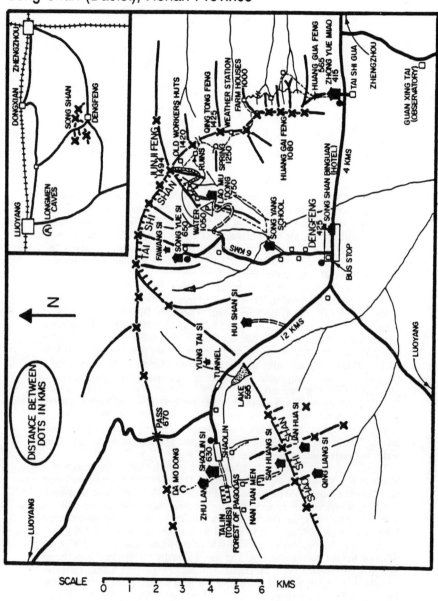

Putuo Shan (Buddhist), Zhejiang Province

Putuo Shan (Pu Island Mountain) is the smallest of all nine sacred mountains in China, but it's an interesting place to visit, nonetheless. The island has a number of temples, all being Buddhist. The best ones are: Puji Si, lying in the center of the only town on the island, Puji; Fayu Si, located at the bottom of the cement staircase leading to the top of the highest peak on the island; Huiji Si, located near the top of the peak at 245 meters (the highest summit is nearby at about 284 meters); and Dacheng Monastery with a large reclining Buddha. There are also many other small monasteries and pavilions.

Putuo Shan is located off the east coast of China, almost due east of Ningpo. It's very near the center of the Zhoushan Archipelago. There are two ways to get to the island, both involving ferry boats. There's a daily boat from Ningpo departing at 08 30, and this takes about 5 hours to reach Huang Fo An. The same service leaves Putuo at 07 00 daily for Ningpo. But rather than take a train to Ningpo, then the boat, you might try the nightly ferry from Shanghai. This is about a 12 hour ride and saves buying a hotel room for the night. Both of these boats are clean and comfortable, and the cruise is enjoyable as all passengers are pilgrims (now called tourists).

From the harbour walk in a northerly direction, first on a road, then a cement path to the hotel located beside the Puji Si (temple) pond. This converted monastery is clean, comfortable and inexpensive. It's apparently the only accommodation on the island for foreign tourists. There are many street vendors and small restaurants in the market street of Puji.

There's one main road on the island running north-south. One branch of it winds its way to near the top of Putuo Shan. The few small buses on the island take old and handicapped people to the Huiji Si and other temples on the island. But the vast majority of people walk along the road then up the cement staircase to the top of the mountain. One could walk from Puji to the top of Putuo Shan and back in a couple of hours, but to see all the temples will require a full day.

There are also beaches on the east side of the island. Lots of people on the beaches, but not many swimming. The author actually put up a tent on the larger beach (night only) in front of the Dacheng Monastery, and took it down early. No one objected, mainly because few people saw it. If you use black and white film, there are people on the street who will develop it on the spot, in little boxes. Best to buy your ticket in advance, the day before departure if possible. Putuo is a foggy place, so to see it all, one might stay several days.

Map: You can buy maps on the ferry boat, or from vendors in Puji.

Putuo Shan (Buddhist), Zhejiang Province

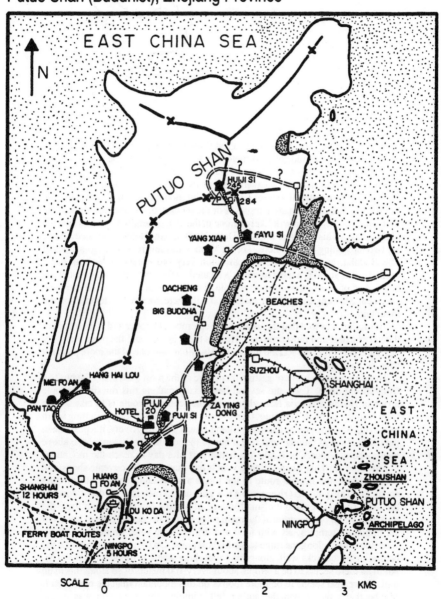

Jiu Hua Shan (Buddhist), Anhui Province

This map shows one of the four sacred Buddhist mountains in China, Jiu Hua Shan, reaching an altitude of 1341 meters. It's located not far to the west of Huang Shan, and even further to the west of Hangzhou. It's south of Tongling, Wuhu and Nanjing, and is in the southern part of the province of Anhui.

As is the case with all nine of China's sacred mountains, Jiu Hua Shan (Nine Flower Mountain) has many temples. For the modern day tourist or pilgrim, the first temple to be visited will likely be one in the area generally known as Jiu Hua Shan village. This is where the new Dong Ya Binguan (Hotel) is located. There are two interesting temples here. The Qi Yuan Si has several very large statues of The Buddha, and the Hua Cheng Si has a very old library as well as many artifacts. Bai Sui Si is a must to see. It's located on the first ridge to the east of the hotel. And of course the top-most temple, Tian Tai Si, at about 1300 meters and very near Shiwang Feng (1341 meters). In all, there are over 50 temples on the mountain.

The author was told that the months of September, October and November are the very busiest and most crowded. He was there in June and the place was very quiet and peaceful. In fact, the trek to Jiu Hua Shan was one of the more pleasant trips he had in China.

There are various ways of getting there, one of the most used being the bus trip from Huang Shan. There are several buses daily making this run (most people arrive at Huang Shan via Hangzhou). Another common route is to take a train from Nanjing south to Tongling, then use one of several daily buses running south to Jiu Hua Shan. If you're using the Chang Jiang (Yangtze River), it's possible to get off the boat at Guichi and ride a bus to the mountain. On any of the above mentioned bus routes it'll take the better part of a day to reach the mountain.

From the Jiu Hua Shan village, which has many small souvenir shops and eating places, the normal route to the top is a stone and cement path running southeast. This path first rises up to a low pass at 735 meters, then drops down to the main river valley and the small village of Middle Minyuan. From there the trail rises steeply to the crest of the main ridge. In the steeper part, there are about six important temples, all with food and drinks being sold. From Tian Tai Si, walk south west along the ridge to the highest point. On the return (or perhaps the beginning of the trek) walk along the small ridge where is found the Bai Sui Si. All in all there seems to be a temple about every 100 meters or so along this main trail. There also seem to be more monks on this mountain than the other eight. Maybe that's the reason the author felt climbing this mountain was a real pilgrimage.

Map: There are good maps available in the little market street between bus stop and hotel.

200

Jiu Hua Shan (Buddhist), Anhui Province

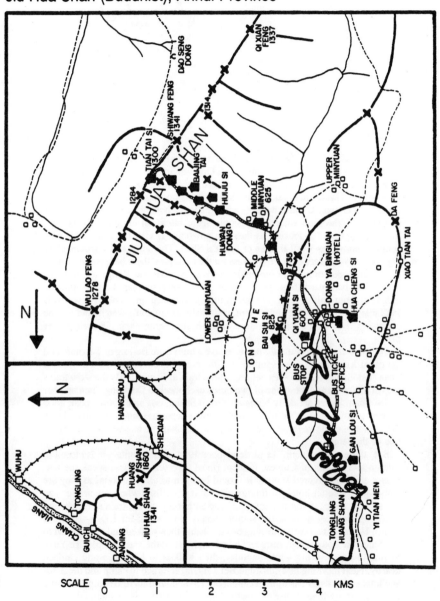

SCALE 0 1 2 3 4 KMS

Wu Tai Shan (Buddhist), Shanxi Province

Wu Tai Shan •

Wu Tai Shan, at 3058 meters, is the most northerly of the four Buddhist mountains in China. Wu Tai, along with Omei Shan, are the two highest of the nine; they being nearly equal in altitude. Wu Tai Shan is located not far south of the northern Daoist mountain, Heng Shan, and is north of the Shanxi Provincial capital of Taiyuan. It's also west of Beijing, about 7 hours by train. Wu Tai is one mountain of the nine where few people seem intent on climbing to the top. Instead, pilgrims (or tourists as they are now called) visit the town or temple complex known as Wu Tai Shan or just Tai Shan. This village is surrounded by high peaks which are covered by grass for the most part, there being pine trees on the north slopes only. The mountains here in the Wu Tai Range are rounded peaks with hardly a difficult pitch in sight. As you use this map keep in mind the temples (about half at least) are not in their exact locations. The map which is available, and used by the author here, isn't really a map, but a sketch, and may be confusing. But the peaks and ridges of the higher summits are in their proper places.

The normal way to Wu Tai Shan is to take a train from Beijing or Taiyuan and get off at Xin Xian, a town southwest of the range. From there take a bus to Tai Shan. Another route involves getting off the train at Fanshi (only the slow trains stop at Shahe), and taking one of two buses each *week* to Dochong, then another to Tai Shan. There are daily buses also from Shahe, but unless you speak good Chinese (putonghua), it's difficult to get correct departure times. All buses leave in the mornings however. There's a hotel in Tai Shan, or maybe you can stay at one of the temples.

But there's a problem. As of September 1984, this mountain was closed to foreign tourists not of Chinese descent (most Overseas Chinese speak the language, thus the favored status). It should be open to all very soon, as they are working on a better hotel for foreigners. But if it's closed when you arrive you can still get there, if you're persistent. The author got off the train at Fanshi and ended up sleeping there at the station (hotels always ask for I.D.'s--so avoid them). He caught an early morning bus to Shahe then walked and hitch-hiked to Tai Shan. He bought souvenirs and maps and visited the main temple, Ta Yuan Si (the one with a big white pagoda), then walked to KM 30.5 and camped nearby. Next morning he climbed to Bei Tai Din, returned to camp and the road, and hitched back to Fanshi, then caught the 23 00 hour train to Beijing. Hitching is very good in China, so use this method instead of busing if the mountain is still closed. Climbing here is best from May through October.

Map: Better maps will surely be made when Wu Tai Shan is open for all. Buy at Tai Shan shops. A very good county map is hanging on a wall at Fanshi Station.

Wu Tai Shan (Buddhist), Shanxi Province

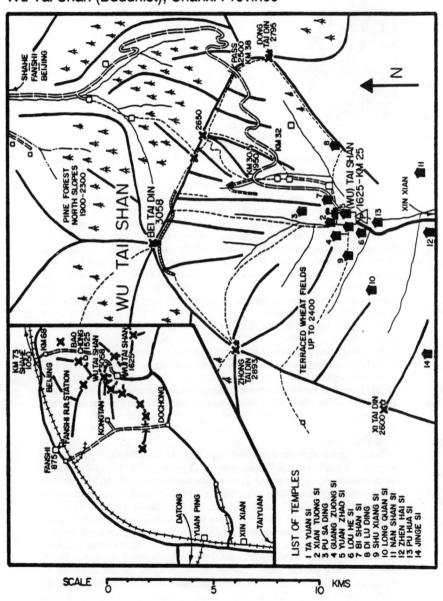

LIST OF TEMPLES

1 TA YUAN SI
2 XIAN TUONG SI
3 PU SA DING
4 GUANG ZUONG SI
5 YUAN ZHAO SI
6 LOU HE SI
7 BI SHAN SI
8 DI LU DING
9 SHU XIANG SI
10 LONG QUAN SI
11 NAN SHAN SI
12 ZHEN HAI SI
13 PU HUA SI
14 JINGE SI

SCALE 0 ——— 5 ——— 10 KMS

Emei Shan (Buddhist), Sichuan Province

Peak of Emei Shan, south of Chengdu.

Emei (always pronounced Omei Shan, but usually spelled Emei) Shan is probably the most famous of the four Buddhist mountains in China. And of the nine sacred mountains in China, Omei Shan is the highest. The highest summit is called Wan Fo Feng, and is 3099 meters. Most people however stop at the first of the three main summits, the Golden Peak, or Jin Ding Feng, at 3077 meters.

Omei Shan is the most popular mountain in China among foreign tourists. One reason for this is it's located on the main rail line running between Kunming and Chengdu (buy your ticket to Emei Shan--which is actually the Emei Station, as shown). It's popular because it's an excellent hike, the scenery is very fine, there are temples all along the way and there are thousands of other tourists or pilgrims on the mountain. The first temple was built in the second century, but many were built in the sixth century. At one time there were 151 temples on the mountain but today most have disappeared.

The normal route to the top of Omei Shan is via the Bao Guo Si (Temple), 6 kms southwest of the town of Emei. From there to the highest summit is about 61 kms, a rather long hike for most. Because of that extra long hike, many people nowadays use other routes requiring less time and energy. Jin Shui is perhaps the most used beginning point on the mountain, but some begin below the Qing Yin Ge Si. Then there are others who ride buses, small vans or trucks, the 49 kms from Emei town to the place called Shuanghuijing, and walk the few remaining kms from there. So from Shuanghuijing to the top is only a couple of hours, and if one could make the proper connections, the mountain could be climbed in one day from Emei Town.

But if a hiker uses the motorized way, then the main point of going to the mountain is totally missed. The enjoyment of the visit to Omei Shan is to witness the thousands of pilgrims walking the cement and stone stair-trails, to stop at any of the hundreds of food stalls along the way and stay overnight in the temples or monasteries; and to really enjoy the hike, one must do the whole hike in 3 to 4 days. The recommended route is to begin at Bao Guo Si, walk to Qing Yin Ge, then to the Xian Feng Si and spend the night. Then on to the top on the second day, returning down the ridge in the direction of Wan Nian Si, spending one more night on the mountain. This first day would be long. It's best to stay at Bao Guo Si one night and get the latest information about where people sleep on the mountain, then go from there. Take an umbrella-it's wet. Plastic rain covers are sold on the mountain. Take as small a pack as possible--all lodging includes bedding; and food is sold everywhere.

Map:　You can buy several different maps at Bao Guo Si, and sometimes along the trail.

Emei Shan (Buddhist), Sichuan Province

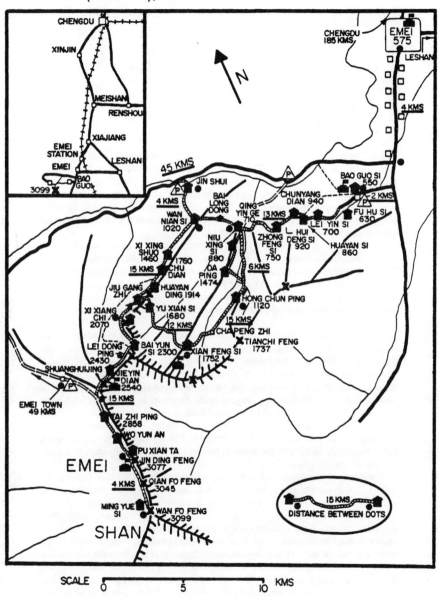

Great Wall--Shanhaiguan, Hebei Province

The Great Wall of China is certainly one of the man-made wonders of the world. The wall snakes its way from east to west a total of about 5000 kms. It runs through the provinces of Hebei, Beijing Municipality, Shanxi, Nei Mongol, Ningxia and Gansu. At one time, or rather at several times throughout history, the wall has been together as one unit. But today some parts are missing; in some places mother nature has taken her toll, and in other places the stones have been carried away by man as building material.

Most tourists, mostly Chinese, see the Great Wall at one of three locations. Most of the hordes visit the place called Badaling, about 60 kms north of Beijing. The wall there has been restored for distances of about 2 kms on either side of the highway. Also, many tourists visit the western end of the wall at Jiayuguan (Jiayu Pass). This is in western Gansu, and is conveniently located on the main rail line running to Xinjiang. A third place is at the eastern end of the wall, Shanhaiguan (Shanhai Pass).

Some adventurous travelers take a late afternoon bus or train to Badaling, then hike up one side of the wall, and sleep overnight in one of the watchtowers. Then they return to Beijing as the crowds come in for the mid-day viewing. But it's all very touristy. So the best place to visit the wall and hike without tourists is at Shanhaiguan. This is where you can see the wall entering the sea. The author spent two days at Shanhaiguan, staying in the one hotel or binguan (it's Chinese class--no showers, but otherwise comfortable). The first day he walked to the sea-end of the wall along a country road, then meandered back to town along the top of the wall. The wall along this section is 7 or 8 meters high, giving one a tree-top view of farms and gardens. At the very end of the wall, huge blocks of granite lie on the beach.

The town of Shanhaiguan has the best preserved city wall ever seen by the author. It's about 8 to 10 meters high and has been kept in good condition. Near the centre of the walled city is a fortress-like building, often seen in photographs. This is where Chinese tourists often visit. Another good part to visit, and a place devoid of tourists, is the wall as it climbs up the mountains northwest of town. The author walked from town to the peak marked 500 meters, along the top of the wall. The part of the wall that is most interesting is that part between the sea and up to the Jiao Shan, 460 meters. Beyond, the wall is crumbling and was never made to the same size as that part built on the more vulnerable plain. Several people could sleep in the watch tower at 260 meters. Take water to drink on any part of this wall hike.

Map: National Geographics map. *The Peoples of China,* and map of Shanhaiguan at hotel.

Great Wall--Shanhaiguan, Hebei Province

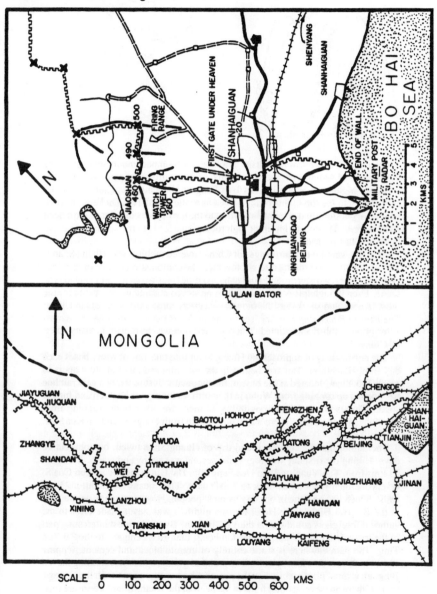

Huang Shan, Anhui Province

Mt. Lotus in Huangshan

Huang Shan or Yellow Mountain is a small and compact mountain range lying in the south of Anhui Province. There are four major groups of peaks or pinnacles here, the highest of which is Lian Hua Feng at 1860 meters. There's a stone-carved path to the top of this peak, as well as to the top of Tian Du Feng, at 1810 meters, and a stone and cement paved trail to the top of the peak with an altitude of 1820 meters. The fourth group of high rock pinnacles is to the south of Tian Du Feng and has no trail.

Of all the small mountain ranges of China covered in this book, Huang Shan is perhaps the most interesting and photogenic. The combination of clouds and fog, rock pinnacles and spires, and oddly shaped pine trees make for a fairyland type scene. Even though this is not one of the nine sacred mountains, it is probably the most famous and surely has the mountain scenery most used by artists in China. The *Pine in Beckoning Posture,* seen near the Yu Binguan is the one scene most often photographed and painted. This one scene is viewed by tourists in many hotels of China.

The normal way of approaching Huang Shan is to take one of many buses each day from Hangzhou. This trip begins in the morning and takes about 8 hours to reach Tao Yuan, located at the base of the mountain. Just recently a new rail line has opened up running from Wuhu in the north to the city of Shexian and further south. This is another route possibility as there are other buses running from Shexian to Huang Shan. There's also bus service from Tongling and Jiu Hua Shan to Tao Yuan.

The author made a circular round-trip of Huang Shan twice, on consecutive days. Hiking the first day was foggy; the second was sunny and warm. It's about 23 kms from Tao Yuan, to Lian Hua Feng, Bei Hai Binguan, and to Yun Goa Si (everyone then rides a bus back to Tao Yuan). This means it's about a 23 km walk which can be done in one day by most people. However, many people stay at the Bei Hai Binguan or Hotel for one night. It was never made clear to the author if foreigners could stay at the Yu Binguan? By far the most interesting part of the trip is from Tao Yuan, to Tian Du Feng, Lian Hua Feng and to the Pai Yun Ting. The pathway here is made entirely of granite block and cement stepping stones with very few level places. The group of granite spires surrounding the Yu Binguan is most photogenic. For the person who has more time than the average tourist, there are several other trails in the heart of the Huang Shan. There are food and drink stalls all along the main route, but carry a water bottle if it's a warm day. Carry an umbrella too as this is one of the wettest parts of China.

Map: Several maps and booklets can be bought at the Tao Yuan Hotel.

Huang Shan, Anhui Province

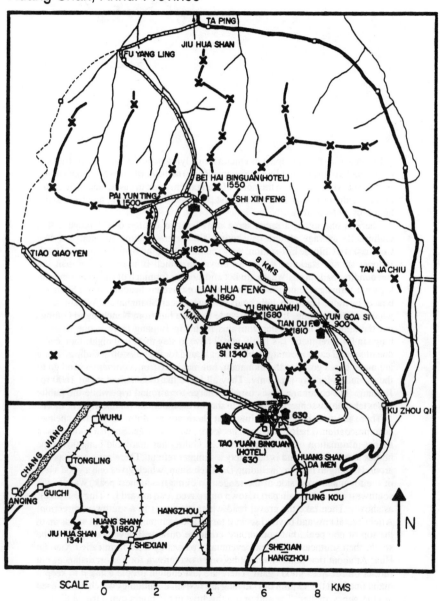

Lu Shan, Jiangxi Province

Lu Shan is a small compact mountain range lying between the cities of Jiujiang on the banks of the Chang Jiang (Yangtze River) to the north, and Nanchang to the south. The whole area is in the north of Jiangxi Province in east China. The entire range is called Lu Shan, but the highest peak is called Hanyang, and rises to the height of 1474 meters.

There is one town, a rather large one, lying at the top of the range called Guling. Its average altitude is about 1000 meters. Guling (pronounced like Cooling) is a Chinese hill-station, very reminiscent of the British India and Dutch Indonesian hill stations. It's at an elevation which is much cooler than the surrounding padi-lands which are hot and steamy for much of the year. One can arrive at Jiujiang, the normal starting point for travelers heading for Lu Shan, by boat or by train. There are daily boats sailing between Shanghai and Wuhan, all of which stop at Jiujiang. It's also possible to ride a bus from Nanchang to Guling, but the author is not familar with this route. In Jiujiang there is one hotel or binguan for foreigners. It's likely you'll have to stay there one night, then catch one of several early morning public buses bound for the bus stop at Guling. There are many buses going to the mountain, but many are from communes and go to the mountain for day-trips only. They all leave the mountain at about 1600 for Jiujiang. The commune buses usually charge for a round trip, while the public buses take the passengers who want to stay on the mountain for one night or more.

There are two hotels at Guling, but there are no dorm rooms for cheaper accommodation. There's one good bookstore with maps and English books, and a tourist information office called C.I.T.S. Guling has many old bungalow type homes and buildings and is definitely a summer retreat. There are several peaks around Guling to hike to, including Da Yueh Shan, which gives one a good view of the town and west side of the range. To climb the highest peak, walk to the southwest out of the main part of town on a paved road toward Lu Ting Hu (lake), as shown. Then take the gravel road which also goes in a southwest direction. After several kms and beyond several farms and communes the road winds up to the top of one peak, but you should continue on a well-developed path to the south, then southeast. This trail eventually passes by a tea farm called Xiao Qi Hua. At about that point the trail becomes overgrown for a short distance, but further on becomes good again. There are just enough people using it to keep it maintained. At the summit of Hanyang are two small buildings which can be used as emergency shelter. The author did this hike in 6½ hours round trip in the rain carrying an umbrella all the way. Take a lunch and water and get an early start.

Map: Two different maps can be bought at the bookstore on the main street of Guling.

Lu Shan, Jiangxi Province

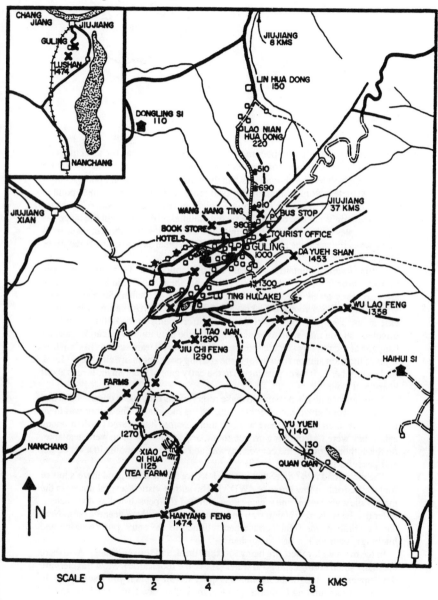

CHANG JIANG
JIUJIANG
GULING
LUSHAN 1474
NANCHANG

JIUJIANG 8 KMS

LIN HUA DONG 150

DONGLING SI 110

LAO NIAN HUA DONG 220

510

690

910

WANG JIANG TING

BUS STOP

JIUJIANG 37 KMS

980

BOOK STORE

TOURIST OFFICE

HOTELS

GULING 1000

DA YUEH SHAN 1453

JIUJIANG XIAN

1300

LU TING HU (LAKE)

WU LAO FENG 1358

LI TAO JIAN 1290

JIU CHI FENG 1290

HAIHUI SI

FARMS

1270

YU YUEN 140

130

NANCHANG

XIAO QI HUA 1125 (TEA FARM)

QUAN QIAN

N

HANYANG FENG 1474

SCALE   0   2   4   6   8   KMS

Qian Shan, Liaoning Province, China

Qian Shan is a small, compact mountain range located near the steel mill city of Anshan, in China's northeastern province of Liaoning. This mountain range is not high by world standards, but the mountain base or entry point is only a mere 100 meters altitude, making the local relief fairly high. The highest point in the range is called Immortal Terrace in English, and its height is about 670 meters. This mountain is not one of the nine sacred mountains of China, but the range has many temples and some stone carvings and even a few Buddhist monks, so in many ways it's the same experience visiting Qian Shan as to visit the Buddhist or Daoist mountains.

Getting to this mountain is very easy and uncomplicated. There are many daily trains running from Beijing to the northeast and Shenyang. From Shenyang there are also many trains heading south to the port city of Dalian. Stop at Anshan, which has one hotel about half a km east of the train station (take any trolley going east about 3 stops). This hotel does not offer rooms or beds for the budget travelers, so you may want to head straight for the mountain. You can leave extra baggage at the railway storage room as is the case in all train stations in China. In front of the train station (east side) is the starting point for many city buses. Look for bus number 8. It takes passengers to the entry gate of Qian Shan. It runs about every half hour.

At the entry gate it's possible to make reservations for a room or possibly a bed at one of several small hotels or binguans on the mountain. The author was there for an hour, then was told there were no more rooms. It appeared (in their phone calls) they were looking for a private room, and apparently none were available. So the author went into the canyon anyway and ended up camping in a very quiet and peaceful place.

The main road into Qian Shan is paved as are all the roads, and there's lots of foot traffic (only a few buses or 4WD's). The author visited several places in the main valley above the entry gate then climbed the peak listed as 485 meters. After that he walked to Naiquanan and camped south of there near the pass. Next day he climbed Immortal Terrace and returned to the entry gate (walking and hitching), then took a bus to Anshan.

In the main valley there are many food and drink and souvenir stalls. Also there are many small springs and good water (above the foot traffic). Most travelers are day-trippers, so at night the mountain is quiet and all yours if you're camping. In the valleys surrounding Immortal Terrace, the author saw fewer vendors, so take food from the main valley.

Map: At the entry gate and at other places up valley one can buy maps of Qian Shan.

Qian Shan, Liaoning Province

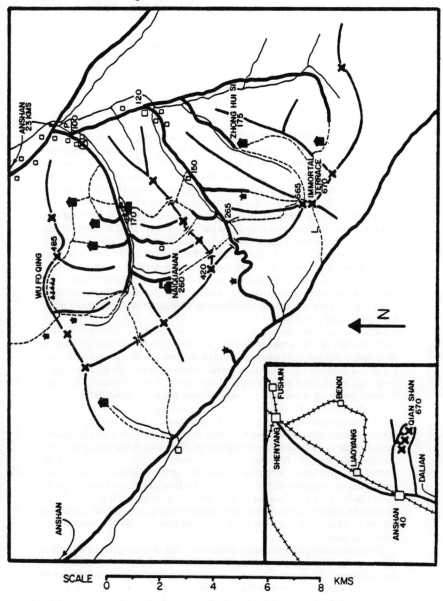

Changbai Shan, Jilin Province, China-Korea

Want to go to a mountain that "no one else knows about"? Then this is it, Changbai Shan. This mountain lies on the Chinese-Korean border, almost due south of Jilin and Mudanjiang in China's Dong Bei or East North (North East). The thing that makes this mountain unique is that it is the remains of an old volcano. At one time in the distant past the volcano erupted, thus making a huge caldera or crater. Within the crater is a rather large fresh water lake 8 or 9 kms in length. Surrounding the lake are the jagged peaks on the crater rim. The highest point is Bai Yun Feng (peak) at 2744 meters. Most of the other high summits are of similar altitude. The mountain and the lake are about evenly divided between China and Korea (a very friendly border). On the Korean side there's a dirt road running to the top of Jiang Jin Feng where a communications station is located. China also has one on the north side of the crater. There is one outlet to the lake (called Tian Chi or Heavenly Lake) that drains to the north and is the source of the Songhua River. Changbai Shan is a kind of National Park or Natural Wildlife Reserve.

Of all the mountains covered in this book this one might be the most difficult to reach, but don't be discouraged. Part of the difficulty is that it lies off in a corner of the country. First, get your permission to visit the area by having *Antu County* put in you travel permit. Then take a train to Jilin and on to the Korean town of Antu, as shown. Most of the people inhabiting this part of China are Koreans. There is one hotel or binguan in Antu (on some maps it's called Mingyuegou). Take one of about five daily buses running to Erdao, all of which leave before noon. The trip takes about 6 hours. If you're stopping in Shenyang, inquire there about the trains going all the way to Erdao-another possibility. There are several small Korean *yogwan* or hotels near the train station, but walk the 4 kms to the Ba Ho Ji Binguan. In this same building complex is the headquarters of the national reserve. Since there is no regular bus service (1984) to the mountain, you'll have to hang around the hotel and/or the headquarters and look for a ride (better learn Chinese fast! no one spoke english when the author was there). There are vehicles going to the mountain daily, and the hotel is one of the better places to find them. One could also walk to the road junction just east of town and hitch hike from there.

On the mountain is one new binguan; or you could camp, as this is a wilderness type country. There's a trail and a road to the com. station, which is very near one peak of about 2680 meters. Another trail runs up the canyon from the hotel to a 60 meter high waterfall, then on to the lake. There are one or two small shops selling food near the hotel. To hike around the rim would take two days. If you're out to hike or climb, do it in the months of June through September.

Map: A booklet with map can be bought at the Bai Shan Binguan.

Changbai Shan, Jilin Province

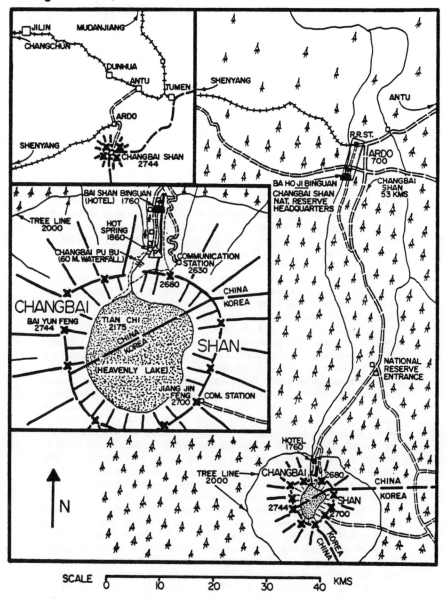

Siguniang, Hengduan Shan, Sichuan Province

Siguniang means *Four Girls*. The peaks stand together in one line running north-south. The elevations are 6250m, 5664, 5454 and 5355. There is a number of other peaks in the surrounding mountains that rise to 5500m also. This whole massif, not far north of Gongga Shan, is part of the Hengduan Shan (mountain). It is also just west of Chengdu, capital of Sichuan Province. For those interested in pandas, the Wolong Panda Reserve is one the same route as the Siguniang peaks.

Officially, Siguniang is open, but permission is required. Since it's considered an expedition type mountain, foreigners are required to have guides or liaison officers in the group, the same as with the other big name mountains such as Everest. Getting to the mountain is reasonably easy. It's a one day ride (280 kms) from Chengdu to the Tibetan commune of Rilong, located at 3150m. (It is very likely that one or two people could hitch hike into this area, but bus stations would likely not sell tickets to foreigners without permission. So if you have a few words of Chinese, and are the adventurous sort, might try the thumb trick - but with no promises by the author. With each passing day more and more of China is being opened to visiting foreigners . Another possible route, one that involves 3 to 4 days of driving (625 kms), is the one shown on the map insert. It goes north through Wenchuan, Lixian and to near Maerkang, then south to Xiaojin, and to Rilong. If you have the time, this would be an interesting trip, as all the villages are Tibetan. Doing this would require using a 4WD, but may be well worth it. Once at Rilong there will be horses or mules to hire as Tibetans normally own livestock of various kinds. It's one day from Rilong to the foot of the mountain on horses. Or the trekkers can walk to the base camps as shown or make other trips into various valleys. This map does not show trails into other valleys, but it's a populated region, so one can assume there are summer grazing trails in all canyons. This map was created from a copy of a topographic map given to the author by the Chinese Mountaineering Association. So there are good maps of the region, but you'll only be given photocopies of them. They have a couple of other simple sketch maps as well. Several of the routes are shown on the map, all from one of two base camps located in the Chang Ping Go (Valley), on the west side of the Siguniang. Take snow and ice climbing equipment as this is a glaciated and difficult peak. Climb here from July and into October. Take all food from Chengdu, although basic foods can be bought in the lower valleys.

Map: As mentioned above, from the Chinese Mountaineering Association.

Siguniang, Hengduan Shan, Sichuan Province

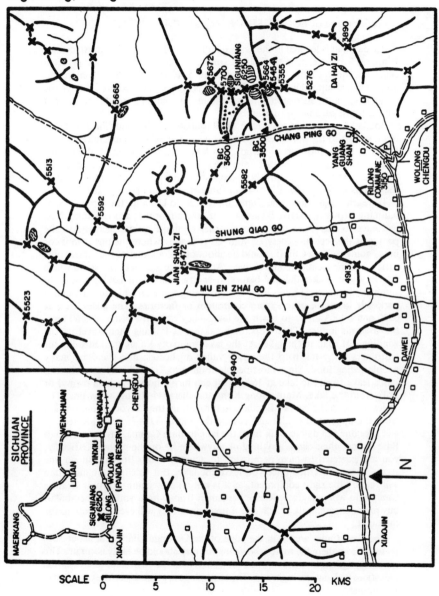

Bogda Shan,

Tian Shan, Xinjiang Province

• Bogda Shan

For a picture of BOGDA SHAN, see page 184.

Bogda Shan is located in the eastern half of the Tian Shan, in north central Xinjiang Province. It is the highest summit in that part of the range often called the Bogda Uula. At an elevation of 5447 metres, it stands high and mighty like a sentinel in the sky. This peak is highly glaciated even though the range lies in a desert region. The mountains surrounding Bogda are covered with a forest of pine, spruce and fir.

Bogda Shan is within easy reach of all tourists, foreign and Chinese. There is a lake just to the northwest of the main summit called Tian Chi (Heavenly Lake) to where most people head. This lake, at an elevation of about 1900 metres, is a real tourist attraction in the summer months where one can take boat rides on the lake. At the bus stop is a resthouse. At the southern end of the lake is a "Yurt Hotel", open in summer only and run by Kazaks.

To reach Bogda Shan and Tian Chi, first go to Urumqi, the capital city of Xinjiang Province. Arrive by air or by train from other parts of China. You will have to stay there one night in order or make arrangements. Ask the people at the reception desk of your hotel exactly where the bus stop is for buses going to Tian Chi. It should be about one block east of the central post office, but the location could change. At that place is a small taxi stand where you buy your ticket the day before to assure yourself of having a seat. In summer time, several buses leave each morning for Tian Chi, some from this park-side location, others from communes or factories. The buses leave at 0700 and take 3 hours to reach the lake. They claim the distance is 60 kms, but it seems longer. They stop for breakfast at Fukang then travel up the winding dirt road to the lake. At the lake are many Kazak men hustling for customers to be taken to the upper valley on horses; also there are many people selling food. Since most people coming to Tian Chi are day-trippers, buses leave from the lake at 1600. You can hire a horse (with its owner) or walk from the lake. Many Hong Kong travellers ride to the snow line. The easiest route to the base of Bogda is to turn left up the canyon, about one km from the upper end of the lake (where the Kazak Yurt Hotel is located). It will take one full day to walk from the lake to Base Camp. Anyone can go to Base Camp, then climb anything or anywhere he or she wishes. Officially, you are expected to have permission to actually climb Bogda, but no one seems to be concerned once you leave the lake. But to climb the mountain will require the right equipment, as it is not an easy climb. Enroute to Base Camp you will encounter Kazak herdsmen from whom you may be able to buy meat, cheese, milk or tea. For a small price they will even put you up for the night.

The Base Camp area is at the edge of the Daweigu Glacier, at about 3650 meters. From there the routes shown on this map should be fairly accurate. This north slope gets a lot more rain and snow, thus there's a coniferous forest at lower elevations and glaciers higher up. The south slope is much drier. Most rain comes in summer.

Map: Book-*High Mountain Peaks in China*, Chinese Mountaineering Association. Also, mountaineering map of Xinjiang Province, from Xinjiang Mountaineering Association, Urumqi (Sports Complex).

Bogda, Tian Shan, Xinjiang Province

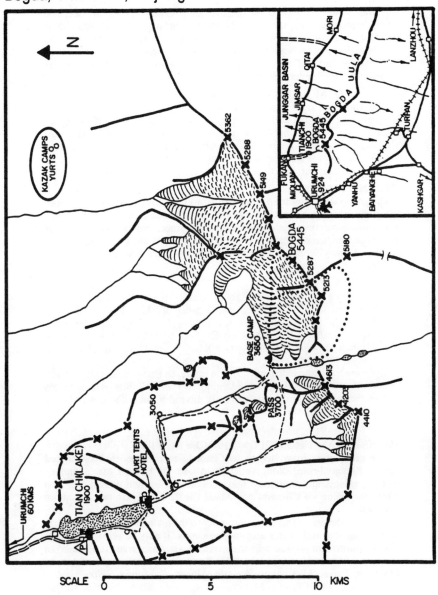

TREKKING ADVENTURES (Organised treks)

Some companies in the West arrange treks to the mountains in China. As arrangements are made by them through the Chinese Mountaineering Association which charges high prices, these costs must be borne by the trekkers.

A trek leader, employed by the overseas trekking outfit, oversees the arrangements, the equipment and the food. Reaching the mountains entails stopovers in some cities. While there, sightseeing tours are arranged. The approximate costs shown below include the use of equipment, food, intra-China flights and land transportation and tours in the cities. Some trekking adventures available include:

TIBET and QOMOLANGMA (Mt. Everest)

The group flies from Beijing to Chengdu then to Lhasa where a few days are spent acclimatizing and sightseeing. You travel by road to Xigatse and Xegar, towns on the Tibet-Nepal trade route, then southward to Rongbuk Monastery near the foot of Qomolangma. You spend about five days trekking in the base camp area before returning via Lhasa and Chengdu to Beijing. The total number of days in China is 22; the cost is about US $6000.

MT. ANYEMAQEN

The group travels by train from Beijing to Lanzhou, a city on the former Silk Road, then to Xining and by road to Xue Shan Xing. From here you trek into alpine country through forests of spruce, cypress and pine. You may chance to see brown bears, gazelles, goats, jackals, wild donkeys and possibly a snow leopard. The days spent in China total 22; the cost is US$3800.

MT. BOGDA

After visiting Beijing you will go to Xian then travel by train through Lanzhou to Urumqi. You will spend a week trekking in the Tianshan (Mountains) in. the shadow of Mt. Bogda. You will encounter both wilderness and villages. The Kazak herders live here in yurts. After returning from Urumqi to Beijing by plane you will have spent 22 days in China. The cost is about US$4000.

If you are travelling independently you can reach Bodga Shan (Mt. Bogda) by taking a bus (several daily) from Urumqi to Tian Chi, then walking to the base of the inspiring peak. You can walk around it but without permission you cannot climb on the high peak. See the hiking section of this book for more details.

MT. SIGUNIANG and WOLONG PANDA RESERVE

The group flies from Beijing to Chengdu then drives to Wolong and nearby Rilong. From Rilong you trek toward the base of Mt. Siguniang through villages and wilderness that abound in bird and animal life. You return to Beijing via Chengdu and Xian. The 22 days in China cost about US$3900.

For more details on this excursion, refer to the hiking section of this book. If you plan to travel to this area independently, it may be possible.

For information on who sells these treks in your area write to Himalayan Journeys (Pvt) Ltd., Kantipath, P.O. Box 989, Kathmandu, Nepal or to Mountain Travel, 1398 Solano Avenue, Albany, California, 94706, USA.

In China, the Chinese Mountaineering Association handles foreign mountaineers and hikers. They are located on the second floor of a school building located just south of Tian Tan Park in Beijing. Refer to the Beijing map. For an appointment, telephone 753746. Someone should speak English there.

SPELLING and PRONUNCIATION

China has adopted the Pinyin system of spelling to replace the former Wade-Giles system. Some old and new spellings are shown below.

Old Spelling	New Spelling	Approximate Pronunciation (where necessary)
Canton	Guangzhou	Gwong-joe
Chengchow	Zhenzhou	Jen-joe
Chengte	Chengde	
Chengtu	Chengdu	
Chungking	Chongqing	Chong-ching
Foochow	Fuzhou	Fu-joe
Hangchow	Hangzhou	Hang-joe
Harbin	Harbin	
Hofei	Hefei	
Huhehot	Hohhot	Ho-hot
Kweilin	Guilin	Gway-lin
Kweyang	Guiyang	Gway-yang
Kunming	Kunming	
Kwangchow	Guangzhou	Gwong-joe
Langchow	Lanzhou	Lan-joe
Loyang	Luoyang	Loy-yang
Nanking	Nanjing	Nan-jing
Nanning	Nanning	
Paotou	Baotou	
Peking	Beijing	Bay-jing
Quiquan	Jiuquan	Joo-kwan
Shanghai	Shanghai	
Shenyang	Shenyang	
Shumchun	Shenzhen	Shen-jen
Sian	Xian	She-ahn
Soochow	Suzhou	Sue-joe
Taching	Daqing	Da-ching
Taiyuan	Taiyuan	
Talien	Dalian	
Tientsin	Tianjin	
Tsinan	Jinan	
Tsingtao	Qingdao	Ching-daow
Urumchi	Urumqi	Oo-ruhm-chi
Wuhan	Wuhan	Woo-harn
Wuhsi	Wuxi	Woo-shee
Yangtze River	Chang Jiang	
Yellow River	Huang	

GETTING AROUND

Map	Di too *or* Dee tu
Do you have a map of Kunming?	Yo may yo di tu Kunming?
Bridge	Qiao *or* Chiao
Road	Lu
Intersection or Junction	Su zu ru ko *or* Soo zoo roo ko
Kilometre	Gong li
Half kilometre	Li
One kilometre	Are li
Where	Naali

PLACES, Geographical terms

North	Bei *or* bay
East	Dong
South	Nan
West	Xi *or* Shi
Cave	Dong
Desert	Shamo
Forest	Lin
Garden	Yuan
Harbour	Gang
Lake	Hu
Mountain	Shan *or* San
Pass	Guan
Peak	Feng *or* Fong
River	He *or* Jiang
Sea or very large lake	Hai
Tomb	Ling

PLACES, Sightseeing

Market	Shi
Commune	Gong she *or* Shuh
Factory	Gong chang

Carpet factory	地氈廠
Glassware factory	玻璃廠
Ivory carving factory	象牙彫刻
Jade carving factory	玉器彫刻
Lacquerware factory	漆器廠
Porcelain factory	瓷器廠
Silk factory	絲綢廠
Museum	Bo wu guan
Park	Gong yuan
School	Xue xiao *or* Shueh shiao
University	Da shu
Church	Jiao tang *or* Geo tong
Mosque	Qin din si *or* Chin din suh
Temple	Si *or* Suh
Big Temple	Miao
Pavilion	Ting
Pagoda	Ta
Gate	Men
Reservoir	Siwayku

PLACES, including Government Organizations

Post office	Yu chung zhou
Police	Qing cha *or* ching cha
Public Security Bureau	Gong anghee
Embassy	Da shu guan
Friendship store	友宜商店
Could you tell me where the Public Security Bureau is?	請 問 何 处 是 公 安 局 ?
China International Travel Service	Luxingshe 中 国 国 际 旅 行 社
Chinese Airline booking office (CAAC)	中 国 民 航 預 訂 机 票 办 事 处
Where is the mailbox?	邮 政 箱 在 那 裡 ?
Telephone	电 話
Money exchange	現 款 兌 换

NATIONAL IDENTITY

Australia	Ao da li ya	Japan	Ri ben
Austria	Ao di li	Netherlands	He lan *or* Ha lan
Argentina	A gen ting	New Zealand	Xin Xilan
Belgium	Bi li shi	Norway	Nuo wei
Brazil	Ba xi *or* Ba shi	Soviet Union	Sulien
Canada	Ji ana da	Sweden	Rui dian
Denmark	Dan mei	Switzerland	Rui shi
France	Fa gua	United Kingdom	Eng gua
Germany (FRD)	Xi de gua *or* Shi de gua	United States of America	Mei gua
Hong Kong	Sheng gung		
India	Yin du *or* Ein du		
Italy	Yi da li *or* Ee da li	Overseas Chinese	Hua zhou

GENERAL CONVERSATION

Yes	Shir
No	Bu
Please	Ching
Thank you (in Cantonese)	Oom gow
Thank you (in Mandarin)	Shay Shay (say it quickly)
I don't understand	Wo budong
I understand now	Wo dongle
Hello	Nee-how
Goodbye	Zai jian
Excuse me *or* I'm sorry	Dui poo chi
Sorry	Nan gooda
Good	How
Bad	Bu how
Okay	How
I have	Yo
Don't have	Mayo
Want	Yao
Don't want	Bu yao
Wait	Dong
Later	Yi ho *or* Ee ho
Photograph	Shang
Bag	Bao
Backpack	Bay bao *or* bei bao
Half a kilogram	Ching
How much?	Duoshao
Please write it down	請 写 下 来 。
Toilet	Cesuo

Men: 男   Women: 女

HOTEL

Hotel	Binguan *or* Bing guan
Where is a (the) hotel?	從那条道路往旅店？
	Ztsay naa li (name) Binguan?
Another hotel	Chi ta binguan
Room	Fung chen
Cheap room	Pian yi *or* Pian ee fung chen
Dormitory room	Tung pu *or* Tung poo
Bed	Puway *or* Pooway
Room key	Fung chen yiao shi *or* Eiao shi
Key	Yiao shi *or* Eiao shi
Shower	Sin yu
Toilet	Cesuo *or* Tsaswo
Sleep	Shuey jao
Noise or Noisy	Zao yin *or* Zao een
Quiet	An jing
I pay	Shi fee
I pay now?	Wo shi fee xian tsy?
I want the cheapest accommodation.	我要最便宜的
Do you have dormitory rooms?	有无宿舍之类的房間？
Do you have one bed in a dormitory room?	Yo may yo yi(e) puway tung pu
How much is that for one night?	每晚多少錢？

HEALTH

Hospital	Yi yuan *or* Ee yuan
Pharmacy	Yao dian
I am sick	Yo bing

226

RESTAURANT

Restaurant or food hall	Fan dian
Food	Fahn
Meal	Fahn
Rice	Fahn
Breakfast	Zao fahn (morning food)
Lunch	Wu fahn (noon food)
Supper	Wang fahn (night or evening food)
Open	Kaida
Closed	Guan
Chopsticks	Kaui zi
Food coupons	Piao (same word as train ticket)
Money	Chen
How much does it cost?	Duo shao chen　多少錢 ?
Expensive	Gui
Cheap	Pian yi *or* Pian ee

QUANTITIES

Bowl	Wan
One each	Ee gaa
Three each	San gaa
Half a bowl	Ban wan
Small bowl	Xiao wan, *or* Shiao wan
Just a little	Ee den den
Too much	Tai doo

FOOD

Rice porridge	Shi fahn
Steamed dumplings	Bao tsa
Boiled dumplings	Siway jiao 湯园
Fish	Yu
Pork	Jew row
Beef	Niu row
Meat	Roe *or* Row
Noodle	Mian tiao 面
Noodles with meat	Roe si miao
Bread	Mian bao
Fried bread	Yu tiao
Peanuts	Washun *or* Wasun
Cucumber	Huangua *or* Huang gua
Tomato	Shi hom shir
Vegetables	Shu tsye *or* Ching tsye 蔬菜
Eggs	Tan *or* Dan 蛋
Fried eggs	Gee dan
Fried rice with eggs	Tan chow fahn 鷄蛋炒飯
Soy sauce	Jao yo 豉汁
Soup	Tahng *or* Tang 湯
Cookies	Bing
Sugar	Bei tung *or* Bay tung

FRUIT AND ICE CREAM

Apples	Ping gua
Apricot	Xiang *or* Shiang
Banana	Xiangjiao *or* Shiang jiao
Melon (water)	Xi gua *or* Shi gua
Melon (honey dew)	Hami gua

228

FRUIT AND ICE CREAM (Continued)

Peach	Lee *or* Li
Yoghurt	Son yu ny
Ice Cream	Bing qi lin *or* Bing chee lin
Icicle	Bing ga *or* Bing gora

BEVERAGES

Water	Siwey *or* Shiway	
Boiled water	Kai siwey	
Cold water	Lung siwey	
Hot (not boiled) water	Re siwey *or* Reh	
Hot drinking water	Kai siwey	热 飲 水
Tea	Chah *or* Chaa	茶
Coffee	Ka fay	
Milk	Nio nung *or* Nio ny	
Beer	Pee jee o	啤 酒
Soda pop	Chee siwey	

ORDERING

I want	Wo yao
I want one bowl of noodles	Wo yao ee gaa wan mian tiao
Give me	Gay wo
Give me one dish of rice	Gay wo e gaa wan mi fahn
Give me one bowl of noodles with meat	Gay wo ee gaa wan row si miao
Do you have _____ ?	Yo may (mei) yo _____ ?
Do you have peanuts?	Yo may yo washun?
Do you have cooked rice?	Yo may yo mi fahn?
I don't like	Wo bu shi kuan

NUMBERS

half	½	Ban
zero	0	Ling
one	1	Yi *or* ee
two	2	Er *or* are *or* ar (*or a new word* liang)
three	3	San
four	4	Si *or* suh (sih)
five	5	Wu *or* woo
six	6	Liu *or* lee-o
seven	7	Qi (Chi) *or* chee
eight	8	Ba *or* bah
nine	9	Jiu *or* jee-o
ten	10	Shi *or shir*
eleven	11	Shiyi *or* shir-ee
twelve	12	Shier *or* shir-ar
twenty	20	Ershi *or* arshir
twenty-one	21	Ershi yi *or* arshir-ee
thirty	30	Sanshi *or* sanshir
thirty-two	32	Sanshi-er *or* sanshir-ar
one hundred	100	Yibai *or* eebay
two hundred	200	Erbai *or* arbai *or* liang bai
one thousand	1000	Yiqian *or* eechian

MONTHS

Year	Nian *or* Neean
Month	Yue *or* Yueh
January	Yi Yue *or* E Yueh
February	Er (Liang) Yue *or* Ar (Liang) Yueh
March	San Yue *or* San Yueh

Refer to Numbers above to establish April, etc.

December	Shi Er Yue *or* Shir Ar Yueh

DAYS

Week	Xing Qi *or* Sing Chi	
Monday	Xing Qi Yi *or* Sing Chi E	星期一
Tuesday	Xing Qi Er *or* Sing Chi Ar	星期二
Wednesday	Xing Qi San *or* Sing Chi San	星期三
Thursday	Xing Qi Si *or* Sing Chi Suh (Sih)	星期四
Friday	Xing Qi Wu Sing *or* Sing Chi Wu	星期五
Saturday	Xing Qi Liu *or* Sing Chi Lee O	星期六
Sunday	Xing Xi Tian *or* Sing Shi Tian	星期日
Day	Tian	
All Day	Chuen Tian	
Today	Jin Tian	今天
Tomorrow	Ming Tian	明天
Day after tomorrow	Houtian	后天
Yesterday	Zuo Tian	昨天
Morning	Zao Shang	晨早
Noon	Zhong Wu	
Afternoon	Xiawu	下午
Evening or Night	Wang Shang	黄昏
Tonight	Jin Tian Wang Shang	
In 3 day's time	San Tian Hou	

HOURS

Hour	Xiao Xi *or* Shiao Shi
Minute	Fun
Three o'clock	San Dian; 0300, 1500
Five o'clock	Wu Dian; 0500, 1700
Five Thirty	0530; Wu Dian Ban
Half or ½	Ban

TRAIN

Where is the train station?	請問車站在何处?
	Ztsay naa li huo che zhan?
Ticket hall	Piao chu ting
Seat	Yiitz
1st Class	Yi done *or* Ee dun
2nd Class	Er done *or* Ar dun
3rd Class	San done *or* San dun
Hard seat	Ying Zhou　　硬座
Hard sleeper	Ying vo *or* Een vo　　硬卧
Could I reserve a ticket from . . . . . to . . . . .?	能否訂位?
I want one (two) hard seats to	我只要一（二）硬座位，往
I want one (two) hard sleepers to	我只要一（二）张硬卧舖，往
One ticket please	Ee piao ching *or* Ee gaa ching

When you are at the ticket window, they know you want a ticket. You can eliminate the word ticket and say one each or Ee gaa.

I go to Datong	Wo chee Datong *or* Wo chiu Datong
What time	Sama shi ho
When	Sama shi ho
What time or when does the train leave? (To help them understand, point to your watch).	請問下一班火车的开車时間?
	Sama shi ho huo che chee oo?
What is the fare?	請問要多少錢?
	Piao duo shao chen
Could you give me the cheapest one?	能否給我最便宜的?
	Pian yi piao (cheap ticket)

TRAIN (Continued)

Is this ticket the cheapest? 是不是最便宜的

Which platform do I go to? 我要到那一处月台？

Note: When you are in Hard Class and you want to find where the conductor is who sells hard berths, show this question to someone:

Comrade: In which carriage may I reserve for hard berths? 同志：到幾號车厢登記硬卧？

Note: When you have found the conductor (usually in car no. 8 or 9) show this question to him.

Comrade: I want to buy one (two) hard berths. Can you help solve this problem? 同志：我要买一（二）张硬卧票。能不能帮助我解决这个問題？

Please tell me when we are about there. 何时抵达？

Where can I leave my luggage? 我的行李放存那一处地方？

Soft sleeper 软卧

AIR

Airport	Fay jee chahng	机场

What time does the plane leave?

飛机 在 什 么 时 间 起 飛？

BICYCLE

Where can I hire a bicycle? 我 往 什 么 地 方 可 以 僱

請 一 輛 脚 踏 车。

BOAT

Harbour	Hwaw cheh jan	海港
Boat terminal		渡 輪 終 点

What time or when does the boat arrive in Wuhan? Sama shi ho chuan da Wuhan?

BUS

Bus	Gung gung chee tsa	公 共 汽 车
Bus station	Chee tsa zhan	巴 士 站

Where is the bus station? Ztsay naa li chee ztsa zhan?

What time does the bus leave? Sama shi no chee cheeo?

巴 士 （ 公 共 车 ） 在 什
么 时 间 开 行

Last stop	Gee ho da
Last station	Gee ho zhan

NOTE: On city buses the conductor will say "May piao, may piao", meaning "Buy ticket, buy ticket". Just say Ee (one) Gaa (each).

TAXI

Where can I get a taxi? 那 里 有 出 租 汽 车？

234

INDEX

BIBLIOGRAPHY

READING GUIDE

- CHINA COMPANION, Evelyne Garside, Andre Deutsh, Ltd., London.
- CHINA GUIDEBOOK, Keijzer/Kaplan, Eurasia Press, New York.
- THE OFFICIAL GUIDEBOOK OF CHINA, CITS (China International Travel Service), Lee Publishers Group, New York.
- CHINA, OFF THE BEATEN TRACK, Schwartz, South China Morning Post Publication, Hong Kong.
- CHINA - A TRAVEL SURVIVAL KIT, Samagalski and Buckley, Lonely Planet Publications, Australia.
- CHINA RAILWAY TIMETABLE, China Railway Publishing House, Beijing.
- A book that gives an indication of life in China is "The Chinese" by David Bonavia, a correspondent in Beijing for "The Times."

MAPS

- THE PEOPLES REPUBLIC OF CHINA (Side one).
- THE PEOPLE OF CHINA (Side two) National Geographic Society, Washington, D.C.

DISTRIBUTORS

"China On Your Own"

AUSTRALIA
Bookwise International, 1 Jeanes Street, Beverley, South Australia, 5007

CANADA
Milestone Publications, P.O. Box 35548, Station E, Vancouver, B.C., V6M 4G8
Tel: (604) 251-7675

GREAT BRITAIN
Cordee Books, 3a De Montfort Street, Leicester, LE1 7HD. Tel: (0533) 543579

HONG KONG
The Book Society, G.P.O. Box 7804

JAPAN
Intercontinental Marketing Corp., IPO Box 5056, Tokyo, 100-31

U.S.A.
Banana Republic, 175 Bluxome St., San Francisco, CA 94107. Tel: (415) 777-0250
Bradt Enterprises, 95 Harvey St., Cambridge, MA 02140. Tel: (617) 492-8776
Pacific Pipeline Inc., 19215 66th Ave. S., Kent, WA. 98032. Tel: (206) 872-5523
Publishers Group West, 5855 Beaudry St., Emeryville, CA 94608. Tel: (415) 658-3453
Quality Books Inc., 400 Anthony Trail, Box 3006, Northbrook, Illinois, 60065-3006